THE
STATUTE OF WESTMINSTER
AND
DOMINION STATUS

THE
STATUTE OF WESTMINSTER
AND
DOMINION STATUS

BY

K. C. WHEARE, F.B.A.

Fifth Edition

OXFORD UNIVERSITY PRESS

1953

Oxford University Press, Amen House, London E.C. 4

GLASGOW NEW YORK TORONTO MELBOURNE WELLINGTON
BOMBAY CALCUTTA MADRAS CAPE TOWN

Geoffrey Cumberlege, Publisher to the University

FIRST EDITION 1938
SECOND EDITION 1942
THIRD EDITION 1947
FOURTH EDITION 1949

Reprinted lithographically in Great Britain
by LOWE & BRYDONE, PRINTERS, LTD., LONDON, from
corrected sheets of the first edition

PREFACE TO THE FIFTH EDITION

SINCE the revision of this book was undertaken in September, 1948, for its fourth edition, some important changes have occurred in the British Commonwealth. Within a few months the parliament of Eire had passed an act to bring to an end its recognition of the King as the symbol of its association with the other members of the Commonwealth, and when that act came into effect on April 18, 1949, the Republic of Ireland ceased to be a member of the Commonwealth, although the other members proposed, through reciprocal arrangements, not to regard Ireland as a foreign country or its citizens as aliens. Within ten days of the Republic of Ireland's leaving the Commonwealth, its members announced that they were prepared to recognize a Republic of India as a member of the Commonwealth in accordance with the terms of India's declaration that, although she would be a Republic, she desired 'to continue her full membership of the Commonwealth of Nations and her acceptance of the King as the symbol of the free association of its independent member nations and as such the Head of the Commonwealth'. Here indeed seemed a contradiction which brought into discussion the whole basis of the Commonwealth.

There were other changes. On March 31, 1949 Newfoundland became the tenth province of Canada, and its separate existence as a Dominion, in terms of the Statute of Westminster, which had amounted to so little, ceased. On December 16, 1949 the royal assent was given to the British North America (No. 2) Act,

1949, which gave power to the Parliament of Canada to alter the Canadian Constitution, though with safeguards for the division of powers and certain other matters, and thus modified the position which had been guaranteed by section 7 of the Statute of Westminster. In South Africa two important events occurred in the judicial sphere. The appeal to the judicial committee of the Privy Council was abolished in 1950. Of far greater importance, however, was the reconsideration in 1951 and 1952 of the whole basis of the South African Constitution, in relation to the Statute of Westminster, culminating in the judgement of the Appellate Division of the Supreme Court in March 1952 in which the case of *Ndlwana* v. *Hofmeyr* was overruled. Finally, on the death of George VI and the accession of Queen Elizabeth II the nature of the Commonwealth was illustrated in the various proclamations that were made in its different members.

Some attempt is made in this fifth edition to consider the significance of these changes in so far as they are relevant to a discussion of the Statute of Westminster and its effect upon status in the Commonwealth. The position of the two republics is considered principally in the chapter on monarchy, while the other changes have been dealt with under the chapters on the countries concerned. The judgement of the Appellate Division of the Supreme Court of South Africa, however, has raised issues of such great importance that it seemed justifiable to deal with it in a new and separate appendix.

In reviewing the development of the Commonwealth and its members since 1931 when the Statute of Westminster was enacted, and since I first attempted to

expound the relation between the Statute and Dominion
Status, it seemed to me that the time had come to
consider whether so much had changed that it was no
longer possible to think profitably in the old terms.
Were the Statute and Dominion Status obsolescent?
I make an attempt to raise this question in a new concluding chapter entitled 'The End of Dominion Status?'

K. C. W.

ALL SOULS COLLEGE, OXFORD
   5 *November* 1952

CONTENTS

TABLE OF CASES

A

TABLE OF STATUTES

United Kingdom

DOMINION STATUTES
Commonwealth of Australia

Dominion of Canada

Irish Free State

I

LAW AND CONVENTION

I

THE first significant fact about the Statute of Westminster, 1931,[1] is that it is a statute. It belongs, that
is to say, to that class of constitutional rules which are
usually described as rules of strict law or juridical constitutional rules; it belongs to the body of law, strictly
so called. These rules of strict law possess the distinguishing formal characteristic that they are those rules
recognized, accepted, and applied by the courts in the
determination of disputes; they alone form the law, as
that term is understood in the courts. Statutes, statutory orders, prerogative orders, and judicial decisions
are all rules of strict law, in the sense in which that term
has been defined above; they will all be accepted and
applied by a court. These constitutional rules of strict
law do not exhaust the whole body of constitutional
rules which regulate the system of government in any
community. There exists in addition a class of non-
legal (though not illegal) constitutional rules, in the
sense that they are rules which do not determine decisions in a court. These rules are described by such terms
as practices, maxims, usages, customs, or conventions.[2]

[1] 22 Geo. 5, c. 4. The Statute is reproduced as Appendix II to this
book.
[2] The best exposition of the nature of these rules is still that of Dicey,
in spite of a few misconceptions which later writers have pointed out.
See *Law of the Constitution* (9th ed.), especially c. xiv. See also W. I. Jennings, *Cabinet Government*, c. i. The misconceptions are pointed out in
W. I. Jennings, *The Law and the Constitution*, c. iii; and in E. C. S. Wade's
Introduction to the 9th ed. of Dicey's book.

B

Their sanction is not necessarily weaker than that of the rules of strict law; their formulation is not necessarily vaguer. The essential characteristic distinguishing the two classes of constitutional rule is that rules of strict law are those rules recognized and applied by a court; non-legal rules are those rules which are not recognized and applied by a court. If and when a court does recognize, say, a constitutional custom, as a rule which it will apply in the determination of a dispute before it, then that custom has ceased to be a non-legal rule, and has joined the body of law strictly so called.[1]

The Statute of Westminster, then, is a constitutional rule of strict law. 'Dominion Status' on the other hand cannot be defined exclusively, or indeed mainly, in terms of strict law. It is an expression used to describe the constitutional and international position of the Dominion of Canada, the Commonwealth of Australia, the Dominion of New Zealand, the Union of South Africa, the

[1] Thus, in *British Coal Corporation* v. *the King*, [1935] A.C. 500, Lord Sankey said: 'But according to constitutional convention it is unknown and unthinkable that His Majesty in Council should not give effect to the report of the Judicial Committee, who are thus in truth an appellate Court of Law, tu which by the statute of 1833 all appeals within their purview are referred.' (At p. 511.)

It is to be noted that Lord Sankey said 'in truth', not 'in law'. The recognition of constitutional custom and convention as law is unusual in the Judicial Committee. It is doubtful whether Lord Sankey's words here should be taken as laying down a new rule of law. But Duff C. J. appears to treat them as doing so in his judgment in the *Privy Council Appeals Reference*, [1940] S.C.R. 49. Perhaps the most extreme example of the recognition of convention as law is found in the judgment of Duff C. J. in Re *Minimum Wage Act*, [1936] S.C.R., 461, espec. at pp. 476–7. But contrast his words in the *Disallowance and Reservation References*, [1938] S.C.R. 71 at p. 78: 'We are not concerned with constitutional usage. We are concerned with questions of law. . . .' Yet, if some conventions are to be recognised, why not all? See Jennings, 52 *L.Q.R.*, at pp. 177–8.

Irish Free State, and Newfoundland,[1] or any one of them. This constitutional and international position may be set out partly in rules of strict law, such as statutes, passed by the United Kingdom Parliament or by the Parliaments of the Dominions, and judicial decisions, and partly in non-legal rules, such as constitutional conventions. The most important of the rules of strict law which define Dominion Status at present are to be found in a statute of the United Kingdom Parliament, the Statute of Westminster itself. The most important of the non-legal rules are to be found in the constitutional conventions between Great Britain and the Dominions agreed upon and declared at the Imperial Conferences of 1926 and 1930, and set out in the reports of these Conferences.[2] This association of constitutional conventions with law, 'has long been familiar in the history of the British Commonwealth; it has been characteristic of political development both in the domestic government of these communities and in their relations with each other; it has permeated both executive and legislative power'.[3] It is proposed in this book to examine the development of Dominion Status in order to analyse out the elements of law and convention, and to discover their interaction upon each other at certain stages in the development. In particular it is

[1] In 1933 Newfoundland surrendered her status as a Dominion. The status of Eire is considered later, pp. 271 ff.

[2] See Report of the Inter-Imperial Relations Committee of the Imperial Conference of 1926; a Committee presided over by Lord Balfour. The Report was adopted by the Conference and is printed as part of the Report of the Conference. Cmd. 2768, pp. 13–30. For 1930, see *Report of the Conference on the Operation of Dominion Legislation and Merchant Shipping Legislation*, 1929, Cmd. 3479, adopted with certain modifications by the Conference of 1930, and made part of its Report (Cmd. 3717, p. 18).

[3] Cmd. 3479, para. 56.

proposed to concentrate attention upon the most important legal rule, the Statute of Westminster, and the most
important collection of non-legal rules, the 1926 and
1930 Reports, and to explain their relation within the
concept of Dominion Status. Neither the Statute of
Westminster alone, nor the Reports alone, can supply
an adequate definition of Dominion Status. The
Statute, taken along with other rules of strict law, could
supply an adequate definition of the legal status of the
Dominions; the Reports, taken along with other non-
legal rules, could supply an adequate definition of the
conventional status of the Dominions; but it requires
a correlation of the two elements to describe the *constitutional* status of the Dominions, and it is this constitutional status which is denoted by the term 'Dominion
Status'. Here, as elsewhere in British constitutional
development, it is not the isolation of law from convention, but the association of law with convention within
the constitutional structure which is the essential
characteristic. This proposition is stated dogmatically
here. But it is believed that the discussion of the Statute
of Westminster and of Dominion Status which follows
will illustrate and justify what has been asserted.

It has seemed necessary at the outset first to distinguish constitutional rules of strict law, as exemplified by
the Statute of Westminster, from non-legal constitutional rules, as exemplified by the conventions declared
in the Imperial Conference Reports, and immediately
thereafter to assert the inter-relation and interaction
of these two classes of rule, as exemplified in the term
'Dominion Status'. For there is a tendency, in the
discussion of British constitutional development, to
underestimate the importance of rules of strict law, and

in particular of statute, in that development; to over-
estimate the importance of non-legal rules; and seriously
to misconceive the relation of the two classes of rule to
each other. It is asserted, for example, that Great
Britain and the British Empire have an 'unwritten' constitution. A constitutional statute is regarded therefore
as something alien to the spirit of the constitution. On
such a view of the nature of the British constitution, and
of the constitution of the British Empire, it was inevitable
that the passing of the Statute of Westminster should
appear to be a mistake. Some members of Parliament,
in the United Kingdom and in the Dominions,[1] objected
to the proposal to pass the Statute, not because of the
terms it contained, but because it was a statute. Lord
Buckmaster, an ex-Lord Chancellor, put this point of
view in the House of Lords during the second reading
of the Statute of Westminster Bill. He said that he intended to support the Bill, but that he felt it was a mistake.

It is not—he said—that its actual terms offend any of the
relationships existing between ourselves and our Dominions.
It is that it is, as I believe, for the first time, an attempt made
to put into the form of an Act of Parliament rules which
bind the various component parts of the Empire, and that
I regard as a grave mistake.[2]

He went on to assert that

the thing which has made this country grow is that it never
has had a written Constitution of any sort or kind, and the

[1] e.g. in Australia, Mr. W. M. Hughes reiterated the view he had
already expressed at the Imperial Conference of 1921 that it was unnecessary to write down the Constitution of the British Empire in black
and white, *Australian Commonwealth Parliamentary Debates*, vol. 131, pp.
4071–6; Sir George Pearce, *ibid.*, p. 4505. In New Zealand, Sir Thomas
Sidey, *New Zealand Parliamentary Debates*, vol. 228, pp. 634 ff.

[2] 83 *H.L. Deb.*, 5 s., 195.

consequence has been that it has been possible to adapt, from time to time, the various relationships and authorities between every component part of this State, without any serious mistake or disaster. That is what I think ought to be the ideal aimed at between ourselves and the various other nations which together make up the British Empire.[1] . . . You should avoid as far as possible putting a definition of what the relationships may be into the unyielding form of an Act of Parliament. That is what this Statute has attempted to do.[2]

2

What validity is there in this argument? It is not possible to answer this question fully at this early stage. It is necessary, however, to make one or two elementary distinctions which may help to put the matter in a true perspective. There may be discovered in any state a collection of rules which establish and regulate the political institutions of that state. It will be convenient to call this entire collection of rules the 'constitutional structure' of the state. It consists of rules of strict law, both written and unwritten, and of rules which are not classed as part of the law strictly so called, and these also may be written and unwritten. In some states, however, a selection from the rules of strict law, which establish and regulate political institutions, is collected in a written document, which is called the Constitution.[3] And, on this definition of 'Constitution', it follows that, first, the Constitution is a part, not the whole, of the constitutional structure; and, secondly, there is no such thing as an 'unwritten'

[1] *Ibid.* 196.
[2] *Ibid.* 195–6. Lord Hailsham, at that time Secretary of State for War, appeared to sympathize with this view. *Ibid.*, 213.
[3] M. Dareste has collected six volumes of them. See F. R. Dareste, *Les Constitutions Modernes* (4th ed.).

Constitution. Adopting these distinctions, it can be said that the United Kingdom has a constitutional structure, but it has no written Constitution. States such as France, the United States, Sweden, the U.S.S.R., Switzerland, or the British Dominions, also possess a constitutional structure, but of this constitutional structure a written Constitution forms part. Lord Buckmaster's statement, then, emphasizes this first point about the system of government in the United Kingdom and it is a point worth making. For it is a usual though not a necessary characteristic of a written Constitution that the rules it contains prevail over all other rules of strict law in so far as the latter are repugnant to the Constitution, and further that the alteration of the rules in the Constitution requires some special process not necessary for the alteration of the ordinary rules of strict law. The existence or not of a written Constitution is for the lawyer and for the politician, therefore, a distinction of practical importance.

But Lord Buckmaster's statement is misleading because it goes on to suggest that not only has Britain had no written Constitution, but that it has had no other written constitutional rules of any importance, and in particular, no constitutional statutes. Changes in its constitutional structure by the method of statutory enactment, it is suggested, are exceptional and abnormal in the British system. This is not true. An important part of the rules which compose the British constitutional structure are written rules of strict law, including statutes, and statutory and prerogative orders. They are collected into books which any one may read.[1] The Bill

[1] e.g. C. Grant Robertson, *Select Statutes, Cases and Documents to illustrate English Constitutional History*.

of Rights (1689),[1] a written statutory enactment of Parliament, lays down, *inter alia*, the fundamental constitutional rule that taxation may not be levied without the consent of Parliament. The Act of Settlement, 1701,[2] the Act of Union with Scotland, 1707,[3] the Act of Union with Ireland, 1800,[4] the Parliament Act, 1911,[5] the Representation of the People Acts, 1832, 1867, 1884, 1918, and 1928,[6] the Ballot Act, 1872,[7] the Judicature Acts, 1873, 1875, and 1925,[8] the Incitement to Disaffection Act, 1934,[9] His Majesty's Declaration of Abdication Act, 1936,[10] the Regency Act, 1937,[11] and the Acts erecting various new ministries, such as the Ministry of Health Act, 1919,[12] and the Ministry of Transport Act, 1919,[13] are all examples of alterations or innovations in the constitutional structure of Great Britain by means of written, statutory, juridical rules. Again, the code of regulations issued under Order-in-Council in pursuance of the Emergency Powers Act, 1920,[14] which confers powers to deal with internal disturbances, is an example of written juridical constitutional rules, issued under statutory powers.

Nor must it be assumed that the class of *written* constitutional rules is confined to the province of the written rules of strict law, such as statutes and statutory orders. There is no necessary reason why a constitutional convention should not take written form. The procedure of

[1] 1 W. & M., sess. 2, c. 2.   [2] 12 & 13, Wm. 3, c. 2.
[3] 5 Anne, c. 8.   [4] 40 Geo. 3, c. 67.   [5] 1 & 2 Geo. 5, c. 13.
[6] 2 Wm. 4, c. 45; 30 & 31 Vict., c. 102; 48 Vict., c. 3; 7 & 8 Geo. 5, c. 64; 18 & 19 Geo. 5, c. 12.
[7] 35 & 36 Vict., c. 33, introducing the secret ballot at elections.
[8] 36 & 37 Vict., c. 66; 38 & 39 Vict., c. 77; 15 & 16 Geo. 5, c. 49.
[9] 24 & 25 Geo. 5, c. 56.   [10] 1 Ed. 8, c. 3.
[11] 1 Ed. 8 & 1 Geo. 6, c. 16.   [12] 9 & 10 Geo. 5, c. 21.
[13] 9 & 10 Geo. 5, c. 50.   [14] 10 & 11 Geo. 5, c. 55.

Parliament, for example, forms part of the constitutional
structure of the United Kingdom, and constitutes a body
of convention. None the less it is in great part embodied
in written form.[1]

The point which Lord Buckmaster made, therefore,
was that Great Britain and the British Empire had no
Constitution. He desired to stress also the fact that many
important constitutional changes had occurred in Great
Britain and in the British Empire without the alteration
of any rule of strict law. It is submitted here, however,
that the form in which he stated this point, and the form
in which it was stated by critics in the Dominion Parliaments, suggested first, that constitutional change in the
British structure by the method of statutory enactment
was abnormal, and secondly that the distinction between
written and unwritten constitutional rules was equivalent to the distinction between statute and convention.
Neither of these propositions can be supported from
British constitutional history.

It is important, on the other hand, to give full weight
to the main point which Lord Buckmaster and other
critics had in mind, and not to concentrate too much attention on verbal inconsistencies. Far-reaching changes
in the British constitutional structure have occurred
without the assistance of statutes; the framework of the
rules of strict law has remained unaltered. Campbell-
Bannerman is reported to have said to M. de Fleuriau,
at one time French Ambassador to the Court of St.
James:

. . . Quand nous faisons une Révolution, nous ne détruisons
pas notre maison, nous en conservons avec soin la façade
et, derrière cette façade, nous reconstruisons une nouvelle

[1] Dicey emphasized this point. *Law of the Constitution* (9th ed.), p. 28.

maison. Vous, Français, agissez autrement: vous jetez bas le vieil édifice et vous reconstruisez la même maison avec une autre façade et sous un nom différent.

And, as M. de Fleuriau remarked: 'Il y a du vrai dans cette boutade.'[1] These non-legal rules are given a variety of names, as has been indicated. It appears convenient to adopt two terms, usage and convention. By convention is meant an obligatory rule; by usage, a rule which is no more than the description of a usual practice and which has not yet obtained obligatory force. A usage, after repeated adoption whenever a given set of circumstances recurs, may for a sufficient reason acquire obligatory force and thus become a convention.[2] But conventions need not have a prior history as usages. A convention may, if a sufficient reason exist, arise from a single precedent. Or again it may result from an agreement between the parties concerned, declared and accepted by them as binding.[3]

Some familiar examples may be mentioned to illustrate the distinction between usage and convention.[2] The rule that the King must assent to a Bill duly passed by Lords and Commons; or the rule that the King must appoint as his Ministers those persons who can command a majority in Parliament; or the rule that the King must act on the advice of such Ministers in the exercise of his powers in ordinary executive government—these are

[1] Recounted by M. de Fleuriau in the Preface to J. Magnan de Bornier, *L'Empire Britannique, son évolution politique et constitutionnelle*, p. 6.

[2] In these cases, the term 'convention' is equivalent to 'custom'.

[3] Here the meaning is equivalent to that attaching to 'convention' in international relations, and it describes most accurately, too, the origin and nature of most of the conventions which regulate Dominion Status, e.g. those declared in the Imperial Conference Reports.

all constitutional conventions. They have acquired obligatory force for some sufficient reason, after, and usually to some extent because of, repeated adoption on successive occasions. Each has had a period in its history when it might be described as a mere usage. It is, indeed, much easier to find usages in certain matters in the British constitutional structure than it is to find conventions.[1] Almost all the rules which regulate the King's exercise of his legal power to dissolve Parliament or his legal power to appoint a Prime Minister amount in truth to little more than usages. It is not possible to say, for example, that there is a convention that the King must grant a dissolution to his Prime Minister, if the Prime Minister asks for it. The grant of a dissolution by George V to Mr. Ramsay MacDonald in 1924 proves no more than that in that particular case the King felt obliged to grant a dissolution. There is no evidence that he recognized an obligatory rule or enunciated any such rule. Groups of cases can be collected to illustrate several points of view on this question.[2] They constitute a collection of usages; they describe what the practice has been; they are instances, not obligatory rules.

In the same way it is not possible to say that there is a convention that the King must appoint as his Prime Minister a member of the House of Commons. The most that can be said is that since Lord Salisbury resigned the Prime-Ministership in 1902, no member of the House of Lords has been appointed Prime Minister, and that in

[1] Mr. Justice H. V. Evatt's *The King and His Dominion Governors*, establishes this point beyond doubt. He does not adopt the term 'usage', but he illustrates the variety of practices that exist and the absence of a defined convention in many matters of fundamental importance.

[2] Evatt, *op. cit.*, c. viii. Cf. Jennings, *Cabinet Government*, c. xii and Appendix IV, especially views of Lord Hugh Cecil and A. V. Dicey.

1922 Mr. Baldwin was appointed Prime Minister at a time when Lord Curzon might have been appointed. There were definite reasons for that appointment in 1922. It was the King's view, we are told, that 'since the Labour Party constituted the official opposition in the House of Commons and were unrepresented in the House of Lords, the objections to a Prime Minister in the Upper Chamber were insuperable'.[1] But there is nothing to suggest that George V in appointing Mr. Baldwin accepted or enunciated an obligatory rule to the effect that the Prime Minister for the future must be a member of the House of Commons. The most that can be said is that he followed the practice usual since 1902. There is a usage, no more. It is obvious that the existence of a variety of usages without any single obligatory convention must lead to vagueness, confusion, and misunderstanding in the exercise by the King of some of his most important powers.[2] But the fact remains that the number of genuine, accepted conventions in this sphere is few. In the opinion of some writers there should be more of them.

For, as has been said, conventions can be created by agreed declaration, and can be written down in an agreed form. The parliamentary procedure of the House of Commons and House of Lords has for the most part been adopted in this form, and now comprises an important body of conventional rules regulating the entire legislative process.[3] These rules exercise an important

[1] Ronaldshay, *Life of Lord Curzon*, vol. i, p. 352.

[2] This is the paramount conclusion of Mr. Justice Evatt's book. His remedy would be not to commit agreed conventions to writing in a non-legal form (which, in the view of the present writer, has much to commend it), but to enact the appropriate rules, to translate them into strictly legal form. See *op. cit.*, p. 289.

[3] See G. F. Campion, *Introduction to the Procedure of the House of Com-*

effect upon the working of the system of responsible
government in Great Britain, and must be ranked as
equal in importance to the other usages and conventions which have also assisted in the development of that
system. Such a rule, for example, as that embodied in
Standing Order 63 of the House of Commons is a major
constitutional principle:

This House will receive no petition for any sum relating
to the public service, or proceed upon any motion for a
grant or charge upon the public revenue, whether payable
out of the consolidated fund or out of money to be provided
by parliament, unless recommended from the crown.[1]

And there are rules which regulate the committee system
in the House of Commons, which regulate the discussion
of public affairs, and which govern the relations between
the executive and the legislature. All these rules are non-
legal, in the sense that they do not receive recognition in
an ordinary court of law.

The view that constitutional change in Great Britain
takes place solely or almost entirely through the operation of usage and convention, leaving the façade of strict
law unaltered, is due very largely to the great promi-
nence given—and rightly given—by constitutional his-
torians to one very important constitutional change
which did take place, in the main, by this method, viz.
the development of the system of Cabinet Government.

-mons; Sir T. Erskine May, *A Treatise on the Law, Privileges, Proceedings and
Usage of Parliament* (14th ed., 1946). The present writer has classified
such rules as the standing orders of the House of Commons under the
heading of conventions. Cf. Dicey, *op. cit.*, p. 28. Jennings appears to
favour a classification which includes such rules under a separate heading
of 'the law and custom of parliament'. *The Law and the Constitution*, p. 55.

[1] This rule, or something like it, has been in operation since the begin-
ning of the eighteenth century.

While France experimented with the twelve 'written' constitutions which have been framed for her since 1789,[1] and, as Campbell-Bannerman's remark suggests, really altered nothing fundamental; in England the transition was made from the system of a royal executive to that of a parliamentary executive, without the formulation in a single rule of strict law of the essential principles involved. But while in no constitutional structure are usage and convention more obviously and more extensively operative than in the British structure, none the less rules of strict law, and in particular statutory enactments, are an integral part of the structure, and are an increasingly important medium through which changes in it are brought about. The Reform Act of 1832, the Ballot Act of 1872, and the Parliament Act of 1911, are each as important and as fundamental as any conventional rule.

One further elementary point may be mentioned to assist in placing the relation of rules of strict law and non-legal rules in its true perspective. Those who stress the fact that Great Britain has no written Constitution, appreciate the importance of non-legal rules, such as usages and conventions, in such a constitutional structure. But they often overlook the fact that in states which possess a written Constitution, not only are many constitutional rules of strict law to be found outside the terms of the Constitution, but also non-legal constitutional rules, in the form of usages and conventions, occupy an important place in the constitutional structure.[2] In other words, such critics tend to overlook the fact that in all states, as has been said, there is a constitutional

[1] Adopting Dicey's enumeration of them in *Law of the Constitution* (9th ed.), p. 129.   [2] Dicey, *op. cit.*, pp. 28–9.

structure, a collection of rules which regulate and establish political institutions, and these rules are in part rules of strict law, and in part non-legal rules. Usages and conventions are no less necessary in a constitutional structure of which part is inscribed in a Constitution, than they are in a constitutional structure which contains no Constitution. In France,[1] Sweden, and the United States, for example, where there is a Constitution, there exists also an additional body of rules of strict law in the form of statutes, executive orders, and judicial decisions. There exists, further, a body of non-legal rules in the form of usages and conventions. Thus in France and the United States the unique position occupied by committees of the two Houses of the Legislature in the conduct of legislative business is based upon the rules of parliamentary procedure adopted by these houses.[2] Usage and convention govern the exercise in France of the legal powers explicitly conferred upon the President in the Constitution of 1875. His right of dissolving the Chamber, with the consent of the Senate, has fallen into disuse; his legislative veto has never been exercised; his extensive powers as chief executive are exercised on the advice of ministers. Usage and convention have initiated and established in Sweden a system of cabinet government, where the principle of the responsibility of the executive to the two Houses of Parliament jointly is gradually being recognized. In this way the elaborate Swedish Constitution of 1806 has been considerably modified, and the preponderating power

[1] The references here and throughout are to the Third Republic.
[2] For France see, e.g., Joseph-Barthélemy, *Essai sur le travail parlementaire et le système des Commissions*; and R. K. Gooch, *The French Parliamentary Committee System*. For the United States see W. F. Willoughby, *Principles of Legislative Organisation and Administration*.

within it is now the legislature rather than the executive. In the United States the most striking case of constitutional change through the operation of convention is found in the exercise of the powers of the presidential electors. Their function, as provided in the Constitution, was intended to be one of deliberation, but they act now merely as an automatic register of the wishes of the electorate. Indeed, as Dicey remarked, 'it may be asserted without much exaggeration that the conventional element in the constitution of the United States is now as large as in the English constitution'.[1]

3

It is then the interaction and co-operation of rules of strict law and non-legal rules which is characteristic of all constitutional structures, and of none more than the British. This interaction and co-operation take a variety of forms. Sometimes the two kinds of rule supplement each other in the regulation of a given sphere, without impingeing upon or modifying or nullifying the operation of each other. A good example of this in the United Kingdom is the position of such institutions as those of Prime Minister, Cabinet, Leader of the Opposition and Party. All four are recognized and, to a small degree, regulated, in the Ministers of the Crown Act,

[1] *Op. cit.*, p. 28, note 1. The whole subject of the place and importance of convention in the American constitutional structure has been discussed illuminatingly by H. W. Horwill in *The Usages of the American Constitution*. He excludes any discussion of the rules regulating the committee system and similar topics on the ground that they are mere rules of parliamentary procedure and cannot be ranked as conventions. *Op. cit.*, p. 197. This distinction does not appear to the present writer to be justified.

1937, but their status and functions otherwise remain governed largely by usage and convention alone.[1] In a similar way the legislatures in France and the United States are regulated as to their powers and composition by rules of strict law set out in the Constitution and in statutes, and, as to their procedure and relations with each other, by non-legal rules in the form of rules of procedure and other usages and conventions.

The two kinds of rule again may impinge upon each other in such a way that the operation of the rule of strict law is modified by the operation of the non-legal rule. A power which, juridically, is conferred upon a person or body of persons may be transferred, guided, canalized by the operation of non-legal rules. In this way a non-legal rule may decide the ends for which and the organs through which some power, which owes its existence to a rule of strict law, may properly be exercised. The rule of strict law is not completely nullified. It is combined with a non-legal rule to make a new constitutional rule. The working of the cabinet system in Britain illustrates this type of co-operation. The legal power in the hands of the King, by prerogative or under statute, to perform certain (not very extensive) functions in the administrative government of the country is exercised, by usage and convention, through and on the advice of ministers responsible to Parliament. In the same way the exercise of the legal executive powers of the President in France has, largely as the result of usage and convention, been transferred to ministers in Parliament, and the effective exercise of the legal power of the College of Electors in the United States to choose a president has been transferred to the electorate.

[1] The Act is 1 Ed. 8 & 1 Geo. 6, c. 38.

Or again a rule of strict law may be nullified by convention in such a way that the powers which the rule of strict law conferred may cease to operate altogether. It would appear that the legal power of the President in France to dissolve the Chamber of Deputies, with the advice and consent of the Senate, is now by convention constitutionally inoperable. It was thought, too, before 1909 that the legal power of the House of Lords to reject or amend a money Bill duly passed by the Commons had been rendered constitutionally inoperable. Redlich wrote in 1907:

... It is now both true in fact and accepted as a principle of constitutional law that the House of Lords is excluded from influence on money matters and it can never expect to reassert a claim to possess any. The immensely important constitutional reform ... was completed without alteration or enactment of a single rule of law, and its establishment vividly illustrates the incomparable elasticity of the British constitution and its contempt for juristic construction and dogmatic formulation.[1]

This comment by Redlich, coming so soon before the passing of the Parliament Act, directs attention at once to the limitations upon non-legal rules as a medium of constitutional change. In the first place, they cannot always nullify or modify a rule of strict law. In the second place, though they may nullify a rule of strict law, they do not and cannot abolish it. They may 'paralyse'[2] a limb of the law, but they cannot amputate it. Or, to

[1] J. Redlich, *The Procedure of the House of Commons*, vol. iii, p. 118.
[2] The word is used by Professor J. J. Chevallier. He writes: 'Sans détruire le droit strict, les conventions constitutionnelles le paralysent, l'écartent en fait, le cantonnent dans la théorie.' See his article 'Les Origines et le sens du Statut de Westminster' in *Revue de Droit International*, No. 2, 1936.

return to the metaphor which Campbell-Bannerman used, non-legal rules may do much to convert an old rambling mansion into a modern house, but they cannot make new windows in the old façade to let in necessary light and air. But it is often just such alterations as these in the old façade which are absolutely essential if the alterations behind the façade are really to be effective. A statute may be needed, for example, to carry a constitutional change, initiated and partially established by convention, to an effective conclusion. The passing of the Parliament Act in 1911 is an example of this translation and extension of a conventional ruling by its embodiment in the juridical form of a statute. It was not enough to have a convention that the Lords ought not to interfere in money Bills. The experience of 1909 showed that it was necessary, if the principle was to be effective, to lay down the further rule that, if they did interfere, their interference would have no effect in strict law. And a rule of strict law was necessary to effect this change.

The choice between rules of strict law and non-legal rules, and in particular between statute and convention, is determined by a variety of considerations. It is clear that some constitutional rules are not translatable into statutory terms; it is clear that others, for the sake of flexibility, ought not to be translated. But in many cases the choice is determined by the question: What sort of change is contemplated? Is it a change which, to be effective, must be recognized by the Courts and enforceable through judicial process? Or is it a change which can be made effective without such recognition, and perhaps could not be effectively enforced through judicial process? In accordance with the answer to this sort of question, it will be decided whether a statute is or is not necessary to effect the change. In many cases it becomes clear that, given the intention to make a change, a convention is not enough. The convention must be translated into or supplemented by a statute.

It cannot be pretended that this emphasis on the association and interaction of rules of strict law with non-legal rules is a new principle in the study of the British constitutional structure. It was already set out in classic form by Dicey as long ago as 1885 in the first edition of his *Law of the Constitution*. But the old misconceptions flourish, and when the Statute of Westminster was proposed, there were many critics who professed to see in it something repugnant to 'the spirit of the constitution', not because of the terms of the Statute but because it was a statute. It has seemed necessary therefore to assert that there is no prima facie reason to condemn the making of a constitutional change in a British system by means of a statute.

II
DOMINION STATUS IN 1926—I

I

'WHAT does "Dominion Status" mean?' asked Mr. Lloyd George in the House of Commons on December 14, 1921.[1] He was speaking on the motion that the House approve the Articles of Agreement for a Treaty between Great Britain and Ireland, signed on December 6, 1921,[2] in the opening words of which it was stated that 'Ireland shall have the same constitutional status in the Community of Nations known as the British Empire as the Dominion of Canada, the Commonwealth of Australia, the Dominion of New Zealand, and the Union of South Africa. . . .' It was, said Mr. Lloyd George, 'difficult and dangerous to give a definition'. Indeed he explained that at an Imperial Conference held earlier in the year all the Dominion delegates had been anxious to avoid a rigid definition. They had felt that to define precisely was 'not the way of the British constitution'. 'Many of the Premiers delivered notable speeches in the course of that Conference, emphasizing the importance of not defining too precisely what the relations of the Dominions were with ourselves, what were their powers, and what was the limit of the power of the Crown. It is something that has never been defined by an Act of Parliament, even in this country, and yet it works perfectly.'

[1] 149 *H.C. Deb.*, 5 s., 27–8. Part of the speech is printed in Keith, *Speeches and Documents on the British Dominions*, pp. 83–97.

[2] Scheduled to the Irish Free State (Agreement) Act, 1922 (12 Geo. 5, c. 4) and the Irish Free State Constitution Act, 1922 (Sess. 2) (13 Geo. 5, sess. 2, c. 1). Printed in Keith, *ibid.*, pp. 77–83.

It was on the whole true. In 1901 the words 'the British Dominions beyond the Seas' were added to the Royal Titles. 'Dominions' here meant possessions, territories, or lands. It was intended to cover all such British territories and possessions, and it included therefore the non-self-governing communities as well as those which were called 'self-governing'.

At the Colonial Conference of 1907 the representatives of the self-governing communities persuaded the United Kingdom that the phrase 'self-governing Dominions' should be used to describe themselves and to mark them off from the non-self-governing British Dominions beyond the seas.[1] This phrase obtained legal recognition in a few United Kingdom Acts in 1911.[2] Quite soon the phrase was shortened, for brevity's sake, to 'Dominions' with 'self-governing' understood, and, so far, undefined. In 1917 the Imperial War Conference passed a resolution that the readjustment of the constitutional relations of the component parts of the Empire was too important and too intricate a subject to be dealt with during the war, and 'should form the subject of a special Imperial Conference to be summoned as soon as possible after the cessation of hostilities'. That readjustment, they declared,

while thoroughly preserving all existing powers of self-government and complete control of domestic affairs, should be based upon a full recognition of the Dominions as autonomous nations of an Imperial Commonwealth, ... should recognise [their] right to an adequate voice in foreign policy and in foreign relations, and should provide effective arrangements for continuous consultation in all important

[1] See discussion in Cd. 3523, especially pp. 78–83.
[2] e.g. 1 & 2 Geo. 5, cc. 46 and 47.

matters of common Imperial concern, and for such necessary concerted action, founded on consultation, as the several Governments may determine.[1]

But in 1921 no action was taken. The majority of the Conference appeared to acquiesce in the view of Mr. W. M. Hughes, the Prime Minister of Australia, that there was no need 'to set down in black and white the relations between Britain and the Dominions'. 'In effect', he said, 'we have all the rights of self-government enjoyed by independent nations. That being the position, what is the Constitutional Conference going to do?' 'Let us leave well alone. That is my advice.' 'What other worlds have we to conquer? ... I know of no power that the Prime Minister of Britain has, that General Smuts has not.'[2]

General Smuts could not afford to be so contented. He had said in 1917 that

although in practice there is great freedom, yet in actual theory the status of the Dominions is of a subject character. Whatever we may say, and whatever we may think, we are subject Provinces of Great Britain. That is the actual theory of the Constitution, and in many ways which I need not specify to-day that theory still permeates practice to some extent.[3]

The position had not changed in 1921, and General Smuts had not changed his view that 'too much ... of the old ideas still clings to the new organism', and that a careful restatement of theory could do no harm, and might do good. Indeed, as he told the Conference of

---

[1] Cd. 8566, p. 5. Printed in Keith, *British Colonial Policy*, vol. ii, pp. 376–7.
[2] Cmd. 1474, pp. 22–3. Printed in Keith, *Speeches and Documents on the British Dominions*, pp. 54–6.   [3] Cd. 8566, p. 47.

1921, he had fought in 1920 and in 1921 two elections on the issue of South Africa's secession from the Empire[1] and had attempted to counter the secession movement by explaining to the people of South Africa 'that they were no longer in the position of a subordinate British colony as they had been before'. Theoretical politics were and are practical politics in South Africa. These inequalities of strict law did not appear to General Smuts or to South African politicians as 'figments', or 'a few ancient forms', as Mr. Hughes called them.[2] But the majority of the Conference was passive. The proposal for a constitutional conference lapsed.

In 1921, therefore, the Dominions could be defined only in terms of the 1917 Resolution as 'autonomous nations of an Imperial Commonwealth', entitled to a voice in the conduct of foreign relations. Further than that it was possible to define Dominion Status only by enumeration. Dominion Status was, that is to say, the Status enjoyed by Canada, Australia, New Zealand, South Africa, and Newfoundland. And Mr. Lloyd George found himself in the end reduced to this definition. 'All we can say', he said, 'is that whatever measure of freedom Dominion status gives to Canada, Australia, New Zealand or South Africa, that will be extended to Ireland . . .'[3] So the position rested in 1921.

By 1926 there had come a change. Australia, New Zealand, and Newfoundland, it is true, still showed no taste for theoretical questions. But they were prepared to acquiesce. In South Africa, General Smuts had been out of office since 1924. He had been succeeded by General Hertzog, his opponent in the elections fought

[1] S. G. Millin, *General Smuts*, vol. ii, pp. 296–7.
[2] Cmd. 1474, p. 22.   [3] 149 *H.C. Deb.*, 5 s., 28.

on the issue of secession, the protagonist of South Africa's right to secede from the British Empire. General Hertzog came to the Conference of 1926 pledged to obtain the declaration and assertion of this right.

From Canada came Mr. Mackenzie King, a Liberal Prime Minister, convinced by two recent events that theoretical issues could become practical politics. He had been refused a dissolution by Lord Byng, the Governor-General, and had resigned office on June 28, 1926. Mr. Meighen, the Conservative Leader, had assumed office; a vote of censure had been passed upon him; he had asked the Governor-General to grant him a dissolution, and the dissolution had been granted. In the event Mr. Mackenzie King won the election and resumed office. Mr. Mackenzie King thought that the refusal of a dissolution to him and the grant of a dissolution to Mr. Meighen was a breach of the constitutional convention which had governed the relation of the Sovereign and his ministers in the United Kingdom and which, if Canada enjoyed equal status in its internal affairs with the United Kingdom, should govern the relations of the Governor-General and his ministers.[1] No less an authority than Professor Berriedale Keith had declared that

Lord Byng, in refusing the dissolution of Parliament advised by Rt. Hon. Mackenzie King, has challenged effectively the doctrine of equality in status of the Dominions and the United Kingdom, and has relegated Canada decisively to the colonial status which we believed she had outgrown.[2]

There occurred also in 1926 the judgement of the Judicial Committee of the Privy Council in *Nadan* v. *the King*,[3]

[1] See speech during election campaign, printed in Keith, *Speeches and Documents on the British Dominions*, at p. 152.
[2] Keith, *ibid.*, pp. 152–3.   [3] [1926] A.C. 482.

in which it was held that legislation of the Canadian Parliament purporting to abolish the appeal in criminal cases to the Judicial Committee of the Privy Council by special leave of the Judicial Committee was invalid. It was held first, that such legislation was repugnant to Imperial legislation extending to the Dominion and was therefore void under the Colonial Laws Validity Act, 1865; and secondly, that such legislation could only be effective if construed as having an extra-territorial operation, and according to the law as it was in 1926 the Dominion statute could not have extra-territorial operation. These, then, were four points of subordination in theory which, in General Smuts's words 'still permeates practice to some extent'—the status of the Governor-General, the operation of the Colonial Laws Validity Act, the lack of power to legislate with extra-territorial effect, and the existence of the appeal by special leave to the Privy Council.

There was a third important difference in the personnel of the Conference of 1926 from that of 1921. The Irish Free State was now a member. Its representatives were inevitably concerned in Canadian inequalities because Ireland's status in the British Commonwealth, though stated in general to be the same as that of all the other Dominions, had been linked in particular with that of Canada in so far as its relations to the Crown, the Imperial Parliament, and the Imperial Government were concerned. The Irish representatives objected particularly to the existence of the appeal by special leave to the Privy Council, and they came to the Conference of 1926 determined to do all they could to remove this particular inequality.

In 1926, then, the task of readjustment and redefinition which had been envisaged in 1917, which had been shelved in 1921, and which had lain dormant in 1923, was at last taken in hand. It might be that, as Mr. Lloyd George said in 1921, 'it is difficult and dangerous to give a definition', but it was felt that it was still more dangerous not to give a definition. The Dominions and Great Britain, therefore, began the task of definition in 1926; they continued it in 1929, and in 1930, and they enacted some portion of their definitions in the Statute of Westminster, 1931. But the end of their definitions is not yet.

2

They began in 1926 with that element in the concept of Dominion Status which could be described in non-legal rules. On October 25 the Conference appointed a Committee under the chairmanship of Lord Balfour, to investigate all the questions on the Conference agenda affecting 'Inter-Imperial Relations'.[1] In their Report to the Conference[2] the Committee stated that they were of opinion that 'nothing would be gained by attempting

[1] The term 'inter-imperial relations' has been commonly used in official and unofficial publications to describe the relations between parts of the British Empire. The term is inaccurate. The relations it purports to describe are not relations between empires—which is what 'inter-imperial' means—but relations between parts of a single empire. It would seem therefore that the word 'imperial' would be sufficient, but if a contrast is to be made with 'international relations', the word 'intra-imperial' might be used. When it is proposed to describe the relations of those parts of the British Empire which are associated as Members of the British Commonwealth of Nations, i.e. of Great Britain and the Dominions, it seems best to speak of 'British Commonwealth Relations' or of 'Commonwealth Relations'—clumsy terms, it is true, but accurate. Professor A. J. Toynbee has done a service in popularizing these terms in his *British Commonwealth Relations*, a record of an unofficial conference held in Toronto in 1933.

[2] Cmd. 2768, pp. 13–30; Keith, *Speeches and Documents on the British Dominions*, pp. 161–70, 380–91.

to lay down a Constitution for the British Empire.' But
they went on to say that there was one important element
in the British Empire, which, from a strictly constitutional point of view, had now, as regards all vital matters,
reached its full development—they referred to the group
of self-governing communities composed of Great
Britain and the Dominions. 'Their position and mutual
relation may be readily defined.' The definition followed in italics:

*They are autonomous Communities within the British Empire,
equal in status, in no way subordinate one to another in any aspect
of their domestic or external affairs, though united by a common
allegiance to the Crown, and freely associated as members of the
British Commonwealth of Nations.*[1]

It has never been absolutely certain what this Declaration meant. It had all the advantages of flexibility and
ambiguity, and all the disadvantages. It could be all
things to all men. It embodied with admirable skill the
difference of emphasis which each Dominion wished to
place upon the terms of its status. On the one hand,
for South Africa and the Irish Free State, they were
autonomous communities—but, on the other hand, for
New Zealand and Australia, say, they were within the
British Empire; they were equal, there was no subordination, but they were united by a common allegiance to
the Crown; they were free, but they were also associated.
The full implications of the definition were not realized
in 1926. It was not until an attempt was made to translate some aspects of its non-legal terms into rules of strict
law, that its true significance came to be estimated. The
importance of the Balfour Report was under-estimated

[1] Cmd. 2768, p. 14.

in 1926, and in consequence the importance of the
Statute of Westminster was over-estimated in 1931.

It may be worth while, in spite of the ambiguity of the
declaration, to set down a few propositions which seem
to be asserted, and about which there can be little
doubt. It is to be noted that there is no reference in the
Declaration, or indeed anywhere in the Report, to the
phrase 'Dominion Status'. The Declaration does not
define 'Dominion Status'. It defines the status of a
Member of the British Commonwealth of Nations, and
it declares that this status is enjoyed by Great Britain and
the Dominions. But it is possible from a study of the
Declaration to discover what sort of status is conferred
upon the Dominions.[1]

There appear to be three distinguishing characteristics of the Dominions. First, they were marked off from
the rest of the political world by the characteristic that
they were territorial communities, other than Great
Britain, which shared with Great Britain a common
allegiance to the Crown; they all had the same king. It
was not quite certain what this meant. It might mean
that George V, and any successor, was in a separate
capacity King of Great Britain, King of Canada, King
of South Africa, and so on; that the same man was King
of Great Britain and of each of the Dominions inasmuch
as and insofar as each of these units agreed to owe
allegiance to this man as King. On this theory the
Dominions and Great Britain formed a personal union,
much as Hanover and Great Britain had formed a personal union under George I. Or, it might mean, on the

---

[1] Dominion Status has been analysed shortly and clearly by Professor
R. Coupland in a letter to *The Times*, Feb. 20, 1935 and reprinted as a
postscript to his *The Empire in These Days*, pp. 275–6.

other hand, that George V and any successor was recognized as King, in a single capacity, of Great Britain and the Dominions; that there was one Kingship and not seven Kingships. The Conference of 1926 gave no guidance on this point. General Hertzog, as General Smuts had done before him,[1] might adopt the first view; the Prime Minister of New Zealand perhaps might adopt the second view; the representative of the Irish Free State would do well to show no interest in kings. But whatever it meant, the first essential of Dominion Status was clearly the acceptance by each territorial community concerned of allegiance, along with Great Britain, to the same King.

By this criterion the Dominions were distinguished in status from foreign nations in international law and relations. They were shown to be 'within the British Empire'. But, thus far, they are not distinguished from other portions of the British Empire. India equally with Great Britain and the Dominions owed allegiance to the Crown; all the territorial communities within the British Empire owed allegiance in some form or another. How were the Dominions to be distinguished from these other communities? There was a second criterion. The Dominions were all equal in status to Great Britain; and, consequently they were all equal in status to one another. They were 'in no way subordinate one to another in any aspect of their domestic or external affairs'. Equality is a difficult term. It is not certain what are its full implications here. Put positively, how-

---

[1] Millin, *op. cit.*, vol. ii, p. 301. In 1919 General Smuts had said: 'My view is that the British Empire is an alliance of free states in which we have one king, and that is the bond which keeps us together. . . . He is the King of England, King of India and King of South Africa and other parts.'

ever, it may be suggested that equality of status meant that whatever the Parliament and Government of Great Britain could do, constitutionally and in international law, to regulate its domestic and external affairs, that also the Parliament and Government of each Dominion might do, subject of course to any limitations of legal power which each community might see fit to impose upon its Parliament or Government.

Put negatively, it meant that the Parliament and Government of each Dominion, in conducting its domestic and external affairs, was to be in no way subject to control by the Parliament and Government of any other Dominion or of Great Britain; that, in other words, each Dominion was to possess sole and exclusive responsibility for the conduct of its domestic and external affairs. That is to say, the Dominions were not necessarily to have the same constitutional structure as Great Britain;[1] but, whatever their constitutional structure, they were to be free from external control by the constitutional structure of Great Britain. The Dominions acquired the same rights as Great Britain in this sense only and to this extent only, that they acquired those rights which Great Britain enjoyed to conduct her

[1] Mr. Mackenzie King and Professor Keith in their criticism (already referred to) of Lord Byng's action in 1926 in refusing a dissolution to Mr. Mackenzie King suggest that because Lord Byng did not act in relation to his ministers in Canada as the King would have acted in relation to his Ministers in the United Kingdom, therefore Canada was unequal in status to the United Kingdom. This does not follow unless, as was not the case, Lord Byng's action had been carried out under orders from the United Kingdom Government. Provided there was no external control the alleged fact that Lord Byng acted differently in Canada from the King in the United Kingdom is no more relevant to the question of equality of status than would be the fact that Lord Byng acted differently from the President of France in similar circumstances. Identity of structure is to be distinguished from equality of status.

domestic and external affairs upon her own responsibility, in no way subordinate to any other community. Great Britain had autonomy; the Dominions too had autonomy. Equality of status meant therefore not necessarily identity of structure, but autonomy for each and all. And for this reason, it would appear, the Declaration speaks of the Dominions and Great Britain as 'autonomous communities', and it follows the words 'equal in status' with the explanatory clause, 'in no way subordinate one to another in any aspect of their domestic or external affairs'. It was made clear, too, that this was a declaration of constitutional capacity to acquire and exercise rights, and not of political capacity or intention to acquire and exercise these rights. Constitutionally, that is, each had an equal right to autonomy, an equal right to equal rights. But it need not exercise the right unless it chose.

. . . The principles of equality and similarity, appropriate to *status*, do not universally extend to function. . . . For example, to deal with questions of diplomacy and questions of defence, we require also flexible machinery—machinery which can, from time to time, be adapted to the changing circumstances of the world.[1]

And when later the Committee came to report their conclusions upon foreign affairs, they said:

It was frankly recognised that in this sphere, as in the sphere of defence, the major share of responsibility rests now, and must for some time continue to rest, with His Majesty's Government in Great Britain.[2]

There was a third undoubted criterion of Dominion Status. It was not enough to say that the Dominions

---

[1] Cmd. 2768, pp. 14–15.   [2] *Ibid.*, pp. 25–6.

shared with Great Britain allegiance to the same King; and that they were equal in status to Great Britain. Something must be said to describe the kind of aggregate which they formed. Was it a federation, a confederation, an alliance, a union? It was described as a 'free association'. What did that mean? Did it mean that the Dominions and Great Britain agreed to describe their relationship as it then existed in 1926 in this way: Of our own free will, we are associated together in the British Commonwealth of Nations? Or did it imply more than that? Did it mean on the one hand, we here and now, of our own free will, permanently associate ourselves into an indissoluble British Commonwealth of Nations? or did it mean on the other hand, we are associated in this British Commonwealth because, of our own free will, we have decided to be so associated, and for so long as, of our own free will, we decide to be so associated? In other words, was the right to secede implicitly denied or explicitly declared in the words 'freely associated'? General Hertzog maintained that the right to secede had been accepted and declared. He was satisfied. The wording was flexible and ambiguous. There was no definite pronouncement upon the point. It could be left to look after itself. On one fact, however, there was no ambiguity or disagreement. The relationship between Great Britain and the Dominions and between one Dominion and another was one of free association. If at any time that association ceased to be a free association, if it was maintained against the free will of a Dominion, then, to that extent that Dominion lacked complete Dominion Status.

In 1926, therefore, an attempt was made to define Dominion Status in non-legal terms, and the essentials of this definition are to be found concentrated in the italicized portion of the Balfour Report. It laid down three indisputable elements in Dominion Status. A Dominion was a territorial community, other than Great Britain, which, first, owed allegiance to the King in common with Great Britain; and secondly, was equal in status to Great Britain; and thirdly, was freely associated with Great Britain. All these three elements were essential. But, of the three, it was recognized that one was fundamental—equality of status. The Committee said: 'Equality of status, so far as Britain and the Dominions are concerned, is thus the root principle governing our Inter-Imperial Relations.'[1]

This equality of status, however, had been declared and accepted in non-legal terms only. The rules of strict law remained unaltered, though not unaffected, by this conventional rule. Secondly, the declaration had been made in general terms only, and there still persisted particular conventional rules regulating certain aspects of the relations of Great Britain and the Dominions which were inconsistent with the general conventional declaration of equal status. 'Existing administrative, legislative, and judicial forms', said the Committee, 'are admittedly not wholly in accord with the position as described in . . . this Report.'[2] Could these legal and non-legal inequalities be made to co-operate easily and without friction with the general convention of equality? The Committee investigated this question: 'Our first task', they said, 'was to examine these forms with special reference to any cases where the want of adaptation of practice to principle caused, or might be thought to cause, inconvenience in the conduct of Inter-Imperial Relations.'[3]

[1] Cmd. 2768, p. 14.   [2] Ibid., p. 15.   [3] Ibid., p. 15.

The eight inequalities of status which the Committee recognized and discussed may be set out briefly here. To some of them reference has already been made. There was first a legal inequality of status which was held to arise from the form of the title of His Majesty the King. The King was described, in the title proclaimed under the Royal Titles Act of 1901 as follows:

George V, by the Grace of God, of the United Kingdom of Great Britain and Ireland and of the British Dominions beyond the Seas King, Defender of the Faith, Emperor of India.

This reference to 'the United Kingdom of Great Britain and Ireland' was not in accordance, it was felt, with the separate existence of the Irish Free State as a Dominion. There was, in the second place, an inequality of status, by law and convention, in the position of the Governor-General of a Dominion. There appear to be two points here. There was, first, the status of the Governor-General in relation to his ministers in the Dominion. By what constitutional rules was a Governor-General to be guided in his relations with his ministers? Was he to be guided by the same rules as those by which the King was guided in his relations with His Majesty's ministers in the United Kingdom or not? This did not necessarily involve any question of inequality of constitutional status in the relations of the Dominions and the United Kingdom. It was a question of difference in the constitutional structures of the Dominions as compared with the constitutional structure of the United Kingdom. The second aspect of the problem of the Governor-General's status did, however, involve a question of inequality of status as between the Dominions and the United Kingdom. In

strict law the Governor-General was the representative
of His Majesty, But, as His Majesty acted, by law or
by convention, on the advice of His Majesty's Government in the United Kingdom, the Governor-General
might seem to be the representative of that Government.
Therefore a part of the constitutional structure of the
Dominion was under the control, in practice, of a part
of the constitutional structure of the United Kingdom.
Thirdly, another legal inequality of status arose from
the power in the hands of the King, exercised upon the
advice of His Majesty's ministers in the United Kingdom,
to disallow, within a specified period, acts duly passed by
certain of the Dominion legislatures and assented to by
the Governor-General.[1] A fourth inequality of status
was of a similar kind. It was the power of reservation,
by which the Governor-General of a Dominion, in
certain circumstances, withheld his assent from a Bill
duly passed by the Dominion legislature, and reserved
it for the signification of His Majesty's pleasure; and His
Majesty, acting upon the advice of his ministers in the
United Kingdom, thereafter signified his pleasure. The
fifth element of inequality of status—a legal inequality—
was held to arise from the fact that the parliaments of
the Dominions were, as a general rule, unable to pass
laws possessing extra-territorial effect, whereas laws
passed by the United Kingdom Parliament might
possess extra-territorial effect.[2]

---

[1] The power did not exist in respect of the Irish Free State.

[2] This difference in power did not of itself constitute, in the view of the
present writer, an element of subordination on the part of the Dominion
legislatures to the United Kingdom legislature. The inequality arose
because the difference in power was imposed upon the Dominion legislatures by the United Kingdom legislature, and, as a result of the difference in power, the Dominion legislatures were dependent upon the

Sixthly, an element of legal inequality of status arose from the legislative supremacy of the United Kingdom Parliament, and was expressed, for example, in the Colonial Laws Validity Act, 1865, where it was provided that any colonial law repugnant to the terms of an Act of the United Kingdom Parliament extending to the colony (and in the law the Dominions were still colonies) by express words or necessary intendment, was, to the extent of such repugnancy, but not otherwise, void and inoperative. A seventh inequality of status arose from the existence of a right to ask for leave to appeal, in certain circumstances, from the courts of a Dominion to the Judicial Committee of the Privy Council, a legal inequality imposed by an Act of the United Kingdom Parliament, and in certain cases unalterable and irremovable by the Dominion legislatures. Finally, there was a legal[1] and conventional inequality of status in that in the conduct of foreign relations, His Majesty's Government in the United Kingdom might still advise His Majesty to commit the whole Empire to international obligations, though their freedom to do so had already, and especially in 1923, been restricted by conventions in certain respects.

Certain of these inequalities—for example reservation, disallowance, the operation of the Colonial Laws Validity Act, and the lack of extra-territorial power—were illustrated and were found in practice to be most irksome in the merchant shipping legislation of the

United Kingdom parliament to legislate for them with extra-territorial effect. See p. 81 below.

[1] It was legal because in this, as in the other acts of the King mentioned above, the King could not act with legal effect unless he had the co-operation of a minister. See e.g. Great Seal Act, 1889. Cf. Dicey, *op. cit.*, c. xi.

Empire. This whole subject therefore required consideration along with the wider question of inequalities in general.

The Inter-Imperial Relations Committee of 1926 was able to arrive at certain conclusions upon some of the inequalities which have been enumerated. It put forward agreed recommendations upon the subject of the Title of His Majesty the King, upon the subject of the status of the Governor-General, and upon the subject of the appeal to the Judicial Committee of the Privy Council. It devoted a whole special section of its Report to the rules which should regulate the conduct of foreign relations in accordance with the principles of equality of status, common allegiance to the Crown, and free association.[1] For the remaining problems, the Committee felt unable to do more than lay down general principles which, in the light of the convention of equality, ought to govern their solutions. 'We felt that, for the rest, it would be necessary to obtain expert guidance as a preliminary to further consideration by His Majesty's Governments in Great Britain and the Dominions.'[2] The recommendations which the Committee put forward on all these points were adopted by the Conference. It is proposed to postpone a discussion of them until a later chapter,[3] when the whole question of the method by which all these legal and non-legal inequalities were removed will be considered. For the present it is necessary to narrate the next step which the Conference of 1926 felt obliged to take. The Committee proposed[4] and the Conference adopted the recommendation that a Committee, representative of Great Britain

[1] Cmd. 2768, pp. 20–31.
[2] *Ibid.*, p. 17.   [3] Chapter V.   [4] Cmd. 2768, p. 18.

and the Dominions, should be set up to inquire into,
report upon, and make recommendations concerning
reservation; disallowance; the Dominions' lack of power
to legislate with extra-territorial effect and 'the practicability and most convenient method of giving effect to the
principle that each Dominion Parliament should have
power to give extra-territorial operation to its legislation
in all cases where such operation is ancillary to provision
for the peace, order, and good government of the Dominion'; and finally the principles of the Colonial Laws
Validity Act, 1865, and the extent to which any provisions of that Act ought to be repealed, amended or
modified in the light of the conventional rules already
laid down in the Report. At the same time the Conference adopted a recommendation from the Inter-
Imperial Relations Committee that a special Sub-
Conference should be set up

to consider and report on the principles which should
govern, in the general interest, the practice and legislation
relating to merchant shipping in the various parts of the
Empire, having regard to the change in constitutional
status and general relations which has occurred since existing laws were enacted.[1]

When the problems referred to these two bodies came
to be examined more closely, it was realized that it would
be more convenient if the Committee and the special
Sub-Conference were organized in a single Conference.
After consultation between the respective Governments
this view was accepted, and, accordingly, the Conference
on the Operation of Dominion Legislation and Merchant
Shipping Legislation met in London from October 8 to
December 4, 1929. The Conference presented its Report

[1] Cmd. 2768, p. 19.

in January 1930,[1] and in it were set out in precise terms the extent of the restrictions imposed upon the Dominions, in so far as the Conference had been authorized to investigate them. The Report contained further a series of recommendations designed to remove, so far as was thought necessary, certain of these inequalities. Before considering these recommendations, however, it is proposed in this and the succeeding chapters to set out as briefly as possible the origin, nature, and extent of the legal and non-legal inequalities which the Conferences of 1926 and 1929 investigated and discussed, in order that these recommendations may be placed in their proper perspective, and, above all, that the true relevance of the Statute of Westminster to the task of removing legal inequalities, may be correctly displayed. It will be convenient to consider the overseas Dominions first, and thereafter the Irish Free State.

3

How was it possible for the Imperial Conference in 1926 to declare that Great Britain and the Dominions were 'equal in status, in no way subordinate one to another in any aspect of their domestic or external affairs,' and immediately thereafter to declare that 'existing administrative, legislative, and judicial forms' were not wholly in accordance with this position? This is the fundamental question in our inquiry.

The student of political institutions who reads the more important documents illustrative of constitutional developments in the British Empire from the Quebec Act

[1] Cmd. 3479. Referred to hereafter as *O.D.L. Report*. Extracts are printed in Keith, *Speeches and Documents on the British Dominions*, pp. 173–205.

of 1774 to the Statute of Westminster, 1931,[1] will conclude that statesmen in Great Britain and in the Colonies
were confronted during this period with three distinct
though not disconnected constitutional problems. There
was, first, the problem of finding a satisfactory constitutional structure through which to regulate the domestic
affairs of each separate colony. There was, secondly,
the problem of finding a satisfactory constitutional
structure through which to regulate affairs which,
though affecting the domestic interests of each separate
colony, affected also the interests of a group of such
colonies, territorially adjacent or contiguous—affairs,
that is to say, which though not domestic to a single
colony, were domestic to a group of colonies, as for
example the British North American colonies, the
Australian colonies, or the South African colonies.
There was, finally, the problem of finding a satisfactory
constitutional structure through which to regulate
affairs which, though affecting the domestic interests of
separate colonies or of a group of colonies territorially
adjacent or contiguous, affected also some other part of
the Empire or of the world, and were therefore 'external'
or 'imperial' affairs, and not merely colonial or inter-
colonial affairs. It is not suggested that these three
problems were chronologically separated, or that the
statesmen who attempted to solve them considered
them in logical separation.[2] They were connected and

[1] Professor Keith has collected these documents in *British Colonial
Policy, 1763–1917* (2 vols.) and *Speeches and Documents on the British
Dominions, 1918–1931*. Where possible, references are given in this book
to these collections of documents.

[2] Earl Grey, Secretary of State for Colonies, writing in 1847 to Sir
Charles FitzRoy, Governor of New South Wales, did, however, state the
three problems clearly. See K. N. Bell and W. P. Morrell, *Select Documents on British Colonial Policy, 1830–1860*, p. 94.

contemporaneous; they were attacked piecemeal, as time and opportunity determined.

The history of the attempt to solve the first problem is the history of the development of self-government in the domestic affairs of each separate colony through a system of responsible (i.e. cabinet) government; the history of the attempt to solve the second problem is the history of the establishment of a federation of the colonies in Canada and in Australia and of a union of the colonies in South Africa, and of the development therewith of self-government in respect of affairs domestic to the federations and the union through a system of responsible government; and the history of the attempt to solve the third problem is the history of the development of a free association of autonomous nations each entitled to co-operate upon a basis of equal status in the regulation of affairs external to each nation, that is to say of Commonwealth affairs. It is irrelevant to the purpose of this book to trace in even the broadest outline these three distinct but connected histories. But what is relevant is the method by which the changes took place, and the consequences of that method as displayed in the concept of Dominion Status in 1926. In the attempt to solve each problem it is found that rules of strict law and non-legal rules co-operated. Usage and convention combined with statute and prerogative to regulate existing institutions, to develop new institutions, to transform, to direct, and to nullify. And yet, when usage and convention have been allowed the fullest possible scope for their operation, the rules of strict law remain, unused or useless, it may be, but unrepealed also.

Consider then the attempt made to solve the first problem—that of finding a satisfactory form of constitutional structure through which to regulate the domestic affairs of each separate colony. What took place may be described in general terms, and subject to one or two exceptions, in this way. By the rules of strict law—in statutes, or in prerogative instruments,[1] as letters patent, the commission to the Governor, or the instructions to the Governor—the institutions of 'representative government' were established in the colony. By 'representative government' was not meant government by representatives. It was a system in which the administrative functions of government were placed in the hands of a Governor, appointed and removable by the Sovereign acting on the advice of the Secretary of State for the Colonies, and this Governor was required, except in certain matters, to act with the advice of an executive council, the members of which were appointed and, in most cases, were dismissible by him. The Governor was not required to act only with the consent of the executive council; indeed he was expressly instructed in some colonies to act in opposition to their advice if he thought fit.[2] The legislative functions of government were placed in

[1] e.g. representative government was established by prerogative instruments in Nova Scotia, Prince Edward Island, New Brunswick (see Houston, *Constitutional Documents of Canada*, pp. 7–23), and Newfoundland. In Upper and Lower Canada, on the other hand, the legislative institutions—including a representative assembly—were established by a statute, the Constitutional Act, 1791 (31 Geo. 3, c. 31), and the executive council was established and regulated by the prerogative instruments. In United Canada similarly an Act of 1840 established representative legislative institutions, whereas the prerogative instruments established the executive council. The same combination was found in the Australian colonies and in New Zealand when representative government was conferred there. In Cape Colony (1853) and in Natal (1856) representative government was established under the prerogative.

[2] See, e.g., instructions to Sydenham, Aug. 30, 1840. Printed in *Report of Canadian Archives*, 1905, vol. i, Sessional Paper No. 18, p. 116.

the hands of the Governor acting with the advice and consent of a nominated legislative council, and of an elected legislative assembly. There were some cases in the early development of representative government where legislation was carried on by the Governor acting with the advice and consent of a legislative council only, and this council was so constituted that a majority of its members were elected.[1] But the usual plan was that of the bicameral legislature, empowered with the Governor to make laws for the peace, order or public welfare, and good government of the colony. Representative government meant, that is to say, that elected representatives shared in the process of legislation, and their consent was necessary to legislation. On the other hand, the Governor was empowered to refuse his assent to Bills duly passed by the legislature, and to summon, prorogue, and dissolve the legislature.

As a general rule, so far as the elected portions of the legislature were concerned, there was a separation of personnel between executive and legislature. In some cases of representative government the executive council and the nominated legislative council consisted of the same persons, though by usage the executive council was a smaller body than the legislative council.[2] In some cases, too, where executive and legislative councils were separated a connexion between legislature and executive was maintained by the provision that members of a

[1] e.g. in New South Wales from 1842 to 1855 under 5 & 6 Vict., c. 76; and in South Australia, Victoria, and Tasmania as a result of the Australian Colonies Government Act, 1850 (13 & 14 Vict., c. 59) until the grant of responsible government in 1855-6.

[2] e.g. in Nova Scotia from 1758, when a representative assembly was first called, to 1838 when Lord Durham separated the executive and legislative councils. See Houston, *op. cit.*, p. 24, note 12.

nominated legislative council might be members also of
the executive council.[1] But in no case was it laid down
in the rules of strict law that members of the elected
branch of the legislature might be members of the
executive council.

The difference between the system of representative
government and the system of responsible government
may be shortly expressed by saying that under responsible government the Governor is obliged to appoint as
members of his executive council persons who can command a majority in the elected branch of the legislature,
and to carry out his administrative and legislative functions through and upon the advice of these persons, in
conformity with the wishes of the elected branch of the
legislature. It follows from this fundamental proposition that, as a corollary, the members of the executive
council to whom the Governor entrusts the administration of domestic affairs in the colony will usually be or
will soon become members of the legislature, and thus a
connexion is made between the executive council and the
elected branch of the legislature. It does not follow that
a Governor may not appoint as members of his executive council persons who cannot command a majority
of the elected legislature, but he must not entrust the
administration of the colony to such persons.

The change from representative government to responsible government could be brought about quite
simply, as Lord Durham said,[2] by a dispatch to a

[1] e.g. in Upper and Lower Canada under the Constitutional Act,
1791. See dispatch of Grenville to Dorchester, October 20, 1789, Keith,
British Colonial Policy, vol. i, pp. 91–2; and instructions to Dorchester, Sept.
16, 1791, *Report of Canadian Archives*, 1905, vol. i, Sessional Paper No. 18.

[2] *Report on the Affairs of British North America*. See extract in Keith,
British Colonial Policy, vol. i, p. 137.

Governor instructing him 'to secure the co-operation
of the Assembly in his policy, by entrusting its administration to such men as could command a majority'. It
would not be necessary to enact the conventional rules
of responsible government in terms of strict law. On the
other hand the change could have been brought about
by a statute. It could have been enacted that 'the official
acts of the Governor should be countersigned by some
public functionary';[1] that executive councillors should
be or should within some specified period become
members of the legislature; that the executive council should be composed of certain specified officers and
of no more; that executive councillors should resign
upon a vote of no confidence in the assembly, and so on.
The detailed rules would have been difficult to draft,
and much would have had to be left to usage. But the
fundamentals could have been enacted. In fact, however, no such process occurred. Responsible government was initiated in the colonies by dispatch from the
Secretary of State, and it was established and operated
by usage and convention. In Canada, for example, the
Act of Union of 1840[2] simply re-established the institutions of representative government which the Constitutional Act of 1791 had conferred. The initiation of
responsible government was made possible by a dispatch
from Lord John Russell to Poulett Thomson, the
Governor-General of Canada,[3] in which he stated that

[1] Durham, *op. cit.*, printed in Keith, *ibid.*, p. 137.

[2] 3 & 4 Vict., c. 35. Printed in W. P. M. Kennedy, *Statutes, Treaties
and Documents of the Canadian Constitution* (2nd ed., 1930), No. cxxi.

[3] Oct. 16, 1839. See Kennedy, *op. cit.*, No. cxiii. Russell had stated
quite clearly in his dispatch of Oct. 14, 1839 that responsible government
in a colony was impossible. Printed in Keith, *British Colonial Policy*,
vol. i, pp. 173–8, and in Kennedy, *op. cit.*, No. cxii.

the tenure of colonial offices held during Her Majesty's pleasure, will not be regarded as equivalent to a tenure during good behaviour; but that not only will such officers be called upon to retire from the public service as often as any sufficient motives of public policy may suggest the expediency of that measure, but that a change in the person of the governor will be considered as a sufficient reason for any alterations which his successor may deem it expedient to make. . . .

This dispatch, which was a circular dispatch to all the Governors, was intended merely to increase the Governors' control over their executive councils, but it gave an opportunity for Poulett Thomson and his successors, and for the Lieutenant-Governors of other British North American colonies, to experiment with the composition of their executive councils, until finally in 1847 Lord Elgin, as Governor-General of Canada, was able to establish the system of responsible government in Canada, in agreement with the dispatch and instructions of the Secretary of State for Colonies, by that time Earl Grey.[1] A similar dispatch from Grey to the Lieutenant-Governor of Nova Scotia in 1846 had initiated responsible government there.[2] The same process was adopted in the other colonies. A dispatch initiated the system, but it gave no detailed explanation of its working. The operation of responsible government was left to usage and convention. In this way a system of responsible government was initiated in Prince Edward Island in

[1] The story is told, with full documentation, in J. L. Morison, *British Supremacy and Canadian Self-Government*; *Cambridge History of the British Empire*, vol. vi, cc. xi and xii (also by J. L. Morison); Chester Martin, *Empire and Commonwealth*, cc. iv and v; W. P. M. Kennedy, *The Constitution of Canada*, cc. xii–xvi.

[2] Kennedy, *Statutes, &c.*, No. cxliii.

1851, in New Brunswick in 1854, in Newfoundland in 1855, in New Zealand in 1854, in the Australian colonies of New South Wales, Victoria, South Australia, and Tasmania in the years 1855-6, in Queensland in 1859, in Western Australia in 1890.[1] In the South African Colonies responsible government was initiated in Cape Colony in 1872, in Natal in 1893, and, after the Boer War, in the Transvaal in 1906 and in the Orange River Colony in 1907.

The extent to which responsible government was initiated and operated in the colonies by the use of non-legal rules must not be exaggerated. While it is true that the fundamental principle of responsible government, that the Governor should entrust the conduct of adminis-tration to executive councillors who could command a majority in the elected legislature, was nowhere enshrined in the Constitutions of the colonies, it is not true to say that in no case did the introduction of re-sponsible government involve consequential alterations in the rules of strict law. Quite apart from the necessity of passing legislation to provide for a Civil List, in certain colonies some minor statutory provisions were enacted as a result of the introduction of responsible government. In New South Wales[2] and Victoria,[3] for example, the Constitutions drawn up in anticipation of the establish-ment of responsible government drew a distinction between 'officers liable to retire from office on political grounds' and officers not so liable. The appointment of the latter officers was vested in the Governor with the

[1] The relevant dispatches to the Governors of the Australian colonies are printed in E. Sweetman, *Australian Constitutional Development*, Ap-pendix A.

[2] s. 37 of the Constitution Act, scheduled to 18 & 19 Vict. ,c. 54.

[3] s. 37 of the Constitution Act, scheduled to 18 & 19 Vict., c. 55.

advice of the executive council, while the appointment
of the former was vested in the Governor alone. This was
a distinction obviously consequential upon the establishment of an executive council the members of which
retained control of the administration inasmuch as and
for so long as they retained the confidence of the elected
legislature.[1] A substantially similar provision appeared
in the Constitutions of South Australia, Queensland, and
Western Australia.[2] The Constitutions of Victoria and
South Australia went further. They contained provisions[3]—amended and enlarged by subsequent legislation
—that a certain number of the officers of the government
were to be or were within a given period to become
members of the legislature. These provisions in the
Constitution of Victoria were sufficient to convince
Chief Justice Higinbotham, of the Supreme Court of
Victoria, that responsible government in Victoria was
established upon a statutory basis, and that it did not owe
its existence merely to a dispatch and to usage and convention.[4] But it seems clear that the fundamental rules
of responsible government are nowhere laid down in the
Victorian Act; such rules as are enacted occur conse-
quentially and refer only indirectly to the system of
responsible government.

When the second problem, that of finding a satisfactory constitutional structure to regulate the domestic
affairs of a group of territorially adjacent or contiguous

[1] Executive councillors in Victoria did not cease to be executive
councillors when they went out of office. They merely ceased to be
summoned by the Governor to attend the meetings of the executive
council.

[2] Quick and Garran, *The Annotated Constitution of the Australian Commonwealth*, p. 46.   [3] ss. 18 and 32 respectively.

[4] *Toy* v. *Musgrove*, 14 Victorian Law Reports, 349 at pp. 392–4.

colonies, came to be dealt with, a similar process occurred. An imperial statute[1] was necessary to create the new political units, and, in the case of the federations, to mark off those matters of common concern to the federating colonies, which it was agreed were to be confided to the authority of the central parliament and government, from those matters of domestic concern to each separate colony, which it was agreed were to be confided to the authority of the parliaments and governments of each separate colony. This division of powers is the essential feature of a federal system. It is a division which must obtain recognition in and which requires interpretation by the Courts, and it was inevitable therefore that it should be set down in terms of a rule of strict law.

Along with this there went the grant of responsible self-government. In general, the statute establishing the new unit conferred little more than the institutions of representative government. Power to make laws for peace, order, and good government was vested in the Sovereign, and a bicameral legislature,[2] the Lower House of which was elective, and the Upper House in Canada nominated, in Australia elective, and in South Africa partly nominated and partly elective. Executive power in Canada[3] and Australia[4] was vested in the Queen and was exercisable by a Governor-General; in South

[1] The Imperial statutes were:—Canada: British North America Act, 1867 (30 & 31 Vict., c. 3); Australia: Commonwealth of Australia Constitution Act, 1900.(63 & 64 Vict., c. 12) section 9 of which contains the Constitution; South Africa: South Africa Act, 1909 (9 Ed. 7, c. 9).

[2] British North America Act, 1867, s. 91; Australian Constitution, ss. 1 & 51; South Africa Act, s. 59.

[3] British North America Act, 1867, s. 9.

[4] Australian Constitution, s. 61.

Africa[1] it was vested in the King, and was exercisable either by His Majesty in person or by a Governor-General. The Governor-General was empowered to appoint an executive council (in Canada described as a Privy Council) to advise him in the government, and its members were to hold office during the pleasure of the Governor-General.[2] In Australia and South Africa it was provided that ministers should be members of the executive council, and that ministers should be or become members of the legislature.[3] But at the same time there was no rule that ministers alone should constitute the executive council, or that their tenure of office as executive councillors should be determined by their capacity to command a majority in the legislature. Responsible government was initiated and operated by usage and convention.

When the federations of Canada and Australia were set up, responsible government continued in the constituent Provinces and States, respectively, and was extended to the new Canadian Provinces of Manitoba, Alberta, and Saskatchewan when they were established. Certain consequential alterations in the rules of strict law were obviously necessary, especially in the terms of the Letters Patent, Commission, and Instructions to the Lieutenant-Governors of the Canadian Provinces and to the Governors of the Australian States. The executive councils of Ontario and Quebec, too, were placed upon a statutory instead of upon a prerogative basis. But in no case was the relationship of Governor, executive council,

[1] South Africa Act, s. 8.
[2] British North America Act, 1867, s. 11; Australian Constitution, s. 62; South Africa Act, s. 12.
[3] Australian Constitution, s. 64; South Africa Act, s. 14.

and legislature, as it exists under responsible government, translated further into terms of strict law. The South African colonies, on the other hand, upon union in 1909, relinquished their systems of responsible government and became provinces under the control of an Administrator and a provincial council. Meanwhile, as these federal dominions and the union came into existence and new examples of responsible government thereby appeared in the Empire, the system of responsible government continued to operate and develop in New Zealand and Newfoundland.

4

The account which has been given above of the method by which an attempt was made to solve the first two problems confronting Imperial and colonial statesmen has been over-simplified. And that in two respects. In the first place it has proceeded on the assumption that the system of responsible government, though nowhere enacted in detail in a statute, was a well-understood system, and that once the decision had been taken to confer responsible government on the separate colonies or upon the federations and union, no controversy was likely to arise about what responsible government really meant. But, as Mr. Justice Holroyd said in the Supreme Court of Victoria in 1888, 'we must not be misled by abstract terms. ... There is no cut-and-dried institution called responsible government, identical in all countries where it exists.'[1] In the second place it has been assumed that when responsible government was conferred upon the separate colonies and the federations and union, the scope of that government's activity was recognized to be

[1] In *Toy* v. *Musgrove*, 14 Victorian Law Reports, 349, at p. 428.

coextensive with the domestic affairs of these colonies or of the federations and union. In other words it has been assumed that self-government in domestic affairs was initiated, and that this self-government was to be carried out through a system of cabinet government, identical with the system prevailing in the United Kingdom. But in truth neither of these assumptions is borne out by the facts. Lord Durham, it is thought, had recommended a system of cabinet government in domestic affairs for United Canada.[1] Robert Baldwin had expressed the same idea in as clear terms as could be desired when he urged that

the Provincial Government as far as respects the internal Affairs of the Province, should be conducted by the Lieutenant-Governor, with the Advice and Assistance of the Executive Council, acting as a Provincial Cabinet;—and that the same Principle on which His Majesty's Cabinet in this Country is composed, should be applied and acted upon in the formation, continuance in office and removal, of such local Provincial Cabinet; . . .[2]

The idea was that a line should be drawn marking off domestic from imperial affairs; that in respect of domestic affairs the Governor, as the representative of His Majesty, should exercise his legal powers in relation to his executive council and the legislature in accordance with the same set of rules as His Majesty recognized in similar circumstances in the United Kingdom; and

[1] See, e.g., Durham Report, extract printed in Keith, *British Colonial Policy*, vol. i, pp. 137–41. The subject is controversial.

[2] Letter from Baldwin to Glenelg, July 13, 1836. Printed in Bell and Morrell, *Select Documents on British Colonial Policy, 1830–1860*, p. 32. Cf. Buller, *Responsible Government for Colonies*, c. 3, p. 107; Joseph Howe, *Letters to Lord John Russell*, in Kennedy, *Statutes, Treaties and Documents on the Canadian Constitution*, p. 399.

that in respect of imperial affairs the Governor, as the representative of His Majesty, should exercise his legal powers upon the instructions of His Majesty as advised by His Government in the United Kingdom. But in fact this plan was not adopted. No line was drawn between domestic affairs and imperial affairs. Lord John Russell held that it was impossible to draw such a line.

. . . There are some cases of internal government,—he said —in which the honour of the Crown or the faith of Parliament, or the safety of the state, are so seriously involved, that it would not be possible for Her Majesty to delegate her authority to a ministry in a colony.[1]

This view prevailed, in spite of later attempts to enact some kind of distinction of spheres.[2] The consequences were threefold. In the first place the United Kingdom Government was able to interfere in respect of domestic affairs in a colony. In other words self-government in domestic affairs was not established by the rules of strict law or by convention. In the second place, and as a consequence of the first proposition, responsible government as understood and practised in the United Kingdom was not established in the domestic affairs of a colony inasmuch as the Governor legally might act in domestic affairs not upon the advice of his ministers in the colony but upon the advice of His Majesty's Ministers in the United Kingdom. And in the third place even within that sphere in which the colonial government was

[1] Russell to Poulett Thomson, Oct. 14, 1839. Keith, *British Colonial Policy*, vol. i, p. 175; Kennedy, *ibid.*, No. cxii, p. 422. The date of the dispatch is given by Keith as Oct. 11 instead of 14.

[2] e.g. by Sir William Molesworth, supported by Gladstone in 1850. See Molesworth's speech 108 *Parl. Deb.*, 3 s., 567–79; Morrell, *Colonial Policy of Peel and Russell*, pp. 490–7; Knaplund, *Gladstone and Britain's Imperial Policy*, pp. 72 ff.

admittedly legally entitled to act and did in fact act
without interference from the United Kingdom Government, responsible government as understood and practised in the United Kingdom was not established in the
colony because it was not laid down anywhere in legal
or non-legal rules, that the Governor, as the representative of His Majesty, would be required to act in accordance with the rules which His Majesty obeyed in similar
circumstances.

This refusal to distinguish at the outset domestic
affairs from imperial affairs, and to define the kind of
responsible government which was to operate in the
colonies, directly affected and therefore explains the
terms in which Dominion Status was enunciated in 1926.
The coexistence of a general convention of equality with
legal and non-legal inequalities arose from this indefinite
expedient adopted when responsible government was
first initiated.

Consider first the working of responsible government
within that sphere, never precisely demarcated, in which
the colonial governments were admitted to have legal
authority, and in which in fact the United Kingdom
Government did not interfere. The Governor acted
here as representative of His Majesty. As such he
possessed a certain executive and administrative power
coextensive with the legislative power of the colonial
legislature. But the Governor possessed also certain
personal prerogatives or reserve powers in relation to the
executive council and legislature in the colony comparable with those which His Majesty possessed in the
United Kingdom. The Governor, in strict law, could
appoint and dismiss his executive council, summon,
prorogue, and dissolve the legislature, nominate members

to the Upper House of the legislature where such houses
were non-elective, and refuse his assent to a Bill duly
passed by the legislature. In the performance of these,
as of all other functions, the Governor in most cases was
required by his instructions to be guided by the advice
of his executive council, subject often to the qualification
that in matters of great urgency or in matters of a very
trivial nature or in matters where consultation with the
executive council might result in harm, the Governor
might act without consulting the executive council,
though he was required to report such action and the
reasons for it to the executive council.[1] In some colonies
there was the additional[2] or alternative instruction that
the Governor might, according to his discretion, act in
opposition to the advice of his executive council,[3] report-
ing at once such action and the reasons for it to the
Secretary of State.

The conventional rule which regulated the exercise of
these powers conferred in strict law upon the Governor
was that the Governor 'in matters of purely local politics
. . . is bound, except in extreme cases, to follow the advice
of a ministry which appears to possess the confidence of
the legislature'.[4] What of 'extreme cases'? The rule

[1] See, e.g., instructions to Governor of Newfoundland, Keith, *Responsible Government in the Dominions* (1912 ed.), vol. iii, Appendix.

[2] e.g. in case of Newfoundland.

[3] Such a provision occurs in instructions to the Governor-General
of Canada to 1878 (see *Report of Canadian Archives*, 1905, vol. i, Sessional
Paper No. 18); in instructions to the Governor of Newfoundland up to
1934; to the Governor-General of New Zealand and to the Governors of
the Australian States up to the present time. Where such provisions
were omitted there was no positive instruction to the Governor that he
must act only with the consent of his executive council.

[4] Secretary of State for the Colonies to Governor of Queensland,
March 26, 1862. Quoted in Todd, *Parliamentary Government in the British
Colonies*, p. 433.

adopted here seems to have been that, while the acts of
the Governor in matters of purely local politics must
be clothed in ministerial responsibility, the Governor
possessed a discretion to refuse the advice of his ministers
for the time being, if he was able to obtain other ministers
able and willing to accept office and take responsibility
ex post facto for his actions. This doctrine of discretion
was not always accepted by colonial ministers and its
exercise gave rise to numerous controversies, chiefly upon
the question of the grant of dissolution.[1] It was discussed
in relation to this question at the Colonial Conference
in 1887[2] and a majority of the colonial premiers approved
it. In 1914 it was clearly enunciated by Mr. Harcourt
in a dispatch to the Governor of Tasmania, where it was
stated that in all cases in which a Governor may have
found himself unable to accept the advice of his ministers, 'the Ministers either acquiesce in the Governor's
action, in which event they accept responsibility for it,
or leave the Governor to find new Ministers who will
accept the responsibility'.[3]

Granted that the Governor possessed this discretion,
was his status in relation to his ministers in the colony the
same as the status of the King in relation to his ministers
in the United Kingdom? Did the King possess a similar
discretion? Here the authorities differed. Some maintained that the King did possess a discretion. Anson
wrote in 1913[4] that 'if the King should determine, in the
interests of the people, to take a course of action which

[1] The cases are discussed in Keith, *Responsible Government in the Dominions* (ed. 1928), vol. i, part 2, c. iv.   [2] C. 5091, pp. 555 ff.

[3] Printed in Keith, *British Colonial Policy*, vol. ii, pp. 137–8.

[4] Letter to *The Times*, Sept. 10, 1913. Printed in Jennings, *Cabinet
Government*, Appendix IV, and discussed *ibid.*, c. xii. See also Evatt, *op.
cit.*, espec. c. x.

his Ministers disapprove, he must either convert his
Ministers to his point of view, or, before taking action,
must find other Ministers who agree with him'. Dicey
approved this view.[1] As late as 1924 Lord Oxford and
Asquith, who had been concerned in these pre-war controversies in which the obligation of the King to take the
advice of his ministers for the time being had been at
issue, supported the view that the King possessed a discretion in the grant of a dissolution. On this view, the
position of a Governor in a colony or Dominion was
similar to that of the King in the United Kingdom.

Other authorities, and notably Professor Keith, took
a different view. '. . . Save in the narrow sphere of the
bestowal of honour', wrote Professor Keith, there was
a 'rigid application of the rule that . . . the King shall
accept the advice of his Ministers in all matters of the
exercise of his powers. In the Dominions no such rule
has yet been accepted. . . .'[2] The same view was reiter-
rated in 1927 in *Responsible Government in the Dominions*.[3]
'In the Dominions', he wrote, '. . . the discretion of the
Governor is still constitutional and real, however much
it may be deemed preferable that the British plan should
persist, and however clearly events are moving in that
direction.'[4]

There was thus considerable room for controversy.
There was controversy whether or not the Governor had
a discretion; whether or not the King had a discretion;
and whether or not the Governor should have the same
status in this respect as the King. In 1926 all three

[1] See also Lord Hugh Cecil in same correspondence. These and other
letters are printed in Jennings, *ibid.*, Appendix IV.
[2] *British Colonial Policy*, vol. i, Introduction, p. x.
[3] Vol. i, p. 154–6.   [4] *Ibid.*, p. 156.

questions were discussed when Lord Byng refused a
dissolution to Mr. Mackenzie King and granted one
shortly afterwards to Mr. Meighen. On this occasion
Professor Keith took the view that 'the duty of the
Governor-General was to act on the same principles as
would have applied to the King' and that therefore he
possessed no discretion in granting a dissolution.[1] It is
difficult to avoid the conclusion that Professor Keith
here contradicts the view expressed in the same book
that the status of the Governor was essentially different
from that of the King.

It is not possible to discuss the Byng episode in detail
here.[2] Two comments only will be attempted. In the
first place it may be remarked that the question at issue
was not simply whether or not the King would have
granted a dissolution automatically in similar circumstances and if so, whether or not Lord Byng was obliged
to follow that rule. The question at issue was whether
or not the King would have refused a dissolution to a
Prime Minister in such circumstances, and would have
granted it to a succeeding Prime Minister within a short
space of time when that Prime Minister had failed to
command a majority in Parliament; and if so, whether
or not Lord Byng was obliged to follow that rule. It
appears that Lord Byng's error (if one may speak of
errors in a matter where rules conflict so much) lay in
refusing to one party in Parliament what he granted
shortly afterwards to their opponents.[3] In later com-

[1] *Ibid.*, vol. i, pp. 147–8.
[2] The fullest treatment is in E. Forsey's *Royal Power of Dissolution of
Parliament in the British Commonwealth.* See also Evatt, *op. cit.*, c. vii.
[3] Mr. Mackenzie King based his criticism on this point. He said:
'Though I am unable to admit that either the refusal to myself of a dissolution or the granting of a dissolution immediately thereafter to Mr

ments on the incident Professor Keith was inclined to base his criticism of Lord Byng more on this double aspect of the question than upon the single aspect of the refusal to Mr. Mackenzie King.[1]

In the second place it is difficult, as has already been suggested, to regard the incident as raising the question of equality of status. Lord Byng's action involved no inequality of status for Canada in relation either to Great Britain or to the other Dominions. His refusal of a dissolution did not imply that the Canadian Government was subordinate to the United Kingdom Government, as Professor Keith suggests.[2] It is true that Lord Byng was the representative of His Majesty's Government in the United Kingdom as well as the representative of His Majesty, and that he was, as Mr. Mackenzie King said 'under instructions' from the British Government. This might suggest that in refusing a dissolution he was acting as the servant of the British Government. But it is clear that in Lord Byng's case no such interpretation was possible. He specifically refused to ask advice

Meighen was a constitutional course of procedure, I am prepared to say that there may be circumstances in which a Governor-General might find subsequent justification for a refusal to grant a dissolution of parliament.' See Keith, *Speeches and Documents on the British Dominions*, p. 153.

[1] e.g. letter to *The Scotsman*, May 10, 1927. Printed in *Letters on Imperial Relations, Indian Reform, Constitutional and International Law*, p. 69.

[2] *Responsible Government in the Dominions* (ed. 1928), vol. i, p. 146. Professor Keith introduces here a distinction between the constitutional rights of a Governor of an Australian State or of Newfoundland and the Governor-General of a Dominion. The former possesses a discretion; the latter acts in accordance with the rules which are obeyed by the King and possesses no discretion. Surely this distinction at any rate between Newfoundland and other Dominions was not warranted. And it appears to conflict with what Professor Keith had said *ibid.*, p. 156. Nor does the distinction between the Australian States and the Dominions seem justified on this point.

from the Secretary of State for Dominion Affairs when
Mr. Mackenzie King suggested that course.[1] He acted
throughout upon his own discretion. There was no
subordination of the Canadian Government to the
United Kingdom Government.[2]

Enough has been said, however, to explain why the
question of the status of the Governor-General in relation to his ministers in a Dominion was one of controversy in 1926 and why it came up for discussion at
the Imperial Conference. Where usages conflicted so
much, it was necessary to adopt and declare some
obligatory rule.[3]

---

[1] *Canadian Debates (House of Commons)*, 1926–7, vol. ii, pp. 1651–4.

[2] Mr. Mackenzie King appeared clearly to realize this. '. . . My
resignation,' he said, 'was in no way due to a difference between the
British Government and the Canadian Government.' *Ibid.*, p. 1654.
But he had maintained at the same time and inconsistently the view
that an issue of status was involved. See election speech, already
referred to, and printed in Keith, *Speeches and Documents on the British
Dominions*, p. 152.

[3] Actually when it came to the point at the Imperial Conference only
part of the question was settled by the adoption of obligatory rules. The
rest was left with conflicting usages as before. See below, p. 126 and
note 1.

III
DOMINION STATUS IN 1926—II

THE problem of the proper relations between a Governor and his ministers in a Dominion in respect of matters in which the United Kingdom Government did not interfere, and in which therefore the Governor acted as the representative of His Majesty alone, did not raise the question of equality of status as between the Dominion Governments and the United Kingdom Government. But when we consider those legal powers vested in the Governor and exercised by him on instructions from His Majesty as advised by the Government in the United Kingdom, the problem of inequality of status emerges. It is proposed to examine now the nature and extent of these legal powers and the rules according to which they were exercised. They extended, as has been said, to the control of domestic as well as to the control of external or imperial affairs. A study of their exercise reveals therefore the method by which the solution to the problem of regulating domestic affairs, whether in separate or in united colonies, already initiated by the establishment of responsible government, was developed and extended; and it reveals also the solution which was attempted *pari passu* to the problem of regulating imperial affairs.

There was first the power of reservation.[1] This was really two powers. There was the power of the Governor, when a Bill duly passed by the two Houses of the legislature was presented for his assent, to declare that he

[1] *O.D.L. Report*, paras. 26–36.

reserved the Bill for the signification of the Sovereign's
pleasure. There was, next, the power of the Sovereign,
upon the advice of the United Kingdom ministers, to
declare his pleasure in regard to the Bill by giving or
refusing assent to it. If assent had not been given within
a specified period, usually two years from reservation by
the Governor,[1] the Bill lapsed. Each power will be considered separately. The Governor's power to reserve
was of two kinds, discretionary and obligatory. The
Governor was empowered to reserve Bills 'according to
his discretion', in most of the early colonies. When the
South African colonies united, the power was vested in
the Governor-General of the Union; in Canada, at
federation, the power in respect of provincial Bills was
vested in the Lieutenant-Governors, but since they reserved Bills for the signification of the Governor-
General's pleasure and not of the Sovereign's pleasure,
the element of subordination to the United Kingdom
Government disappeared.[2] In 1926 the power existed
in the Constitutions of the Australian States, which thus
preserved a link with the United Kingdom Government, and in the Constitutions of the Dominions of
Canada,[3] Australia,[4] New Zealand,[5] South Africa,[6] and
the Irish Free State.[7]

Obligatory reservation required the Governor to

[1] One year in the Union of South Africa. South Africa Act, s. 66.
[2] B.N.A. Act, 1867, s. 90. It was decided unanimously by the Supreme
Court of Canada in 1938 that this power to reserve provincial Bills and
the power of the Governor-General to disallow provincial Acts (see
below, p. 71) were still subsisting powers. [1938] S.C.R. 71.
[3] B.N.A. Act, 1867, ss. 55 and 57.
[4] Australian Constitution, ss. 58 and 60.
[5] Constitution Act, 1852 (15 & 16 Vict., c. 72), ss. 56 and 59.
[6] South Africa Act, ss. 64 and 66.
[7] Constitution, Art. 41. See below, pp. 118.

reserve bills dealing with certain specified classes of subject-matter. This obligation to reserve was found either in a prerogative instrument, such as the instructions to the Governor,[1] or in a statute, sometimes in the constitutional statute of the colony, sometimes in a general statute extending to all colonies. Instructions to reserve were issued in most of the early colonies. They disappeared for the provinces in the Union of South Africa. When the British North American colonies united in 1867 to become provinces in a federation, the power to issue instructions to the Lieutenant-Governors was vested in the Governor-General and not in the Sovereign, and subordination to the United Kingdom disappeared.[2] This power has been exercised. In 1926 the power to issue such instructions was in existence on a statutory basis in the Australian States,[3] and in the Dominions of Canada,[4] New Zealand,[5] and South Africa.[6] In fact no instructions to reserve had been issued to the Governor-General of Canada since 1878, to the Governor-General of New Zealand since 1907, nor to the Governors-General of Australia and the Irish Free State at any time. But such instructions were issued to the Governor-General of South Africa,[7] and to the Gover-

---

[1] In Transvaal and Orange Free State it is found in Letters Patent, ss. 49 and 51 respectively.   [2] B.N.A. Act, 1867, s. 90.

[3] The Australian States Constitution Act, 1907 (7 Ed. 7, c. 7).

[4] B.N.A. Act, 1867, s. 55.

[5] Constitution Act, 1852, s. 56.   [6] South Africa Act, s. 64.

[7] Paragraph VII of the instructions read: 'The Governor-General shall not assent in our name to any bill which we have specially instructed him through one of our principal Secretaries of State to reserve; and he shall take special care that he does not assent to any bill which he may be required under the South Africa Act, 1909, to reserve; and in particular he shall reserve any bill which disqualifies any person in the Province of the Cape of Good Hope, who, under the laws existing in the Colony

nors of Australian States.[1] In Newfoundland reservation strictly speaking did not exist. However, the Governor was instructed to refuse his assent to Bills dealing with certain classes of subject-matter unless such Bills con-

of the Cape of Good Hope at the establishment of the Union, is, or may become, capable of being registered as a voter, from being so registered in the Province of the Cape of Good Hope by reason of his race or colour only.' Keith, *Responsible Government in the Dominions* (ed. 1912), Appendix.

[1] The relevant paragraph in the instructions read: 'The Governor shall not, except in the cases hereunder mentioned, assent in our name to any bill of any of the following classes:

'1. Any bill for the divorce of persons joined together in holy matrimony.

'2. Any bill whereby any grant of land or money, or other donation or gratuity, may be made to himself.

'3. Any bill affecting the currency of the State.

'4. Any bill, the provisions of which shall appear inconsistent with obligations imposed upon us by treaty.

'5. Any bill of an extraordinary nature and importance, whereby our prerogative, or the rights and property of our subjects not residing in the State or the trade and shipping of the United Kingdom and its Dependencies may be prejudiced.

'6. Any bill containing provisions to which our assent has been once refused, or which have been disallowed by us; Unless he shall have previously obtained our instructions upon such bill through one of our principal Secretaries of State, or unless such bill shall contain a clause suspending the operation of such bill until the signification in the State of our pleasure thereupon, or unless the Governor shall have satisfied himself that an urgent necessity exists requiring that such bill be brought into immediate operation, in which case he is authorised to assent in our name to such bill, unless the same shall be repugnant to the law of England, or inconsistent with any obligations imposed upon us by treaty. But he is to transmit to us by the earliest opportunity the bill so assented to, together with his reasons for assenting thereto.' (Printed in Keith, *ibid.*)

Before federation two further classes of subject-matter were included, viz. Bills imposing differential duties, and Bills regulating the armed forces of the Crown. These two subjects passed to federal control from the states upon the establishment of the Commonwealth. The full list of eight subjects was included in the instructions to the Governor-General of Canada until 1878, and to the Governor of New Zealand until 1907. The office of Governor-General was not created in New Zealand until 1917.

tained a clause suspending their operation until the
Sovereign's pleasure was known, except in certain urgent
cases. The list of subjects corresponded closely with the
list included in the instructions for obligatory reservation
issued to the Governor-General of Canada until 1878,
to the Governor of New Zealand until 1907, and to the
Governors of the Australian colonies before the federation came into existence in 1900.[1]

Obligatory reservation under statute may next be
described. In 1926 the Constitution Acts of Australia,
New Zealand, and South Africa contained provisions
requiring reservation of Bills dealing with certain subjects.[2] In Australia[3] and South Africa[4] Bills limiting the
matters in which the Judicial Committee of the Privy
Council may be asked to grant special leave to appeal
from the highest court of the Dominion must be reserved.
In South Africa, further, it was provided in section 64 of
the Constitution Act that all Bills repealing or amending that section or any of the provisions of Chapter IV of
the Act under the heading 'House of Assembly', and all
Bills abolishing provincial councils or abridging the
powers conferred on them under section 85 of the Act
should be reserved. And in paragraph 25 of the Schedule
to the Act, it was required to reserve Bills to alter or
amend that Schedule (which laid down the conditions
under which the South African Government would
administer the native territories if they were handed over
to the Union). In New Zealand, it was required that
Bills altering the salary of the Governor or the sums

[1] See Note 1 on p. 65. Also Keith, *ibid.*
[2] Australian Constitution, s. 74; New Zealand Constitution Act, s. 65;
South Africa Act, ss. 64 and 106, and paragraph 25 of the Schedule to
the Act.   [3] s. 74.   [4] s. 106.

allocated to native purposes, both of which were set out in the Schedule to the Constitution Act, must be reserved. No obligatory reservation is provided for in the Constitution Acts of Canada or the Irish Free State. In the Australian States, however, there was a statutory obligation to reserve Bills making certain constitutional changes.[1]

Finally, there was obligatory reservation not under constitutional statutes but under general imperial statutes. Section 735 of the Merchant Shipping Act of 1894[2] required in effect the reservation of Bills passed by the legislature of any British possession relating to ships registered in that possession. Section 736 required Bills passed by the legislature of a British possession regulating the coasting trade of the possession to contain a suspending clause providing that they should not come into operation until the Sovereign's pleasure had been signified. Similarly the Colonial Courts of Admiralty Act, 1890[3] required the reservation of Bills or the insertion of a suspending clause in Bills which affected the jurisdiction of, or practice or procedure in these courts of admiralty.

How was the power of reservation exercised? Consider first the Governor's power to reserve. In so far as this power was obligatory under instructions it had been progressively restricted before 1926, for, as has been seen, instructions had ceased to be issued to Canada in 1878,[4] and to New Zealand in 1907; and they had never

---

[1] Australian States Constitution Act, 1907 (7 Ed. 7, c. 7).

[2] 57 & 58 Vict., c. 60.

[3] 53 & 54 Vict., c. 27, ss. 4 and 7.

[4] On the insistence of Mr. Blake, the Canadian Minister of Justice. See *Canadian Sessional Papers*, A. 1877. Up to this date the Governor-General had reserved 21 Bills under instructions.

been issued to Australia and the Irish Free State. But they remained in the Australian States, in South Africa, and (in effect) in Newfoundland and were obeyed. Obligatory reservation under statute continued to exist and was regularly exercised.[1] In the case of discretionary reservation a usage developed that the Governor's discretion should be exercised more and more in accordance with the advice of his ministers in the Dominion. In this way an Australian tariff Bill of 1906 was reserved by the Governor-General according to his discretion and this discretion was exercised on the advice of ministers in Australia;[2] a New Zealand immigration restriction Bill was similarly reserved in 1906,[3] and a New Zealand Nationality Bill in 1923.[4] But there was no established convention.

What action was taken by the United Kingdom Government in dealing with reserved Bills? It would appear that, in the first place, they recognized a convention of consultation. Indeed as time went on 'the veto became little more than a means of securing consultation and delay'.[5] The Imperial and colonial Governments discussed the legislation and endeavoured to find an agreed form in which it could be passed. But while the United Kingdom felt bound to consult the colonies

[1] e.g. in South Africa, Bills Nos. 12, 15, and 31 of 1918 and No. 5 of 1921 were reserved under s. 64 of the South Africa Act (and were all assented to). See *Journal of Comparative Legislation*, 3rd series, vol. ii, pp. 100–3, 117; vol. v, p. 124.

[2] Australian Customs Tariff (British Preference) Bill. See *Parl. Pap.* H.C. 1912, lx, No. 160.

[3] Immigration Restriction Act Amendment Bill, No. 65.

[4] British Nationality and Status of Aliens (in New Zealand) Bill, No. 46 of 1923.

[5] K. H. Bailey, in *Cambridge History of the British Empire*, vol. vii, part i, p. 411.

upon reserved Bills before taking action, it did not feel
bound to consent to such Bills. The veto was exercised
in certain cases. In the Australian colonies between
1856 and 1900 we are told,

assent was often withheld only temporarily, pending amendments. Only some forty bills during these years definitely
failed to receive the royal assent, and of these four-fifths
subsequently passed into law, with perhaps some modification. Purely local bills were vetoed only in the earlier
years, and two thirds of the whole forty fell within the first
half of the period.[1]

Dissent on imperial grounds persisted until 1926, however. Bills affecting immigration, nationality, native
interests, copyright, and merchant shipping for example
were refused assent or were modified from time to time.[2]
The Australian Customs Tariff (British Preference) Bill
of 1906, to which reference has been made, was dropped,
and an amended Bill was passed in 1908.[3] Similarly a
New Zealand Shipping Bill of 1910,[4] after reservation
and consultation, did not receive the royal assent and
lapsed, by agreement between the two governments.
As late as 1923 a New Zealand nationality bill,[5] reserved
on the advice of New Zealand ministers, was objected to
by the United Kingdom. It received the royal assent,
but in 1928 a new Bill[6] was passed repealing the Act of

[1] Bailey, *ibid.* Based upon *Returns of Colonial Bills to which the Royal Veto
has been applied. Parl. Pap.* H.L. 1894, No. 196; H.C. 1901, xlvi, No. 362;
H.C. 1906, lxxvii, No. 184.
[2] See Bailey, *op. cit.*, pp. 411–14; Keith, *Responsible Government in the
Dominions* (ed. 1912), vol. ii, pp. 1054–1100; vol. iii, pp. 1188–1247; or
ed. 1928, part v, cc. i–iv, vi–ix. See also above *Returns* and H.C. 1912–13,
lx, No. 160.   [3] No. 7 of 1908.
[4] New Zealand Shipping and Seamen (Amendment) Bill, No. 85 of
1910. Printed in Cd. 5582, p. 178.
[5] No. 46 of 1923 already referred to.   [6] No. 58.

1923 and adopting part II of the Imperial Act on the subject. This Bill also the Governor-General was advised by his ministers to reserve 'as a matter of policy'.[1] Cases of refusal of assent occurred in Newfoundland, too. In 1906, for example, a Foreign Fishing Vessels Act, directed against fishermen from the United States, was refused assent on the Imperial Government's advice.[2] There appears to be no case since 1900 in which Bills from Canada, South Africa, or the Irish Free State failed to receive assent. But there was no general convention of consent. In domestic affairs perhaps it might be said that assent ought not to be refused. But in imperial affairs it might well be refused, though usually after consultation and agreement between the Imperial and Dominion Governments. There existed, therefore, a subordination of the Dominion legislatures to the United Kingdom Government, and the latter was by no means powerless in 1926 to control Dominion legislation in imperial interests when necessary.

The second element of subordination in a colonial constitutional structure in respect of domestic and external affairs, and, conversely, the second instrument through which the Imperial Government was enabled to regulate domestic and imperial affairs, was found in the power of disallowance.[3] The power of disallowance meant the power of the Sovereign, acting on the advice of ministers in the United Kingdom, to annul within a specified period an Act passed by a Dominion or colonial legislature and assented to by the Governor. The power was found in all the early colonial constitutions. Its

---

[1] *Journal of Comparative Legislation*, 3rd series, vol. xii, p. 138. Cf. also No. 53 of 1912 amending No. 36 of 1909.
[2] H.C. 1912–13, lx, No. 160.   [3] *O.D.L. Report*, paras. 18–25.

scope was described by Sir William Molesworth in 1850 when he said that a colonial legislature may

make any laws whatever, affecting imperial interests in any manner whatever, provided the Colonial Office does not disallow them within a certain period of time. On the other hand, the colonial legislatures cannot make any law which the Colonial Office may not disallow.[1]

The power disappeared in South Africa in respect of provincial ordinances at the establishment of the union; it was transferred to the Governor-General of Canada in respect of legislation by the Provinces when federation occurred in 1867, and subordination to the United Kingdom Government so far as the Provinces were concerned was removed;[2] but it persisted in the Australian States after federation in 1900. In 1926 the power was in existence on a statutory basis in the Australian States[3] and in the Constitutions of Canada,[4] Australia,[5] New Zealand,[6] and South Africa.[7] It was not provided for in the Irish Free State Constitution. In Newfoundland, where the Constitution took the form of Letters Patent, disallowance was provided for in the Letters Patent. The period within which disallowance might occur was two years in the cases of the Australian States, Canada, and New Zealand; and one year in the case of Australia and South Africa. The most interesting provision for disallowance in respect of Dominion and

[1] 108 *Parl. Deb.*, 3 s., 578.
[2] B.N.A. Act, 1867, s. 90. On the exercise of this power and also of reservation, see E. Forsey, *Canadian Journal of Economics and Political Science*, vol. iv, Feb. 1938, pp. 47 ff. See also p. 63 above, note 2.
[3] 5 & 6 Vict., c. 76 and 13 & 14 Vict., c. 59.
[4] B.N.A. Act, 1867, s. 56.   [5] Australian Constitution, s. 59.
[6] New Zealand Constitution Act, s. 58.
[7] South Africa Act, s. 65.

colonial legislation existed as a result of powers conferred on the United Kingdom Treasury by the Colonial Stock Act, 1900.[1] The Act provided[2] that the Treasury might lay down conditions under which colonial stocks would be admitted as trustee securities in the United Kingdom. The third of these conditions laid down by the Treasury was that the Dominion concerned must place on record a formal expression of its opinion that legislation which appeared to the United Kingdom Government to alter any of the provisions affecting such trustee stocks to the injury of the stock holder or to depart from the original contract, might properly be disallowed. All the Dominions except the Irish Free State were able to take advantage of the provisions of the Colonial Stock Act, subject to this condition. The Australian States also were able to do so; but the Canadian Provinces could not, since disallowance of their legislation had passed from the hands of the United Kingdom Government.

How was the power exercised? In the early stages of responsible government its scope was extended to domestic as well as to imperial affairs. Legislation upon primarily local matters was disallowed in one case in New Brunswick in the period 1836 to 1867,[3] and in Newfoundland in a few cases in the period 1850 to 1890, because the Imperial Government disapproved of the policy it embodied.[4] On the other hand there appears to be one case only of disallowance of an act dealing with domestic affairs in the Australian colonies

---

[1] 63 & 64 Vict., c. 62. [2] s. 2.
[3] H.C. 1864, xl, No. 529. See p. 42 for the view of the Secretary of State for Colonies on propriety of refusing assent to such legislation.
[4] See H.L. 1894, No. 196, p. 8.

from 1856 to 1900.[1] In Canada an act of 1873 regulating parliamentary powers was found to be *ultra vires* the Canadian Parliament;[2] by agreement between the Canadian and United Kingdom Governments it was disallowed; an imperial act was passed in 1875 conferring powers on the Canadian Parliament to legislate in the desired direction,[3] and the Act of 1873 was then re-enacted in 1876 and became law.[4] In 1898 a dispatch from Joseph Chamberlain, Secretary of State for the Colonies, to the Governor of Newfoundland, established a constitutional convention that the prerogative of disallowance

is a safeguard for the protection of those interests for which the Secretary of State is responsible to Her Majesty and to the Imperial Parliament. To advise its exercise in cases where only local interests are concerned would involve the Imperial Government in liability for matters of the control of which it has divested itself, and for which the Colony has accepted full responsibility.[5]

Its operation was therefore confined for the future to legislation affecting imperial interests.

But even in imperial affairs its exercise had been infrequent in the latter half of the nineteenth century. From 1856 to 1900 four acts only of Australian colonial legislatures dealing with imperial affairs were disallowed, and all four cases occurred before 1865. In two of the cases the principle of the acts came into operation soon after,

---

[1] See *ibid*. It occurred in 1862 and the principle of the act was embodied in another act in 1864 which was not disallowed.

[2] *Canadian Sessional Papers*, 1876, No. 45.

[3] Parliament of Canada Act, 1875. 38 & 39 Vict., c. 38. It also validated the Act of 1873.　　[4] 39 Vict., c. 7 (Canadian).

[5] C. 9137. Dispatch of Dec. 5, 1898. Cf. Dispatch of March 23, 1898, *ibid*. Also printed in Keith, *British Colonial Policy*, vol. ii, pp. 105–8.

either as a result of imperial legislation or by arrangement with the Imperial Government.[1] In New Zealand two such acts were disallowed between 1855 and 1867, and none since. No cases of disallowance occurred in respect of Canada since 1873, nor at any time in respect of the Commonwealth of Australia, the Union of South Africa or the Irish Free State. In 1926 it could be said that, if we except Newfoundland, there had been no case of disallowance in a Dominion since 1873, and that in that case disallowance had occurred after consultation and with consent. There was, it seems clear, a convention that disallowance might not be used in respect of Dominion legislation.

2

But inequality of status was not confined to the control of the United Kingdom Government over colonial legislation. The prerogative powers of the Crown were supplemented by the over-riding legal supremacy of the United Kingdom Parliament, exercised, in particular, in accordance with the provisions of the Colonial Laws Validity Act, 1865. In the words of Todd, 'the colonial possessions of the British Crown, howsoever acquired and whatever may be their political constitution, are subject at all periods of their existence to the legislative control of the Imperial Parliament.'[2] In 1926 these words, written in 1880, still applied in strict law to all the legislatures of all the Dominions.[3]

The scope and effects of the Colonial Laws Validity

[1] H.L. 1894, xi, No. 196.

[2] *Parliamentary Government in the British Colonies*, p. 172.

[3] This view would not be accepted universally in the Irish Free State. See below, Chap. IV.

Act[1] should be stated in some detail. A word must be said of the circumstances which made the passing of the Act necessary. In the early sixties of last century, Mr. Justice Boothby, of the Supreme Court of South Australia, declared invalid a series of Acts passed by the South Australian legislature upon two main grounds.[2] In the first place he asserted the doctrine that colonial laws repugnant to the law of England were invalid to the extent of such repugnancy, and on this ground he held, for example, that those portions of the Constitution Act of 1855–6 passed by the colonial legislature, which provided for a legislative council which could not be dissolved by the Crown, which contained the rule that the Attorney-General must be a minister and a member of parliament, and which did not require ministers to submit themselves to re-election upon their appointment, were invalid, on the ground that these provisions were repugnant to English law. In the second place he asserted that colonial laws which dealt with classes of subject-matter, legislation upon which the Governor was obliged by his instructions to reserve, were invalid if the Governor had failed so to reserve them and had given his assent to them. On this ground he declared the Real Property Act, the entire Constitution Act, and the Electoral Act invalid. The matter was finally referred to the imperial law officers. In their opinion Mr. Justice Boothby based his doctrine of repugnancy upon too wide a ground. A colonial law was not invalid on the ground of repugnancy to any rule of English law; it was invalid only if and in so far as it was repugnant to a statute of the

---

[1] 28 & 29 Vict., c. 63. *O.D.L. Report*, paras. 45 ff. The Act is printed as Appendix I to this book.

[2] See *Parl. Pap.*, 1862, xxxvii, p. 113.

Imperial Parliament extending to the colony, or repugnant to the fundamental principles of English law. The law officers were 'unable to lay down any rule to fix the dividing line between fundamental and non-fundamental rules of English law', but they spoke of the fundamental principles as those 'equally applicable in the nature of things to all Her Majesty's Christian subjects in every part of the British Dominions', and it would appear that they would have regarded a law permitting slavery or polygamy or prohibiting Christianity as repugnant to these fundamental principles. The law officers held further that the second ground of invalidity which Mr. Justice Boothby had adopted was unacceptable. Failure by the Governor to reserve Bills which he was obliged by instructions to reserve did not invalidate the act when it had received the Governor's assent. On the other hand failure by the Governor to reserve Bills which he was obliged by imperial statute to reserve, would render such legislation void, although it had been assented to by the Governor. And in fact the Electoral Act of 1856 was declared void upon this ground. In consequence all laws passed by the two Houses of Parliament in South Australia, elected under this Act, were invalid, and an Imperial Act was passed validating them in 1862.[1]

The matter was not settled by this opinion, however. In later cases the Supreme Court expressed doubts about the competence of the colonial legislature to amend its constitution.[2] After further correspondence and another validating act[3] of the Imperial Parliament, it was finally decided to pass an Imperial Act clarifying the position.

[1] 25 & 26 Vict., c. 11.
[2] South Australian *Parl. Pap.* 1863, Nos. 23, 129, 130.
[3] 26 & 27 Vict., c. 84.

Each of the three problems—repugnancy, the effect of failure to observe royal instructions to reserve, and the competence of the colonial legislature to amend its constitution—were dealt with in the clauses of the Act, styled the Colonial Laws Validity Act, 1865. Repugnancy was dealt with in sections 2 and 3. One criterion of repugnancy and one only was laid down. Any colonial law which was repugnant to the provisions of an Act of the Parliament of the United Kingdom extending to the colony by express words or necessary intendment,[1] or repugnant to any order or regulation made under the authority of such an Act, was, to the extent of such repugnancy, but not otherwise, absolutely void and inoperative. At the same time the criterion of repugnancy to the fundamental principles of English law, which the law officers had asserted in their opinion, was abandoned, and section 3 asserts the wide proposition that no colonial law shall be declared void on the ground of repugnancy to the law of England, unless it is repugnant to an imperial act as aforesaid. The effect of sections 2 and 3 is well stated by Keir and Lawson in the passage:

The intention of the Act was to quiet doubts which had been suggested by a colonial court concerning the validity of colonial acts which were inconsistent with English law, and having set up its one criterion of repugnancy, the Act at once emphasises the fact that it imposes no other. Its third section is just as important, just as categorical, as the second. The Act is not and was never intended to be a Colonial Laws Invalidity Act.[2]

In the case of *Phillips* v. *Eyre*[3] in 1870 the whole matter was reviewed at length. Invalidity on the grounds of

[1] s. 1.　　　　　　[2] *Cases in Constitutional Law*, 2nd ed., p. 414.
[3] (1870) L.R. 6 Q.B. 1; Keir and Lawson, *ibid.*, at p. 431.

repugnancy either to the English common law, or to
statutes of the United Kingdom Parliament not extending to the colony by express words or necessary intendment, or to the principles of 'natural justice', was expressly rejected, and one criterion of repugnancy, viz.
repugnancy to an Imperial Act extending to the colony
by express words or necessary intendment, was asserted.[1]

The question of the effect of failure by the Governor to
observe the Crown's instructions to reserve was dealt
with in section 4 of the Act. It was provided that no
colonial law passed with the concurrence of or assented
to by the Governor of the colony should be deemed
invalid by reason only of any instructions which had
been given to the Governor. The question of colonial
competence to amend the constitution of the legislature
was dealt with in section 5. It was there provided that
every colonial legislature should have power to establish,
abolish, alter or reconstitute the judicature of the colony
and further that every representative legislature[2]

shall, in respect to the colony under its jurisdiction, have,
and be deemed at all times to have had, full power to make
laws respecting the constitution, powers, and procedure of
such legislature; provided that such laws shall have been
passed in such manner and form as may from time to time
be required by any act of parliament, letters-patent, order
in council, or colonial law for the time being in force in the
said colony.[3]

[1] See also *Riel* v. *The Queen*, (1885) 10 A.C. 675, Lord Halsbury at
p. 687. Quoted in Keir and Lawson, *ibid.*, at p. 413.
[2] 'Representative Legislature' is defined in s. 1 as 'any colonial legislature which shall comprise a legislative body of which one half are
elected by inhabitants of the colony.'
[3] The meaning of s. 5 was at issue in *Attorney-General for New South
Wales* v. *Trethowan*, [1932] A.C. 526, which is discussed below, Chap. VII.

It is clear, then, that the Colonial Laws Validity Act was 'an enabling Act, not a restrictive or disabling Act'.

. . . It took away no power previously enjoyed; it was, in fact, looked upon as one of the charters of colonial legislative independence, next in importance to the famous Declaratory Act, 18 Geo. III, c. 12, in which the British Parliament, profiting by the lessons of the American rebellion, renounced its intention to again tax the colonies.[1]

. . . Even before the passing of the Colonial Laws Validity Act it was recognized in law[2] as well as in practice that a colonial Legislature could not repeal an Imperial Act applicable to the colonies, whether that Act was in force before or came into force after the constitution of such colonial Legislature. That Act limits rather than enlarges the doctrine of repugnancy; it enlarges rather than limits the power of colonial Legislatures (1) by repealing the common law rule that every colonial law repugnant to English law is void, and confining nullity for repugnancy to cases where statutes are expressly intended to apply to the colonies, and (2) by restricting the nullity to the inconsistent provisions only, and not allowing a particular variance to invalidate the whole colonial Act.[3]

But, while the Act was passed to extend rather than to restrict the powers of colonial legislatures, it reasserted, at the same time, in statutory form the overriding supremacy of the Imperial Parliament. To what extent was this legal power exercised up to 1926 to regulate the domestic and external affairs of the colonies and Dominions?[4] In respect of the domestic sphere it had been

[1] Quick and Garran, *The Annotated Constitution of the Australian Commonwealth*, p. 348. It is interesting to notice that so important an Act was passed evidently without any discussion in either house of Parliament.

[2] See, e.g., *Low* v. *Routledge*, L.R. 1 Ch. 42 (1865), decided just before the Act was passed.   [3] Quick and Garran, *op. cit.*, p. 349.

[4] See Keith, *Responsible Government in the Dominions* (ed. 1928), part v, cc. vi–ix, xii, xiii.

laid down as a convention by the Secretary of State for the Colonies, Lord Glenelg, as early as 1839 that

parliamentary legislation, on any subject of exclusively internal concern, in any British colony possessing a representative assembly, is, as a general rule unconstitutional. It is a right of which the exercise is reserved for extreme cases, in which necessity at once creates and justifies the exception.[1]

What exceptions have occurred in practice? In general, where a colonial legislature has lacked power to make laws regulating some domestic matter, the United Kingdom Parliament has legislated for it at the request and with the consent of the colony. Thus the Dominion Parliament of Canada lacks power to amend the British North America Act, 1867, and in consequence the United Kingdom Parliament, at the request and with the consent of the Dominion Government, passed amending Acts in 1871, 1875, 1886, 1907, 1915, 1916, 1930 and 1940.[2] These Acts dealt with matters of domestic concern to the federation and the provinces. Again, colonial acts dealing with domestic affairs, as has already been seen, were sometimes found to be invalid, and it was necessary for the United Kingdom Parliament to pass a validating Act, as was done in respect of South Australian legislation in 1862 and 1863,[3] and again in the Colonial Laws Validity Act itself, in 1865.[4] Similar validating Acts were passed at the request of certain Australian States in 1901 and 1907. The Constitutions

[1] Glenelg to Sir F. Bond Head, Lieut.-Governor of Upper Canada, *Parl. Pap.* 1839, xxxiii, p. 9.

[2] The Acts are respectively, 34 & 35 Vict., c. 28; 38 & 39 Vict., c. 38; 49 & 50 Vict., c. 35; 7 Ed. 7, c. 11; 5 & 6 Geo. 5, c. 45; 6 & 7 Geo. 5, c. 19; 20 & 21 Geo. 5, c. 26; 3 & 4 Geo. 6, c. 36.

[3] 25 & 26 Vict., c. 11, and 26 & 27 Vict., c. 84, already referred to.

[4] s. 7.

of the Dominions of Canada, Australia, South Africa, and the Irish Free State[1] similarly were passed by the United Kingdom Parliament and given force of law because no legislature existed in those territories competent to enact these Constitutions. In each case the Constitution was drawn up in the community concerned and enacted substantially in accordance with its wishes. In domestic affairs the convention seems established that the United Kingdom Parliament might legislate only at such times and in such terms as were consented to by the Dominion.

In imperial affairs, there were some matters which a colonial legislature was unable to regulate because it lacked power to make laws with extra-territorial effect—a limitation upon colonial legislative competence which will shortly be considered. In such cases the United Kingdom Parliament legislated with the consent of the colony, and passed such acts as the Fugitive Offenders Act, 1881,[2] the Colonial Prisoners Removal Acts, 1869 and 1884,[3] and the Extradition Acts, 1870 and 1873.[4]

In imperial affairs the United Kingdom Parliament legislated for the colonies, in the next place, to regulate foreign relations, as in the Foreign Enlistment Act, 1870,[5] the Anglo-French Convention Act, 1904,[6] the International Copyright Acts, 1852 and 1886,[7] and the Geneva Convention Act, 1911.[8] In the third place, it

---

[1] This view would not be accepted universally by Irish jurists. See below, Chap. IV.   [2] 44 & 45 Vict., c. 69.

[3] 32 Vict., c. 10 and 47 & 48 Vict., c. 31.

[4] 33 & 34 Vict., c. 52 and 36 & 37 Vict., c. 60.

[5] 33 & 34 Vict., c. 90.   [6] 4 Ed. 7, c. 33.

[7] 15 & 16 Vict., c. 12 and 49 & 50 Vict., c. 33.

[8] 1 & 2 Geo. 5, c. 20.

legislated where the uniform regulation of some matter of common concern to all parts of the Empire was necessary, and where it was desired to control Imperial interests. The Fugitive Offenders Act, the Colonial Prisoners Removal Acts, and the Extradition Acts, already referred to, were passed by the United Kingdom Parliament as much for this reason as for the reason that the colonies lacked power to legislate with extra-territorial effect. But the best examples of imperial legislation of this kind are found in the Merchant Shipping Acts of 1854 and 1894,[1] the Copyright Acts of 1842 and 1911,[2] the Naturalization Act of 1870,[3] and the British Nationality and Status of Aliens Act, 1914, as amended in 1918 and 1922.[4] And finally, such matters of common concern as the royal style and titles, the succession to the throne, regency, and demise of the Crown were all regulated by Acts of the United Kingdom Parliament, and it was recognized before 1926 that in strict law and in convention that Parliament alone might legislate to regulate such matters.

It is clear that by 1926 a convention had been established that legislation by the United Kingdom Parliament upon imperial affairs might take place only after consultation and with the consent of the Dominions. It came to be accepted that Imperial Acts when passed applied to the Dominions only in so far as the Dominions had consented to their provisions; where consent had not been obtained, the Dominions were left free to adopt or amend the United Kingdom Act in so far as they

[1] 17 & 18 Vict., c. 104; 57 & 58 Vict., c. 60.
[2] 5 & 6 Vict., c. 45 and 1 & 2 Geo. 5, c. 46.
[3] 33 & 34 Vict., c. 14.
[4] 4 & 5 Geo. 5, c. 17; 8 & 9 Geo. 5, c. 38; 12 & 13 Geo. 5, c. 44.

thought fit, or to legislate for themselves, along their own lines. Thus the Copyright Act of 1911, the Maritime Conventions Act, 1911, and the British Nationality and Status of Aliens Act of 1914 were all passed in such terms as were requested and consented to by the Dominions at imperial conferences, and they were made applicable to the Dominions to such an extent only as was consented to by the Dominions. The Copyright Act, for example, did not extend to a self-governing Dominion unless the legislature of that Dominion declared the Act to be in force therein,[1] and the Dominion legislature was empowered to repeal 'all or any of the enactments relating to copyright passed by Parliament (including this Act) so far as they are operative within that dominion', saving all legal rights existing at the time of such repeal.[2] The Maritime Conventions Act[3] did not apply the rules of the convention to the Dominions, but left them free to adopt them or not as they wished; and the British Nationality and Status of Aliens Act, though it created a common status of British subject throughout the Empire, left the Dominions free to adopt Part II of the Act and to declare a local national status upon such terms as they thought fit.[4] In the post-war period legislation giving effect to treaties appears to have been applied to the Dominions only in so far as the Dominions were prepared to accept it; for the most part they were left free to pass their own legislation, wherever they possessed the power to do so. There were certain exceptions, but they were exceptions which broke rather than disproved the rule.

---

[1] s. 25. Contrast Act of 1886, s. 9.   [2] s. 26.
[3] 1 & 2 Geo. 5, c. 57, s. 9. The same principle was followed in the Merchant Shipping (Convention) Act, 1914, 4 & 5 Geo. 5, c. 50, s. 24, and Fifth Schedule.   [4] s. 9.

But the establishment of this convention of consent did not remove entirely the overriding. control of imperial legislation. New laws were passed only with request and consent; but old laws were not entirely repealed. Thus in 1926, as has been mentioned, Canadian legislation purporting to limit the appeal by special leave to the Judicial Committee of the Privy Council was declared invalid on two grounds, one of which was that it was repugnant to the Imperial Acts of 1833 and 1844 which regulated the appeal in Canada, and that in virtue of the Colonial Laws Validity Act, the Canadian legislation was void to the extent of such repugnancy.[1]

The best example of the restrictions which the Colonial Laws Validity Act perpetuated was found in the merchant shipping legislation already referred to. The Merchant Shipping Act of 1894 substantially regulated this sphere of United Kingdom and Dominion economic life. The Act was largely a re-enactment of the Act of 1854, and as was natural in legislation framed at that stage in colonial constitutional development,

it assumes that the general subject of maritime law is exclusively a matter of imperial concern, and that nothing can be safely permitted to the colonies but a minute power of local regulation.[2]

Part III of the Act of 1894, which dealt with emigrant ships, was placed entirely outside colonial legislative competence, and, at the same time, legislation upon subjects covered by the remainder of the Act was required to be reserved.[3]

[1] *Nadan* v. *The King*, [1926] A.C. 482.
[2] H. A. Smith in *Law Quarterly Review*, vol. xliii, 378 at p. 384, 'The Legislative Competence of the Dominions'.
[3] By ss. 735–6 already mentioned above, p. 67.

Thus, although since the Maritime Conventions Act of 1911 maritime legislation of the British Parliament had not been made necessarily applicable to the Dominions, it could be said in 1926 that

these new liberties do not enlarge the general limitations placed upon the Dominions by the Acts of 1890[1] and 1894. The Dominions are now permitted to refuse their assent to new changes in the law initiated by Great Britain, but they have no general power to make new laws according to their own discretion.[2]

There is next to be considered the limitation upon colonial and Dominion legislative competence which is expressed in the rule that colonial or Dominion legislatures lack power to make laws possessing extra-territorial effect. The origin, nature, and extent of the doctrine is obscure and open to controversy.[3] But in so far as the limitation existed, the legislative competence of a Dominion parliament was unequal to that of the United Kingdom Parliament. Now in so far as the limitation arose from the terms of the Dominion Constitution, enacted by the United Kingdom Parliament, and in so far as that limitation made it necessary for the Dominion to rely upon legislation by the United Kingdom Parliament to obtain for its laws extra-territorial effect, to that extent there existed an inequality of legal status as between the Dominion and the United Kingdom.

[1] The Colonial Courts of Admiralty Act.

[2] H. A. Smith, *Law Quarterly Review*, vol. xliii, at pp. 384–5. See the Australian case *Union Steamship Co.* v. *The Commonwealth*, 36 C.L.R. 130.

[3] Lord Sankey in *British Coal Corporation* v. *The King*, [1935] A.C. 500 at p. 520. The controversy is illustrated by the divergence of views expressed by H. A. Smith, supporting a measure of Dominion competence to legislate with extra-territorial effect in criminal matters (*Canadian Bar Review*, vol. i, at pp. 338–50) and A. B. Keith, to the contrary, *Journal of Comparative Legislation* (1923), 3rd series, vol. v, at p. 274.

The O.D.L. Conference of 1929[1] concluded that 'it would not seem to be possible in the present state of the authorities to come to definite conclusions regarding the competence of Dominion Parliaments to give their legislation extra-territorial operation'.[2] And they indicated the inconvenience which arose from this position when they wrote that

it introduces a general uncertainty which can be illustrated by questions raised concerning fisheries, taxation, shipping, air navigation, marriage, criminal law, deportation, and the enforcement of laws against smuggling and unlawful immigration.[3]

Thus, in matters which were often purely of domestic concern, a Dominion lacked power to legislate as it thought fit.

The limitations upon colonial and Dominion legislative competence which arose from disallowance, from reservation, from the supremacy of the United Kingdom Parliament as expressed in the Colonial Laws Validity Act, and from the lack of extra-territorial power were considerable. But it must be emphasized that within the sphere confided to the colony, subject to these restrictions, the colonial legislature was supreme and sovereign. A colonial legislature was 'a Legislature restricted in the area of its powers, but within that area unrestricted, and not acting as an agent or a delegate'.[4] The position is shortly and admirably stated in a passage from *Phillips* v. *Eyre*:

---

[1] For their treatment of the limitation see *O.D.L. Report*, Cmd. 3479, paras. 37–44.

[2] *Ibid.*, para. 39.   [3] *Ibid.*, para. 38.

[4] Sir Robert Collier in *Powell* v. *Apollo Candle Co.*, (1885) 10 A.C. 282 at p. 290.

... A confirmed act of the local legislature lawfully constituted, whether in a settled or a conquered colony, has, as
to matters within its competence and the limits of its jurisdiction, the operation and force of sovereign legislation,
though subject to be controlled by the imperial parliament.[1]

3

There was, next, an element of colonial subordination
to the United Kingdom in the existence of the appeal
from the courts in a colony to the Judicial Committee of
the Privy Council.[2] The extent of that restriction upon
Dominion judicial autonomy should not be exaggerated.
The fact that the appeals were heard by a tribunal sitting
in London and not in the Dominion did not of itself
constitute an element of inequality of status. But there
appear to have been at least two respects in which inequality did exist. In the first place, the Judicial Committee in its personnel was, and is, predominantly a
United Kingdom and not a colonial or Dominion tribunal. It was true that from 1895[3] provision was made
for a fuller representation of Dominion judges upon the
Board, so that in 1926 it comprised the Lord President of
the Council, former Lords President, the Lord Chancellor
and former Lords Chancellor, all members of the Privy
Council who hold or had held high judicial office (that is
to say persons who are or have been Lords of Appeal in

[1] (1870) L.R. 6 Q.B. 1 at p. 20. See also Lord Selborne, *The Queen* v.
Burah, (1878) 3 A.C. 889 at p. 904; Sir Barnes Peacock, *Hodge* v. *The
Queen*, (1883) 9 A.C. 117 at p. 132; Lord Halsbury, *Riel* v. *The Queen*,
(1885) 10 A.C. 675 at p. 678; Lord Loreburn, *Att.-Gen. for Ontario* v.
Att-Gen. for Canada, [1912] A.C. 571 at p. 581.
[2] Keith, *Responsible Government in the Dominions* (ed. 1928), vol ii,
part vi, c. iii.
[3] Judicial Committee Amendment Act, 1895 (58 & 59 Vict., c. 44).
Subsequent Acts were 8 Ed. 7, c. 51, and 3 & 4 Geo. 5, c. 21.

Ordinary, Judges of the Supreme Court in England, or of the Court of Session in Scotland), and in addition to these United Kingdom members, Privy Councillors who hold or had held office as judges of the Superior Courts of the Dominions,[1] or of a High Court in British India (up to the number of two) together with others specially appointed up to the number of four, of whom two must be specially qualified in Indian law. In addition any judge of a Superior Court of a Dominion from which an appeal was being heard might be summoned to sit. But in spite of these provisions the Judicial Committee in hearing appeals from the Dominions remained predominantly a Board composed of Law Lords from England and Scotland. Dominion judges seldom sat, and the Dominion governments for the most part took few steps to ensure permanent representation of such judges upon the Committee.

The second limitation was found in the nature of the appeal itself. Appeals came to the Judicial Committee either by special leave of the Judicial Committee itself or without special leave of the Judicial Committee.[2] The former is usually called the appeal as of grace, and the latter the appeal as of right. The distinction appears to be that in the appeal as of grace the subject has the right, where it is not expressly abridged or abol-

[1] That is to say, of the Supreme Court of Canada, the High Court of Australia, the Appellate Division of the Supreme Court of South Africa, the Supreme Court of New Zealand, the Supreme Court of Newfoundland, the Supreme Courts and other superior courts of the Australian States and the Canadian Provinces. The number of these Dominion judges had been limited to 5 in 1895, and was extended to 7 by 3 & 4 Geo. 5, c. 21. This limitation was abolished in 1928 by the Administration of Justice Act, s. 13.

[2] See Lord Sankey, [1935] A.C. 500 at pp. 510-12. Cf. also Lord Cave in *Nadan* v. *The King*, [1926] A.C. 482 at p. 491.

ished, and subject to any valid conditions laid down, to ask the Judicial Committee for special leave to appeal and the Judicial Committee has the right to grant or refuse leave. In the appeal of right the subject has the right, where it is not expressly abridged or abolished, and subject to any valid conditions laid down, to appeal to the Judicial Committee without asking special leave of the Judicial Committee, and the Judicial Committee has the duty to admit and determine such an appeal.

The right of the subject in His Majesty's Dominions beyond the seas to appeal to His Majesty in Council from any Court in His Majesty's Dominions was 'a privilege belonging to every subject of the King'.[1] It extended to judgements in criminal as well as in civil cases and it was recognized and regulated in a series of statutes, of which the Acts of 1833 and 1844 are the most important. The Act of 1833[2] recited that 'from the decisions of various courts of judicature in the East Indies and in the Plantations, Colonies, and other Dominions of His Majesty abroad, an appeal lies to His Majesty in Council'. It proceeded to constitute a Judicial Committee of the Privy Council to which such appeals should be referred, and regulated the manner in which appeals should be heard. The Act of 1844[3] is more important, for it expressly extends the jurisdiction of the Committee and provides that Her Majesty may provide by general or special Order-in-Council 'for the admission of any appeal or appeals to Her Majesty in Council from any judgements, sentences, decrees, or orders of any Court of justice within any British Colony or Possession abroad'. This was an assertion in the widest form of the right of Her Majesty to hear appeals and of the right of the

[1] Lord Cave, *loc. cit.*   [2] 3 & 4 Wm. 4, c. 41.   [3] 7 & 8 Vict., c. 69, s. 1.

subject to ask leave to appeal. 'These Acts, and other later
statutes by which the constitution of the Judicial Committee has from time to time been amended, give legislative sanction to the jurisdiction which had previously
existed.'[1] The Act of 1833, further, provided that it
should be lawful for His Majesty to refer to the Judicial
Committee for hearing or consideration 'any such other
matters whatsoever as His Majesty shall think fit' and
for the Judicial Committee to hear and consider them
and to advise His Majesty.[2]

The unrestricted right of the subject to appeal to the
Judicial Committee and of the Judicial Committee to
hear and determine such appeals was in fact limited by
statute and Orders-in-Council and otherwise in so far as
the colonies and Dominions were concerned. In the
first place, the right of the subject to appeal without obtaining special leave of the Judicial Committee had been
restricted or abolished by Act of the United Kingdom
Parliament, by Order-in-Council, or by colonial laws
passed under the authority of some Act of the United
Kingdom Parliament. In this way the appeal without
special leave of the Judicial Committee had been made
subject, where it existed, to the requirement that no such
appeal should lie unless the sum in dispute in the case
was of £500 or more; or unless leave to appeal was given
by the court in the colony. In 1926 the appeal without

---

[1] Lord Cave, *ibid.*, at p. 492.
[2] s. 4. The best-known case of this special reference in respect of the
Dominions was that of the Labrador Boundary Dispute between Canada
and Newfoundland when His Majesty was petitioned to refer to the
Judicial Committee the question: 'What is the location and definition
of the boundary as between Canada and Newfoundland in the Labrador
Peninsula under the Statutes, Orders-in-Council and Proclamations?'
(43 T.L.R. 289.)

special leave of the Judicial Committee existed, subject
to such conditions as these, from the Court of Appeal
and the Supreme Court of New Zealand, from the
Supreme Court of Newfoundland, from the Supreme
Courts of the Australian States (in their state jurisdiction, though not in the federal jurisdiction vested in
them by the Commonwealth Parliament), and from the
superior courts of the Canadian Provinces. No such
right of appeal existed from the High Court of Australia
or from the Supreme Court of South Africa,[1] or from the
Supreme Court of the Irish Free State, the right in each
case having been abolished by imperial enactment.[2]
A Canadian Act of 1888 had purported to abolish the
right of appeal with or without special leave of the
Judicial Committee in criminal cases[3] and the parties in
Nadan v. *The King* accepted the view that the appeal
without special leave had been effectively abolished,

presumably on the ground that the Dominion Parliament
having exclusive legislative authority in respect of the procedure in criminal matters throughout Canada, had power
to deprive the Canadian Courts of any jurisdiction to grant
leave to appeal in those matters.[4]

The Judicial Committee was not asked to decide the
question. It was concerned with the appeal by special

[1] One apparent exception was that appeals still lay as of right from
the decisions of the Appellate Division of the Supreme Court of South
Africa in cases arising from colonial Courts of Admiralty, but this was
not really an exception, since that jurisdiction fell directly under Imperial legislation and the appeal lay outside the normal South African
internal jurisdiction. Keith, *Responsible Government in the Dominions* (ed.
1928), p. 1097.

[2] Australian Constitution, s. 73; South Africa Act, s. 106; Irish Free
State Constitution, Art. 66.

[3] 51 Vict., c. 43. Revised Statutes 1906, c. 146, s. 1025.

[4] [1926] A.C. 482 at p. 490.

leave only; and therefore it assumed 'for the purposes of this case, that the leave to appeal granted by the Supreme Court was ineffective', that is to say that no appeal without special leave existed.[1] It is clear then that in 1926 no limitation upon the judicial autonomy of the Dominion of Canada, the Union of South Africa, the Commonwealth of Australia, or the Irish Free State could be held to exist in virtue of any right of appeal from the highest courts of these Dominions to the Judicial Committee without special leave of the Judicial Committee.

'But outside these limits', to quote from Lord Sankey's words in *British Coal Corporation* v. *The King*, 'there had always been reserved a discretion to the King in Council to grant special leave to appeal from a colonial Court irrespective of the limitations fixed by the colonial law.'[2] This right of the subject to ask special leave and of the Judicial Committee to grant such leave was recognized and regulated primarily by the Act of 1844. In 1926 it existed unimpaired in respect of Canada, South Africa, New Zealand, the Irish Free State, Newfoundland, the Australian States, and the Canadian Provinces. In the Commonwealth of Australia, however, it had been restricted by Imperial enactment in express words.

No appeal shall be permitted to the Queen in Council from a decision of the High Court upon any question, howsoever arising, as to the limits *inter se* of the Constitutional powers of the Commonwealth and those of any State or States, or as to the limits *inter se* of the Constitutional powers of any two or more States, unless the High Court shall certify

[1] [1926] A.C. 482 at p. 490.
[2] [1935] A.C. 500 at p. 511.

that the question is one which ought to be determined by
Her Majesty in Council. The High Court may so certify if
satisfied that for any special reason the certificate should be
granted, thereupon an appeal shall lie to Her Majesty in
Council on the question without further leave.[1]

This power has been exercised sparingly by the High
Court of Australia. A certificate has been granted in one
case only.[2] The decision of the Judicial Committee in
this case[3] and its decisions in certain earlier constitutional cases,[4] tended to confirm opinion in favour of
restricting appeals, as far as possible, both by legislation
and by judicial decision.[5] In particular the Commonwealth Parliament, in its amendments to the Judiciary
Act, had prevented any of the *inter se* questions referred
to in section 74 from being dealt with by the Supreme
Courts of the States otherwise than upon the condition that any appeal should be to the High Court
only.[6] Apart from the cases covered by section 74, the
appeal by special leave existed in 1926 in the case of
Australia.

It is necessary to inquire next whether any of these
Dominions possessed any power to restrict or abolish the
appeal by special leave. It was held that there were

[1] Constitution, s. 74.
[2] *Colonial Sugar Refining Co., Ltd.* v. *Att.-Gen. for the Commonwealth*, 15
C.L.R. 182 at p. 234.   [3] [1914] A.C. 237.
[4] e.g. *Webb* v. *Outtrim*, [1907] A.C. 81.
[5] On the other hand, since 1926 opinion has changed a little and it is
stated that the decision in *James* v. *The Commonwealth*, [1936] A.C. 578
'has materially strengthened the prestige of the Privy Council as a final
court of appeal from Australia'. (Australian correspondent in *The Round
Table*, No. 105, p. 199.)
[6] Judiciary Act, 1903–27, ss. 38 A to 40 A. There is considerable
difference of judicial opinion about the validity of these amendments.
See J. G. Latham, *Australia and the British Commonwealth*, pp. 115–17.

three obstacles in the way of restriction or abolition. In the first place, the right of the Judicial Committee to grant special leave to appeal was a prerogative right, and it was established that for a colonial legislature to enact valid legislation restricting or abolishing a prerogative right it was necessary not only that the colonial statute itself should

deal with the prerogative either by express terms or by necessary intendment, but it must be the Act of a Dominion or Colonial Legislature which has been endowed with the requisite power by an Imperial Act likewise giving the power either by express terms or by necessary intendment.[1]

But, in the second place, even if the colonial legislature had this power to deal with the prerogative, any such legislation purporting to restrict or abolish the appeal by special leave would be repugnant to the Acts of 1833 and 1844 and void to the extent of such repugnancy. And finally, it was held, any such legislation, to be effective in restricting the prerogative power to grant special leave, would require to have extra-territorial operation, and, in the absence of an endowment of such a power by the Imperial Parliament, colonial laws did not possess extra-territorial effect. If, therefore, a colonial legislature was to restrict or abolish the appeal by special leave, it must possess powers to overcome all three obstacles.

In 1926 it was decided in *Nadan* v. *The King* that the Canadian Parliament lacked power to overcome at least two of the obstacles, viz. that its legislation would be repugnant to the Acts of 1833 and 1844 and void to the extent of such repugnancy, and that its legislation could only be effective if construed as having an extra-

[1] *British Coal Corporation* v. *The King*, [1935] A.C. 500 at p. 519.

territorial operation, whereas according to the law as it was in 1926 a Dominion statute could not have extra-territorial operation.[1]

It might be argued, too, that on a reasonable interpretation of that judgement, their Lordships implied at least that the Canadian Parliament lacked power to abolish the appeal by special leave because it was an exercise of the prerogative. But in 1935 the Judicial Committee, in explaining the judgment in *Nadan's Case*, held that no actual decision upon this point had been taken in 1926, and they proceeded therefore to decide it.[2] They held that the powers conferred upon the Parliament of Canada by the British North America Act, 1867,[3] to regulate 'the criminal law, except the constitution of courts of criminal jurisdiction, but including the procedure in criminal matters' and to provide for a general Court of Appeal for Canada, were sufficient, not by express words but by necessary intendment, to enable the Parliament of Canada, in the absence of the two fetters already referred to, to restrict or abolish the prerogative power to grant special leave to appeal.

At any rate there existed two obstacles in 1926 to the abolition of the appeal by Canada. The same two obstacles prevented the restriction or abolition of the appeal by New Zealand, Newfoundland, the Australian States, and the Canadian Provinces.[4] The Irish Free State, on the Canadian model, was unable similarly to restrict or abolish the appeal. Australia and South

---

[1] Lord Sankey's words in *British Coal Corporation* v. *The King*, [1935] A.C. 500 at p. 516.   [2] *Ibid.*, at pp. 516 ff.   [3] ss. 91(27), 101.

[4] It is probable that the third obstacle, viz. lack of power to deal with the prerogative, did not exist for these legislatures either, on the argument adopted in the *British Coal Corporation Case*. See especially [1935] A.C. 500 at pp. 520-2.

Africa were in a special position. Their Parliaments[1] were empowered to make laws limiting the matters in which special leave to appeal might be asked, but such laws must be reserved for the Sovereign's pleasure. Further, the appeal could have been abolished by the ordinary process of constitutional amendment. In fact no legislation had been passed by these Dominions to restrict the appeal, and no constitutional amendment had been passed to abolish it.

A word may be said, in conclusion, of the extent to which the right to grant special leave to appeal has been exercised in practice by the Judicial Committee. Here it is found that their Lordships regard themselves as bound by certain rules. First, in respect of criminal cases, the words of Lord Halsbury in *Riel* v. *The Queen* express the customary rule adopted by the Committee. He said:

It is the usual rule of this Committee not to grant leave to appeal in criminal cases, except where some clear departure from the requirements of justice is alleged to have taken place.[2]

This view has often been stated[3] and it restricts the legal power of the Committee to admit appeals by special leave in criminal cases whether they come from the Dominions or from the Colonies.

[1] Australian Constitution, s. 74; South Africa Act, s. 106.
[2] (1885) 10 A.C. 675 at p. 677.
[3] e.g. Lord Cave in *Nadan* v. *The King*, [1926] A.C. 482 at p. 495 and the cases there cited by him. (Keir and Lawson, *op. cit.*, pp. 448–9.) Cf. also Lord Dunedin in *Knowles* v. *The King*, [1930] A.C. 366 at pp. 371–2. In this case leave to appeal was granted from the decision of a judge in Ashanti who, sitting without a jury, convicted and sentenced the appellant to death on a charge of murder, without considering the possibility of manslaughter. The appeal was allowed.

In respect of civil cases, the Committee's rule was laid down clearly by Lord Fitzgerald in *Prince* v. *Gagnon*. He said:

... Their Lordships are not prepared to advise Her Majesty to exercise her prerogative by admitting an appeal to Her Majesty in Council from the Supreme Court of the Dominion, save where the case is of gravity involving matter of public interest or some important question of law, or affecting property of considerable amount, or where the case is otherwise of some public importance or of a very substantial character.[1]

Lord Haldane in 1923 uttered certain *obiter dicta* in the Irish case *Hull* v. *McKenna* which suggested that the Committee granted special leave to appeal from the highest court of a federal Dominion more readily than from the highest court of a unitary Dominion, and further that in granting leave account was taken of the wishes of the Dominion concerned. In fact appeals had been seldom entertained from the Appellate Division of the Supreme Court of South Africa,[2] and the Committee were reluctant to admit appeals from the Irish Free State. Appeals from New Zealand were frequently heard, though New Zealand was a unitary Dominion, but it expressed no objection to the appeal. In the federations, appeals from Australia on certain constitutional matters were effectively restricted by the Constitution

[1] (1882) 8 A.C. 103, at p. 105. Cf. also *Johnston* v. *Minister of St. Andrew's Church, Montreal*, (1877) 3 A.C. 159; *Valin* v. *Langlois*, (1879) 5 A.C. 115; *Montreal* v. *Ecclésiastiques de St. Sulpice*, (1889) 14 A.C. 660; *Daily Telegraph* v. *McLaughlin*, [1904] A.C. 776; *Hull* v. *McKenna*, [1926] I.R. 402, Lord Haldane at p. 404, Lord Buckmaster at p. 409.

[2] Leave to appeal had been given three times only before 1934; in that year leave was given in *Pearl Assurance Co.* v. *Union Government*, [1934] A.C. 570. See South African *House of Assembly Debates*, vol. xxviii, Col. D. Reitz, Minister of Agriculture and Forestry, col. 226.

itself as has been seen, but appeals from Canada were unrestricted and were frequently heard. In the result the Judicial Committee was the final authority in interpreting the Canadian Constitution.[1] It is interesting to notice, in respect of Canadian constitutional appeals, that a power existed in Canada to refer questions to the Supreme Courts of the Provinces and of the Dominion for an advisory opinion. These questions came on appeal to the Judicial Committee. The exercise of this power by the executive to consult the Judiciary was held to be valid in *Attorney-General for Ontario* v. *Attorney-General for Canada*,[2] though Lord Loreburn stressed 'the mischief and inconvenience which might arise from an indiscriminate and injudicious use' of the power. The practice of obtaining judicial opinions beforehand is not favoured on the whole by judges in England.[3] Lord Haldane considered that the Canadian experience had not been satisfactory. 'I have had a long experience of these questions,' he said in 1928. 'I have decided scores and scores of them, and anything more unsatisfactory and more mischievous I do not know.'[4]

[1] The trend of this interpretation is discussed by V. C. MacDonald in *University of Toronto Law Journal*, vol. i, p. 260. See also R. Tuck, *ibid.*, vol. iv; and *Canadian Bar Review*, vol. xv, No. 6.   [2] [1912] A.C. 571.

[3] See, e.g., a debate in the House of Lords in 1928 on the Rating and Valuation Bill, which proposed, by clause 4, to give power to the executive, in certain events, to secure the interpretation of certain questions of rating law by propounding hypothetical cases to the High Court. The majority of judicial opinion in the Lords was against the proposal (see Lord Haldane, 70 *H.L. Deb.*, 5 s., 630; Lord Hanworth, *ibid.* 631; Lord Carson, *ibid.* 626; Lord Merrivale, *ibid.* 636; Lord Atkin, *ibid.* 775), and despite a forceful defence from Lord Birkenhead, the Government withdrew the clause (*ibid.* 917–18). For a discussion of the problem see E. C. S. Wade, *Law Quarterly Review*, vol. xlvi, pp. 169 ff.; a criticism by C. K. Allen in *ibid.*, vol. xlvii, pp. 43 ff., and a reply by E. C. S. Wade, pp. 58 ff.   [4] 70 *H.L. Deb.*, 5 s., 630 and 765.

There remained one most important field in which in
1926 a measure of inequality of status existed between
the Dominions and the United Kingdom, and that was
the field of foreign relations. In this field, usage and
convention had combined before 1914 to render the
exercise of the legal powers of the King conditional in
some degree upon consultation with, and consent from,
the Dominion Governments. That process had been
taken still further by the Imperial War Conference of
1917, the Paris Peace Conference, and the Imperial
Conference of 1923. But the subject is complex, and
it is impossible to treat it adequately or accurately in
a brief space.[1] Moreover, inasmuch as the Statute of
Westminster did not deal directly with the relations of
the United Kingdom Government and the Dominion
Governments, but rather with the relations of the United
Kingdom Parliament and the Dominion Parliaments,
it is submitted that a full discussion of the problem of
equality of status in foreign relations is not strictly relevant to the purpose of this book. The subject is mentioned merely as a further illustration of the general
thesis that the interaction of usage and convention with
rules of strict law is a fundamental characteristic of the
constitutional structure of the British Commonwealth.

---

[1] The best treatment is in R. B. Stewart, *Treaty Relations of the British
Commonwealth of Nations* (1939).

IV

THE SPECIAL CASE OF THE IRISH FREE STATE

I

IT is proposed now to consider the position of the Irish Free State. In what respects did it possess a status of inequality, by law or by convention, to the United Kingdom in 1926? The question cannot be answered without doubt. In 1926 the Constitution of 1922 was in operation in the Irish Free State.

The legal basis of the Constitution of 1922 is a matter of irreconcilable dispute.[1] There are not one but several essential documents to be taken into account. There are the 'Articles of Agreement for a Treaty between Great Britain and Ireland', signed by British and Irish representatives in London on December 6, 1921.[2] There is the Irish Free State (Agreement) Act, 1922,[3] an Act passed by the United Kingdom Parliament, and assented to by the King on March 31, 1922. Section 1 (1) of this Act stated that as from the date of the passing of the Act, the Articles of Agreement, which were scheduled to the Act, should have the force of law. Next there is the Constitution of the Irish Free State (Saorstát Eireann) Act, 1922,[4] described as an 'Act of Dáil Eireann, sitting as a Constituent Assembly, enacting a Constitution for the

[1] See L. Kohn, *The Constitution of the Irish Free State*, and N. Mansergh, *The Irish Free State, its Government and Politics*.

[2] Printed in Keith, *Speeches and Documents on the British Dominions*, pp. 77–83. For a clear and exciting account of the making of the treaty, see F. Pakenham, *Peace by Ordeal*.   [3] 12 Geo. 5, c. 4.

[4] Keith, *op. cit.*, pp. 107–19. The Constitution contained 83 Articles, of which a selection only is printed by Professor Keith.

Irish Free State'. The Act was passed on October 25, 1922, and is referred to as 'No. 1 of 1922'. It consists of a Constituent Act of three sections, and to this Constituent Act are attached two Schedules. The First Schedule contains the Constitution of the Irish Free State, and the Second Schedule contains the Articles of Agreement. The Constituent Act declares[1] that the Constitution set forth in the First Schedule shall be the Constitution of the Irish Free State, and it declares that the Articles of Agreement set forth in the Second Schedule 'are hereby given the force of law'.[2] Finally, there is the Irish Free State Constitution Act, 1922,[3] an Act of the United Kingdom Parliament, which received the Royal Assent on December 5, 1922. This is an Act of five sections, and to it is attached as a Schedule the 'Act of Dáil Eireann' above mentioned,[4] which, in its turn, carried with it, as already mentioned, the Constitution as its First Schedule and the Articles of Agreement as its Second Schedule. This Act of the United Kingdom Parliament declared that 'the Constitution set forth in the First Schedule to the Constituent Act shall, subject to the provisions to which the same is by the Constituent Act so made subject . . ., be the Constitution of the Irish Free State . . . .'.[5]

These are the essential documents. The irreconcilable dispute arises when an attempt is made to decide their legal relation to each other. Two views have obtained judicial recognition. There is first the view that the Constitution of the Irish Free State (Saorstát Eireann) Act or Constituent Act, and the Scheduled Constitution and

[1] s. 1.   [2] s. 2.   [3] 13 Geo. 5 (sess. 2), c. 1.
[4] i.e. the Constitution of the Irish Free State (Saorstát Eireann) Act.
[5] s. 1.

Articles of Agreement owe their legal force in the Irish
Free State to their enactment by Dáil Eireann, which
possessed supreme legislative authority. This view
received its most authoritative expression from the
Supreme Court of the Irish Free State, more particularly
in the case of *The State (Ryan)* v. *Lennon*,[1] decided in
1934, and might therefore be described conveniently,
though not with complete accuracy, as 'the view in
Ryan's Case'. It was elaborated in most detail perhaps
in the judgement of Chief Justice Kennedy in that case,
and also in some passages in his judgement in an earlier
case, *Lynham* v. *Butler*, in 1927.[2] 'The Constitution, or
Bunreacht', said the Chief Justice, 'is the fundamental
structure upon which the State was set up by the Third
Dáil Eireann sitting as a Constituent Assembly. The
Dáil thereby formulated the system or principles, and
created the organs, of government of the State.'[3] On
the other side is the completely opposing view which
received its most authoritative expression from the
Judicial Committee of the Privy Council, more particularly in the case of *Moore* v. *The Attorney-General for the
Irish Free State*,[4] decided in 1935, and might therefore
be described conveniently, though again rather inac-
curately, as 'the view in *Moore's Case*'. This view can
best be stated in a passage from the Board's opinion in
that case.

In their opinion,—said Lord Sankey—the Constituent

---

[1] [1935] I.R. 170.   [2] [1933] I.R. 74.
[3] [1935] I.R. 170 at p. 203. FitzGibbon J. in the same case said that
he was not disposed to quarrel with the statement 'that the Constitution
was proclaimed in the name of the people by Dáil Eireann as an act of
supreme authority, which it alone had the right to do, because it was the
mouthpiece of the people, requiring and receiving no Royal assent'.
Ibid., at p. 226.   [4] [1935] A.C. 484; [1935] I.R. 472.

Act and the Constitution of the Irish Free State derived their validity from the Act of the Imperial Parliament, the Irish Free State Constitution Act, 1922. This Act established that the Constitution, subject to the provisions of the Constituent Act, should be the Constitution of the Irish Free State and should come into operation on being proclaimed by His Majesty, as was done on December 6, 1922. The action of the House of Parliament was thereby ratified; apart from such ratification that body had no authority to make a Constitution. . . .[1]

These views are clearly irreconcilable. The one takes its start from an Irish legislature possessed of supreme authority to enact a Constitution in exercise of its undoubted right, and regards the Acts of the United Kingdom Parliament as valid and necessary only in so far as they give force of law in the United Kingdom to the changes consequential upon the recognition by the United Kingdom of the establishment of the Irish Free State. The other takes its start from the United Kingdom Parliament as the only source of legal authority, and regards the Irish legislature and its enactments as legally valid in the United Kingdom or in the Irish Free State only in so far as they derive such force of law from Acts of the United Kingdom Parliament. The argument proceeds on parallel lines.

It is not possible in this chapter to enter into a detailed discussion of the merits of these two conflicting interpretations of the legal basis of the Free State Constitution. But it is necessary to know what are the principal implications of each interpretation if one is to state precisely the nature and extent of the juridical inequalities of status possessed by the Irish Free State in 1926. To

[1] [1935] A.C. 484 at p. 497.

understand the difference of view it is necessary to go back into the history of Anglo-Irish relations before December 6, 1922, not necessarily to the Battle of the Boyne, but at least to 1918, and to trace the development of the two opposing theories.[1]

At the General Election for the United Kingdom Parliament in December 1918, Sinn Fein candidates in Ireland were successful in almost all constituencies except in the north-eastern counties of Ulster. They were pledged not to take their seats at Westminster. Instead they assembled at Dublin,[2] proclaimed the independence of the Irish Republic on January 21, 1919, constituted themselves a legislature for the whole of Ireland in virtue of their election by an overwhelming majority of the Irish electorate, and appointed a ministry responsible to themselves with Mr. de Valera as Príomh-Aire or First Minister.[3] This body was called the First Dáil Eireann. On the view in *Moore's Case* it was at the least a party meeting in Dublin of a majority of the members of the United Kingdom Parliament elected from Ireland, and at the most an insurrectionary congress. There followed open hostilities between the Dáil Ministry and the Lord-Lieutenant's Government.

In 1920 the Government of Ireland Act[4] was passed. It divided Ireland into two parts, Northern Ireland, to consist of the six counties of north-eastern Ulster—Antrim, Armagh, Down, Fermanagh, Londonderry, and Tyrone—with Belfast and Londonderry; and Southern Ireland, to consist of the remaining counties and

[1] The writer has based the following account on Kohn, *op. cit.*, Mansergh, *op. cit.*, and B. Ó Briain, *The Irish Constitution*.
[2] With the exception of those in prison.
[3] Usually translated 'President'.
[4] 10 & 11 Gco. 5, c. 67.

boroughs. It established separate parliaments for Northern and Southern Ireland, each to consist of a Senate and House of Commons; and it authorized the setting up of a Council of Ireland, to be elected in equal numbers by and from the members of the two Parliaments.

Elections were held in May 1921. On the view in *Moore's Case* these elections were authorized by a proclamation of the Lord-Lieutenant issued under the authority of the Government of Ireland Act, 1920, and the resulting House of Commons for Southern Ireland derived its legal existence and authority from this Act. The First Dáil, however, declared these elections to the Houses of Commons illegal, but decided to regard them as elections to itself. The resulting assembly, in their view, was the Second Dáil Eireann, which derived its legal existence and authority from the resolution of the First Dáil, the latter being dissolved upon the summoning of the newly elected Dáil by Mr. de Valera. The First Dáil refused, also, to recognize the partition of Ireland, and the Second Dáil claimed authority to legislate for the whole of Ireland. Meanwhile a Northern Ireland Parliament came into existence with a ministry, under Sir James Craig (later Lord Craigavon), responsible to it.

The Second Dáil Ministry and the Lord-Lieutenant's Government continued to fight each other until the truce of July 11, 1921. Negotiations for a peace settlement began and a conference opened on October 11, 1921. Throughout these preliminary negotiations, and during the conference itself, the Second Dáil and its Ministry maintained that they represented a separate Irish Republic negotiating with the British Government, a claim which on the British side was never explicitly admitted.[1] The Irish negotiators were nominated by the Dáil Ministry, they received full powers signed by Mr. de Valera,[2] they reported to the Dáil Ministry from time to time,[3] and they signed a *Treaty*, a final proof of their independent national status.[4] On the British view, in strict law the British ministers were negotiating the settlement of a dispute with certain chosen representatives of the Irish people, members of the House of Commons for Southern Ireland, and with them they signed an *Agreement* expressing their intention to take such legislative and administrative steps as were necessary to establish an Irish Free State, which would be a distinct nation, but not a disconnected nation, in the 'Community of Nations known as the British Empire'.[5] Far from recognizing the Second Dáil and its Ministry, the Articles of Agreement provided for the establishment of a Provisional Government in Southern Ireland to conduct administration until the constitution of a Parliament and Government of the new Irish Free State.

. . . Steps shall be taken forthwith—it ran—for summoning a meeting of members of Parliament elected for constituencies in Southern Ireland since the passing of the Government of Ireland Act, 1920, and for constituting a provisional Government, and the British Government shall take the steps necessary to transfer to such provisional Government the powers and machinery requisite for the discharge of its duties, provided that every member of such provisional Government shall have signified in writing his or her

[1] See correspondence between Mr. de Valera and Mr. Lloyd George, Cmd. 1539.   [2] Printed in Mansergh, *op. cit.*, pp. 30 and 31.
[3] Mansergh, *ibid.*, p. 31.
[4] See Kennedy C.J., *In re W. J. Reade* [1927] I.R. 31, at p. 47.
[5] Article 1.

acceptance of this instrument. But this arrangement shall not continue in force beyond the expiration of twelve months from the date hereof.[1]

In this way the British legal view was maintained, but the element of compromise was found in the description of the terms of the settlement as 'Articles of Agreement for a Treaty'.

Northern Ireland, by Articles 11 and 12, was given the opportunity of 'contracting out' of the new Irish Free State if it chose to do so. It was provided that, if, within a month from the ratification of the Agreement by Act of Parliament, the Houses of Parliament of Northern Ireland passed an Address to that effect, the powers of the Parliament and Government of the Irish Free State would not extend to them. And in fact such an Address was passed and Northern Ireland continued to exist as established by the Government of Ireland Act, 1920.

When the Articles of Agreement came to be approved and ratified by both parties, the legal divergence persisted. Article 18 provided that 'this instrument shall be submitted forthwith by His Majesty's Government for the approval of Parliament and by the Irish signatories to a meeting summoned for the purpose of the members elected to sit in the House of Commons of Southern Ireland, and if approved shall be ratified by the necessary legislation'. Here again there was no recognition of the Second Dáil. On the British side, the Agreement had been approved by both Houses of the United Kingdom Parliament on December 16, 1921,[2] though this approval did not give the Agreement the force of law. On the Irish side, the Treaty was im-

---

[1] Article 17.
[2] 149 *H.C. Deb.*, 5 s., 363 and 48 *H.L. Deb.*, 5 s., 217.

mediately submitted by the Dáil Ministry to the Dáil, and was approved by a majority on January 7, 1922, though this approval did not purport to give force of law to the Treaty in Ireland. The Treaty did not confer upon Ireland the status of an independent or even of an associated republic, but merely the status of a Dominion, and Mr. de Valera and his supporters resigned from the Dáil Ministry. Arthur Griffith succeeded him as First Minister.

On the Irish view in *Ryan's Case* the Treaty had now been approved by the competent authority, the Dáil.[1] But Article 18 had not yet been complied with. Griffith therefore called the prescribed meeting of members of the House of Commons for Southern Ireland a week later, January 14, 1922, and the Agreement was approved. In this way the British view was maintained. The Agreement had been approved by a body whose legal existence and authority were derived from the Government of Ireland Act, 1920.

At the same meeting of the House of Commons of Southern Ireland on January 14, a Provisional Government was set up, in accordance with Article 17, with Michael Collins as its chairman, and its personnel almost identical with that of the Second Dáil Ministry.[2] These two Governments functioned side by side for about seven months, an interesting illustration of the two theories whose development we have discussed. The

---

[1] Mr. de Valera and his supporters held that the Dáil was not legally competent to approve a Treaty which violated the Republican Declaration of 1919. They reject therefore the view in *Ryan's Case* of the Treaty and the Constitution. There are thus not one but at least two 'Irish' views, the view in *Ryan's Case* and the Republican view. But the latter was not judicially recognized and is therefore ignored here.

[2] The names of the two ministries are given in Mansergh, *ibid.*, p. 39.

British view was maintained that the Provisional Government in Southern Ireland derived its existence and authority from the Act of the United Kingdom Parliament. The Dáil Ministry was accorded no legal recognition.

So far the Articles of Agreement had not obtained force of law in Ireland or in Great Britain. The United Kingdom Parliament therefore passed the Irish Free State (Agreement) Act, which received the Royal assent on March 31, 1922. This Act was expressly declared[1] not to be that Act of Parliament for the ratification of the Agreement from the date of which the 'Ulster month' provided for in Article 11 was to run. But, with this reservation, the Act, on the British view in *Moore's Case*, gave force of law to the Agreement in Great Britain and Ireland; on the Irish view in *Ryan's Case* it merely gave force of law to the Treaty in the municipal law of Great Britain.[2] It was not, on the latter view, until the Third Dáil passed the Constitution of the Irish Free State (Saorstát Eireann) Act on October 25, 1922, that the Treaty received force of law in the Free State.[3]

The Irish Free State (Agreement) Act, further, gave no recognition to the Second Dáil or the Dáil Ministry. It provided that, within four months of its passage, the Parliament of Southern Ireland should be dissolved, and that steps should be taken for holding

in accordance with the law now in force with respect to the franchise, number of members and method of election and holding of elections to that Parliament, an election of members for the constituencies which would have been entitled

[1] s. 1 (5).
[2] e.g. Kennedy C.J., *The State (Ryan)* v. *Lennon* [1935] I.R. 170, at p. 205.   [3] By s. 2.

to elect members to that Parliament, and the members so elected shall constitute the House of the Parliament to which the Provisional Government shall be responsible, and that Parliament shall, as respects matters within the jurisdiction of the Provisional Government, have power to make laws in like manner as the Parliament of the Irish Free State when constituted.[1]

Elections were held in June, 1922. They were authorized, on the view in *Moore's Case*, by a proclamation of the Lord-Lieutenant, dated May 27, 1922, issued pursuant to the Irish Free State (Agreement) Act. On the view in *Ryan's Case* they were authorized by the Dáil and the Dáil Ministry.[2] The resulting assembly was, on the former view, a House of Parliament owing its existence and deriving its authority from an Act of the United Kingdom Parliament; on the latter view it was the Third Dáil, owing its existence to the decision of the Second Dáil and deriving its authority from the people of Ireland.

There followed an interval of civil war, in which the Dáil Ministry and the Provisional Government on one side fought the Republicans who had refused to accept the Treaty. When the assembly met on September 9, 1922, Arthur Griffith and Michael Collins were dead, and Mr. Cosgrave was First Minister. He announced that the system of dual ministries was at an end,[3] and thereafter the Provisional Government of which he was head functioned alone. The assembly proceeded to draw up a constitution for the Irish Free State. The divergence of view between Irish and British at this stage can best be illustrated by comparing the preamble

[1] s. 1 (2).   [2] By resolution of May 20.
[3] *Dail Debates*, vol. i, col. 56.

to the Constitution of the Irish Free State (Saorstát Eireann) Act, which the Dáil passed, with the preamble to the Irish Free State Constitution Act, which the United Kingdom Parliament passed. The Irish Act begins:

Dáil Eireann sitting as a Constituent Assembly in this Provisional Parliament, acknowledging that all lawful authority comes from God to the people and in confidence that the National life and unity of Ireland shall thus be restored, hereby proclaims the establishment of The Irish Free State (otherwise called Saorstat Eireann) and in the exercise of undoubted right, decrees and enacts as follows:

and in section 1 it is enacted that the Constitution scheduled to the Act shall be the Constitution of the Irish Free State, and in section 2 that the Articles of Agreement 'are hereby given the force of law'.

The United Kingdom Act, which is entitled 'An Act to provide for the Constitution of the Irish Free State', begins:

Whereas the House of the Parliament constituted pursuant to the Irish Free State (Agreement) Act, 1922, sitting as a Constituent Assembly for the settlement of the Constitution of the Irish Free State, has passed the Measure (hereinafter referred to as 'the Constituent Act'), set forth in the Schedule to this Act, whereby the Constitution appearing as the First Schedule to the Constituent Act is declared to be the Constitution of the Irish Free State,

and in section 1 it is enacted that the Constitution set forth in the First Schedule to the Constituent Act shall, subject to the provisions to which the same is by the Constituent Act made subject, be the Constitution of the Irish Free State, and shall come into operation on being proclaimed by His Majesty. On the British view, therefore, the Constituent Assembly was a 'House of

Parliament', not Dáil Eireann; its authority came from
the Irish Free State (Agreement) Act, not from 'God to
the people' nor from 'undoubted right'; its deliberations
were directed to the 'settlement' not the enactment of a
Constitution; it passed a 'Measure', not an Act, though
that measure might be 'referred to as "The Constituent
Act"'; and it merely 'declared' the Scheduled Constitution to be the Constitution of the Irish Free State, it did
not enact it. On the British view, indeed, the Assembly
had no power to enact a Constitution; it had not been
authorized to do so by the terms of the Irish Free State
(Agreement) Act. In Lord Sankey's words: 'This Act
gave no power to "the House of the Parliament" to enact
a Constitution for the Irish Free State'.[1] The Constituent Act and the Scheduled Constitution and the
Articles of Agreement owe their validity in Great
Britain and Ireland to the Acts of the United Kingdom
Parliament. All that the House of the Parliament did
was to 'prepare' a Constitution, in accordance with the
practice which had been followed in the Dominions of
Canada, Australia, and South Africa, and in the Australian colonies. In Mr. Lloyd George's words:

Here we are going to follow the example which has been
set in the framing of every constitution throughout the
Empire.[2] The constitution is drafted and decided by the
Dominion, the Imperial Parliament taking such steps as
may be necessary to legalize these decisions.[3]

2

Such was the process by which these two irreconcilable
theories of the origin and legal basis of the Constitution

[1] *Moore* v. *Att.-Gen. for the Irish Free State* [1935] A.C. 484 at p. 491.
[2] An exaggeration.   [3] 149 *H.C. Deb.*, 5 s., 42.

of 1922 arose. It is necessary to have them in mind in considering, first, the nature and extent of the legal inequalities of status possessed by the Irish Free State in 1926; second, the effect upon that legal status of the Statute of Westminster; and third, the power of the Free State to adopt for itself a new constitution in place of the Constitution of 1922. It is the first of these questions which must be considered in this section. The remaining two are discussed in Chapter XI.

Consider the position first upon the basis of the view in *Ryan's Case*. What legal inequalities of status existed under the Constitution of 1922? On this view the only relevant document is the Constituent Act with its two Schedules. The first point to be noticed is that this Constituent Act was not an enactment of the Oireachtas, or legislature of the Free State. '. . . The Constitution was enacted by the Third Dáil, sitting as a Constituent Assembly, and not by the Oireachtas, which, in fact, it created.'[1] It was indeed the only legislative enactment of the Third Dáil. 'The Oireachtas did not come into existence until after the Constitution itself had come into operation on the 6th of December, 1922.'[2] Now the Third Dáil, though it did confer upon the Oireachtas by Article 50 of the Constitution a power to amend the Constitution, confined this power, in the first place, to 'amendment of this Constitution', and did not therefore confer upon the Oireachtas any power to amend the Constituent Act itself. The Oireachtas is, therefore,

[1] Kennedy C.J., *The State (Ryan)* v. *Lennon*, [1935] I.R. 170, at p. 203.
[2] Kennedy C.J., *ibid.*, at p. 204. The Chief Justice criticized a publication of the Free State Government entitled 'Index to the Legislation passed by the Oireachtas in the years 1922 to 1932', in which at several places (e.g. at pp. 6, 75 *passim*) the Constituent Act was stated to have been enacted by the Oireachtas.

bound by the terms of the Constituent Act; it is power-less itself to alter them.[1]

The terms of the Constituent Act must then be studied. Section 2 is the most important. It lays down the legal relation between the two Schedules, the Constitution and the Treaty, in these terms:

The said Constitution shall be construed with reference to the Articles of Agreement for a Treaty between Great Britain and Ireland set forth in the Second Schedule hereto annexed (hereinafter referred to as 'the Scheduled Treaty') which are hereby given the force of law, and if any provision of the said Constitution or of any amendment thereof or of any law made thereunder is in any respect repugnant to any of the Provisions of the Scheduled Treaty, it shall, to the extent only of such repugnancy, be absolutely void and inoperative and the Parliament and the Executive Council of the Irish Free State (Saorstát Eireann) shall respectively pass such further legislation and do all such other things as may be necessary to implement the Scheduled Treaty.

Dáil Eireann had therefore imposed a second limitation upon the power of the Oireachtas to alter the Constitution, as set out in Article 50.

. . . The supreme legislative authority, speaking as the mouthpiece of the people, expressly denied to the Oireachtas the power of enacting *any* legislation, by way of amendment of the Constitution or otherwise, which might be 'in any respect repugnant to any of the provisions of the Scheduled Treaty', and it reiterated this prohibition in Article 50, which empowered the Oireachtas to make *amendments of this Constitution within the terms of the Scheduled Treaty*.'[2]

[1] *The State (Ryan)* v. *Lennon*, [1935] I.R. 170, Kennedy C.J., at p. 204; FitzGibbon J., at p. 226.

[2] *The State (Ryan)* v. *Lennon*, [1935] I.R. 170, FitzGibbon J., at p. 226; see also Kennedy C.J., at p. 205; and Murnaghan J., at pp. 239, 241.

Dáil Eireann had, therefore, of its own juridical authority
and of its own juridical freewill imposed the Constituent
Act and the Scheduled Treaty upon the Irish Free State
as a form of fundamental law which the Oireachtas
was powerless to alter. But this subordination of the
Oireachtas to the Treaty did not constitute a point of
juridical inequality imposed by the United Kingdom
legislature upon the Free State, any more than the
subordination of the United States Congress to the Constitution is a form of juridical inequality imposed by any
alien legislature. It is, in law, a self-imposed restriction.

But might not this self-imposed restriction result in
legal or conventional inequalities as between the Free
State and other members of the British Commonwealth?
To answer this it is necessary to consider the terms of
the Articles of Agreement. Article 1, as has been mentioned, conferred upon the Free State

the same constitutional status in the Community of Nations
known as the British Empire as the Dominion of Canada,
the Commonwealth of Australia, the Dominion of New
Zealand, and the Union of South Africa. . . .

But, as has been pointed out, the constitutional status of
a Dominion is a relationship which must be described
not only in terms of non-legal rules but also in terms of
legal rules, and while there might be equality of constitutional status between these enumerated Dominions,
there was not always identity in the rules of law or convention which described the status of each particular
Dominion. To which of these models then should the
Irish Free State conform? The answer was found in
Article 2 of the Treaty which provided that, subject to
its later provisions,

the position of the Irish Free State in relation to the

Imperial Parliament and Government and otherwise shall be that of the Dominion of Canada, and the law, practice and constitutional usage governing the relationship of the Crown or the representative of the Crown and of the Imperial Parliament to the Dominion of Canada shall govern their relationship to the Irish Free State.

The later Articles of the Treaty did in fact impose upon Ireland duties and restrictions in relation to Great Britain to which Canada was not made subject, duties in respect of naval defence,[1] restrictions upon the size of the Free State army,[2] guarantees against legislation directly or indirectly endowing any religion, or prohibiting or restricting the free exercise of any religion,[3] and financial obligations in respect of Ireland's share in the National Debt,[4] and compensation to officials who were discharged or who retired as a result of the change of Government.[5] As Mr. Lloyd George said:

There was no use saying, 'You must treat Ireland exactly as you treat Canada or Australia'. There was Ireland, right across the ocean. . . . We had to safeguard the security of this land.[6]

It would appear, then, that subject to these specific provisions in the Treaty which imposed obligations upon the Free State and Great Britain, and which, on the Irish view, were given the force of law in the Free State by an Act of Dáil Eireann, the constitutional status of Ireland in relation to Great Britain was to be the same as that of Canada, and, if any provision of the Constitution or any amendment of it was repugnant to this status,

[1] Articles 6 and 7.   [2] Article 8.
[3] Article 16.   [4] Article 5.   [5] Article 10.
[6] 149 H.C. Deb., 5 s., 32. Cf. Erskine Childers in the Second Dáil: 'This Treaty does not give you what is called Dominion status.' (Debate on the Treaty between Great Britain and Ireland, p. 37.)

as defined in terms of law, practice, and constitutional usage, it was void to the extent of such repugnancy, and the Free State Parliament must pass such further legislation as was necessary to bring these provisions into agreement with the Treaty.

To what extent was the Free State, under the provisions of its Constituent Act and Schedules, subject to those inequalities of status whose nature and extent have been examined in the case of the other Dominions? In the opinion of the writer, if the view of the Constituent Act taken in *Ryan's Case* is accepted, these inequalities may be stated as follows.[1] In the first place the Governor-General of the Free State was, in law, the representative of His Majesty, and in law too he might be regarded as the representative also of His Majesty's Government in the United Kingdom, and to that extent the Free State Executive was subordinate in status to the United Kingdom Government, in the same manner and to the same extent as was the Dominion of Canada. The status of the Governor-General in relation to his ministers in the Free State was the same as that of the Governor-General of Canada in relation to his ministers, and the Free State, therefore, shared with Mr. Mackenzie King an anxiety that this status should be defined. It had been defined to some extent in the Constitution, but in so far as that statement was repugnant to the law, practice, and usage obtaining in respect of Canada, it was void, and in so far as the practice and usage of Canada was vague and ambiguous, to that extent the position in the

---

[1] It cannot be pretended that this summary statement of the inequalities would be accepted by all those who hold this Irish view. Nor that the statement itself is free from inconsistencies. But a short statement inevitably possesses such blemishes.

Free State was vague and ambiguous, in spite of constitutional provisions. Secondly, the Free State was subject, according to Article 41 of its Constitution, to the power of discretionary reservation, though this power, on the Canadian model, would not be exercised except with the consent of ministers. Further, though no provision was made explicitly in the Constitution, there existed in law the power of the Crown to issue instructions to the Governor-General of the Free State to reserve certain classes of Bills, but this power, by the practice and usage obtaining in respect of Canada, could not constitutionally be exercised. Obligatory reservation of specified classes of Bills, which existed in the Constitutions of South Africa, Australia, and New Zealand, but which did not exist in the Canadian Constitution, was not found in the Free State Constitution, again following the Canadian model. Obligatory reservation under the Merchant Shipping Act, 1894, and the Colonial Courts of Admiralty Act, 1890, applied in respect of the Free State, on the Canadian model.

Thirdly, the legislative supremacy of the United Kingdom Parliament extended to the Free State on the Canadian model, and consequently the Colonial Laws Validity Act must apply to the Free State. But, on the Irish view, the provisions of this Act did not apply to the Constituent Act and its Schedules. It is true that this Constituent Act and its Schedules were made part of an Act of the United Kingdom Parliament in the Irish Free State Constitution Act, 1922, and that the Articles of Agreement alone were also made part of a United Kingdom Act in the Irish Free State (Agreement) Act, 1922, but these Acts were necessary only to give force of law to the Free State Constitution and to the

Agreement in the United Kingdom. They were not to be construed as Acts of the United Kingdom Parliament extending to the Free State by express words or necessary intendment. On the above view, then, the United Kingdom Parliament had legislative supremacy over the Free State in law, and the Colonial Laws Validity Act extended to the Free State in law, but this legal power was irrelevant to a consideration of the legal basis in the Free State of the Constituent Act, the Constitution, and the Articles of Agreement. Moreover, the legal power of the United Kingdom Parliament must be exercised according to the practice and usage obtaining in respect of Canada, and that meant that no Act of the United Kingdom Parliament might be passed affecting the Free State except at such times and in such terms as the Free State consented to.[1]

Then there is the question of lack of power to make laws possessing extra-territorial effect. On the Irish view, it would seem that no inequality of status could arise for the Free State even if there was some such limitation in the Constitution upon the powers of the Oireachtas. It would be self-imposed; for on the Irish view the Free State Constitution was not an Act of the United Kingdom Parliament, and no inequality of status could be held to arise on this ground. Actually the Irish courts did not admit that the Oireachtas lacked power to legislate with extra-territorial effect. (See *R (Alexander)* v. *Circuit Judge of Cork*, [1925] 2 I.R. 165, especially FitzGibbon J. at 193, and

---

[1] Cf. Kevin O'Higgins in *Debate on Treaty between Great Britain and Ireland*, p. 47. '. . . These two words "practice" and "usage" mean much more than Mr. Childers was prepared to attribute to them. They neutralize and nullify "law".'

Keeger v. *Dawson*, [1934] I.R. 232, and the same judge at 249.)

In the fifth place, the Free State was made subject, by Article 66 of its Constitution, to the appeal to the Judicial Committee by special leave, though the appeal as of right was abolished. This was in accordance with the Canadian model. It was made clear in 1926, in the decision of *Nadan* v. *The King*, not only that Canada was subject to the appeal, but also that Canada was unable to abolish it. It followed therefore that, for so long as Canada remained subject to the appeal, for so long must the Free State remain subject to it.

There was finally, on the Irish view, an inconsistency and an inequality of status arising from the description of the King in the Royal Style and Titles as King of the 'United Kingdom of Great Britain and Ireland', when that United Kingdom included only a part of Ireland since the establishment of the Free State.

Such were the inequalities, on the Irish view in *Ryan's Case*, and it remains to add that in so far as these inequalities resulted from and were in accordance with the status of Canada, the Free State legislature was unable to remove them, not because they were imposed upon the Free State by an external authority, but because the Third Dáil had imposed them.

What then was the position on the British view? It differed from the Irish view, not so much in its statement of the extent of the legal inequalities but in its statement of their legal origin and validity, and therefore of the capacity of the Free State legislature to abolish them. On the British view the Canadian model was imposed upon the Free State not by an Act of Dáil Eireann but by an Act of the United Kingdom Parliament. Any attempt by the Free State legislature to amend the Constitution in any way repugnant to the Articles of Agreement must be void, first, because section 2 of the Irish Constituent Act, itself part of the United Kingdom Act, said so, and the Constituent Act lay outside the *area* of the powers of the Oireachtas; second, because quite apart from questions of area, the Articles of Agreement had been enacted as part of a United Kingdom Act, which extended to the Irish Free State by express words, and, by the provisions of the Colonial Laws Validity Act, any amendment repugnant to their terms was void.

On the British view then, the Free State was, as the result of an Imperial Act, subject to the inequalities, on the model of Canada, involved in the status of the Governor-General, in discretionary reservation, in the supremacy of the United Kingdom Parliament—as expressed through the Colonial Laws Validity Act which extended to the Constituent Act and its two Schedules— in the lack of extra-territorial power upon the same sort of principles as applied in Canada, and in the existence of the appeal by special leave to the Judicial Committee.[1] These legal powers must be exercised in accordance with the practice and usage applying to Canada, but of their existence there was no doubt in law.

[1] It was so decided in *Performing Right Society* v. *Bray Urban District Council*, [1930] A.C. 377, Lord Sankey, at pp. 394–6. See also *Hull* v. *McKenna*, [1926] I.R. 402 at p. 404, where the 'practice and usage' of the Judicial Committee in admitting appeals was explained.

V

THE SCOPE OF THE STATUTE

I

THE Statute of Westminster is intituled 'an Act to give effect to certain resolutions passed by Imperial Conferences held in the years 1926 and 1930'. In order to understand the function of the Statute in that process of the redefinition of Dominion status which was carried on by the Conferences of 1926 and 1930, it is necessary to examine carefully the resolutions which were passed by the two Conferences. And it will be wise, to begin with, to segregate those resolutions which were *not* given effect in the preamble and clauses of the Statute.

The task before the Conferences of 1926 and 1930 has been made clear. It can be seen what was meant by the Conference of 1926 when, having declared that 'equality of status, so far as Britain and the Dominions are concerned, is thus the root principle governing our Inter-Imperial Relations', it declared immediately thereafter that in practice 'existing administrative, legislative, and judicial forms are admittedly not wholly in accord' with this position. The reason for this disconformity between the declaration of 1926 and certain existing forms of law and convention is also now apparent. It results from the historical fact that, in the words of the Conference of 1926, 'most of these forms date back to a time well antecedent to the present stage of constitutional development'. At the same time it has been seen that there existed by 1926 considerably less constitutional inequality than a study of the mere legal forms would suggest. Usage and convention had operated, in some cases, to modify or nullify the workings of strict law. Thus the power of disallowance had been rendered inoperative, the refusal of assent to reserved Bills had been made conditional upon consultation and consent of the Dominion concerned, the exercise of the supreme legislative power of the United Kingdom Parliament in respect of a Dominion had been made conditional upon request or consent of that Dominion, and the exercise of the Crown's prerogative in foreign affairs in respect of a Dominion had become subject to consultation and consent of the Dominion concerned. And so on. There was, therefore, nothing catastrophic in the declaration of the Conference of 1926 that Great Britain and the Dominions were 'equal in status, in no way subordinate one to another in any aspect of their domestic or external affairs'. To a large extent this declaration represented a generalization from the practice which usage and convention had established in the years which had succeeded the establishment of responsible government in the colonies. The declaration was in great measure a recognition and definition of the existing position. But it was more than that. It was itself a statement not merely of a usage but of a convention; not merely, that is to say, of a usual practice, but of an obligatory rule. It laid down not merely that the powers of strict law had, on the whole, been exercised in accordance with a convention of equality, but that the powers of strict law henceforth must be exercised only in accordance with that convention. And for this reason it was necessary for the Conference of 1926, having declared this convention, to proceed thereafter to examine the disconformities 'with special reference to any cases where the want of adaptation of practice to principle caused, or might be thought to cause, inconvenience in the conduct of Inter-Imperial Relations', and to make recommendations upon the extent to which and the method by which such inconsistencies between practice and the general convention should be removed.

This was the task before the Conference of 1926. As has been seen, it found itself unable to make a full study of or a complete set of recommendations upon all the points in which disconformity existed. Certain questions were confided for study and recommendation to the Conference on the Operation of Dominion Legislation and Merchant Shipping Legislation in 1929. On the basis of the Report of this Conference, the Imperial Conference of 1930 gave further consideration to the question, adopted substantially the *O.D.L. Report* of 1929, and passed a further set of resolutions designed to carry on the process of removing legal and conventional inequalities. It is to these resolutions of 1926 and 1930 that attention must now be directed.

Their most striking characteristic, considered as a whole, is that they advise the removal of these inequalities not by the method of legislative change only, but also by the method of conventional change. They saw that not by statute alone nor by convention alone could 'the want of adaptation of practice to principle' and the resulting inconvenience it caused be most satisfactorily removed. Their recommendations illustrate and confirm the proposition, already asserted in this book, that it is not the isolation of law from convention but the interaction and co-operation of law with convention which is characteristic of the constitutional structure of the British Commonwealth.

Consider first the legal inequality of status which was

held to exist as a result of the title of His Majesty the King. The Conference of 1926 agreed that a small change in the terms of the title was necessary in order to meet the altered state of affairs arising from the establishment of the Irish Free State. It recommended therefore[1] that, subject to His Majesty's approval, the necessary legislative action should be taken to secure that His Majesty's title should henceforward read:

George V, by the Grace of God, of Great Britain, Ireland and the British Dominions beyond the Seas King, Defender of the Faith, Emperor of India.

Here the legal term 'Great Britain', and the geographical term 'Ireland' replace the legal expression 'the United Kingdom of Great Britain and Ireland', and reference to the political partition of Ireland is avoided. It was clear that a change of this kind could be effectively carried out only by an alteration in the proclamation; and for this alteration it was deemed necessary to obtain statutory authority in a new Titles Act. The recommendation was carried out in the Royal and Parliamentary Titles Act, 1927,[2] and by a proclamation issued under the authority of that Act. Not only was the King's title altered, but the title of Parliament also was altered. Thereafter it was to be known as the Parliament of the United Kingdom of Great Britain and Northern Ireland, and the expression 'United Kingdom' in every Act and public document was to mean 'Great Britain and Northern Ireland' unless the context otherwise required.

The problem of the status of the Governor-General

[1] Cmd. 2768, pp. 15–16.
[2] 17 Geo. 5, c. 4. The Act and the proclamation are printed in Keith, *Speeches and Documents on the British Dominions*, pp. 171–2.

and of the inequalities alleged to result from that
status, on the other hand, were dealt with by the Conferences of 1926 and 1930 solely by the adoption of constitutional conventions. There was first the question of
the Governor-General's status in relation to his ministers in the Dominion. It was declared in 1926 that the
Governor-General of a Dominion held in all essential
respects the same position in relation to the administration of public affairs in the Dominion as is held by
His Majesty the King in Great Britain. Thus the
Governor-General must act in accordance with the same
rules as the King recognizes in his relations with his
ministers. No attempt was made to indicate what these
rules were. The problems of discretion still remained
unsolved.[1] The second question—the relation of the
Governor-General to His Majesty's Government in the
United Kingdom—was settled in 1926 by the declaration that the Governor-General was not the representative or agent of His Majesty's Government in Great
Britain or of any department of that Government; he
is the representative of His Majesty alone.[2] In 1930
the matter was taken a step further by a series of declarations to the effect that the Governor-General of
a Dominion should be appointed by His Majesty on
the advice of His Majesty's ministers in the Dominion
concerned, who tender their formal advice after informal
consultation with His Majesty.[3]

The inequalities which arose from disallowance and
reservation, on the other hand, were dealt with by the
Conferences of 1926 and 1930 in recommendations

---

[1] Evatt, *op. cit.*, c. xxi. The Governor-General of South Africa refused
to grant a dissolution to General Hertzog in 1939 and this refusal
aroused controversy.   [2] Cmd. 2768, p. 16.   [3] Cmd. 3717, p. 27.

which combined the declaration of constitutional conventions with the envisagement of legislative action by the Dominions or by the United Kingdom if and when it was considered advisable. The Conference of 1926 began by laying down a general convention in relation to disallowance and reservation in these words:

. . . Apart from provisions embodied in constitutions or in specific statutes expressly providing for reservation, it is recognized that it is the right of the Government of each Dominion to advise the Crown in all matters relating to its own affairs. Consequently, it would not be in accordance with constitutional practice for advice to be tendered to His Majesty by His Majesty's Government in Great Britain in any matter appertaining to the affairs of a Dominion against the views of the Government of that Dominion.[1]

The Conference of 1929 studied the nature and extent of the powers of disallowance and reservation in the Dominion Constitutions and made recommendations upon them in the light of this declaration adopted by the Conference of 1926. These recommendations were adopted by the Conference of 1930.

In respect of disallowance the convention was recognized in 1930 that 'the power of disallowance can no longer be exercised in relation to Dominion legislation'.[2] This was clearly in accordance with the above proposition that no advice should be tendered to the King by the United Kingdom Government against the views of the Government of the Dominion concerned. To adopt this convention was to nullify the power of disallowance, but it was not to abolish it. It was agreed, therefore, that those Dominions which possessed the power to

[1] Cmd. 2768, p. 17.
[2] Adopting the recommendation of *O.D.L. Report*, para. 23.

delete disallowance from their Constitutions were at liberty to do so, by following the prescribed procedure, while in the case of those Dominions which did not possess this power 'it would be in accordance with constitutional practice that, if so requested by the Dominion concerned, the Government of the United Kingdom should ask Parliament to pass the necessary legislation'.[1] There was one qualification to be added to this conclusion. Where a Dominion had taken advantage of the provisions of the Colonial Stock Act, 1900, and had placed on record, in accordance with the third of the rules of the United Kingdom Treasury, a formal expression of its opinion that its legislation in certain circumstances might properly be disallowed,[2] 'the right of disallowance in respect of such legislation must remain and can properly be exercised'.[3]

It was clear that this qualification imposed a certain restriction upon the full formal equality of the Dominion in respect of disallowance. In 1934, therefore, when the Union of South Africa decided to remove disallowance from its Constitution, an alternative procedure was devised to safeguard trustee securities in so far as the Dominions were concerned. By the Colonial Stock Act, 1934,[4] passed by the United Kingdom Parliament, it was enacted that the third of the conditions prescribed by the Treasury under section 2 of the Colonial Stock Act, 1900, should be deemed to have been observed with respect to any stock issued by the Government of a Dominion if either the requirement therein specified had been complied with or if two other requirements were complied

---

[1] Adopting the recommendation of *O.D.L. Report*, para. 23.
[2] See above, p. 72.
[3] *O.D.L. Report*, para. 24.   [4] 24 & 25 Geo. 5, c. 47, s. 1 (1).

with. The first requirement was that the Government of the Dominion had undertaken that legislation which appeared to the United Kingdom Government to alter any of the provisions affecting the stock to the injury of stock-holders or to involve a departure from the original contract in regard to the stock, should not be submitted for the Royal Assent except after agreement with the United Kingdom Government, and that if attention was drawn to any such legislation after the passing thereof by the Dominion Parliament, the Dominion Government would take the necessary steps to ensure such amendments as might be requested by the United Kingdom Government. The second requirement was that the above undertaking should have been confirmed by an Act of the Parliament of the Dominion. South Africa complied with both these requirements in 1934 and disallowance was thereafter repealed from its Constitution (Status Act, 1934, s. 11 (2)), except as provided for in para. 20 of the Schedule affecting native territories.

The power of reservation was dealt with in 1930 by a similar co-operation of convention and strict law. The Conference of 1926 had recognized the distinction between the Governor-General's statutory power of obligatory reservation on the one hand, and his statutory power of discretionary reservation and his power of obligatory reservation under instructions from the United Kingdom Government, on the other. In respect of discretionary reservation it was recognized in 1930 that the Governor-General in virtue of his acknowledged status as representative of the King, must exercise this discretion in accordance with the advice of ministers— though here again there was no certainty that he must take the advice of his ministers for the time being if he could find others to take responsibility for his action *ex post facto*. But no inequality in relation to the United Kingdom Government remained. In respect of obligatory reservation under instructions from the United Kingdom Government, it was declared that 'His Majesty's Government in the United Kingdom will not advise His Majesty the King to give the Governor-General any instructions to reserve Bills presented to him for assent'.[1] Thus by convention the exercise of the power of discretionary reservation was brought under the control of Dominion ministers, and the inequality in the power of obligatory reservation under instructions was nullified. The exercise of the power of obligatory reservation under statutory provisions was, however, incapable of control through a convention; the Governor-General had a statutory duty and he must perform it.

So much for the exercise of the Governor-General's power to reserve, in so far as and for so long as it existed in respect of a Dominion. But what rules should regulate the inequality which arose not only from the exercise of this power but from its existence also? Here statutory alteration would be necessary. It was agreed in 1930 that where Dominions possessed the power, by amending their Constitutions, to abolish provisions in these Constitutions either for discretionary reservation or for obligatory reservation, it was open to these Dominions to take the prescribed steps to that end if they so desired.[2] In the case of Dominions which required the co-operation of the United Kingdom Parliament in order to amend the provisions in their Constitutions relating to reservation, the convention was adopted

[1] *O.D.L. Report*, para. 32. [2] *Ibid.*, para. 35.

that the United Kingdom Government, if so requested by the Dominion concerned, should ask the United Kingdom Parliament to pass the necessary legislation.[1]

There remained the provisions for obligatory reservation not in the constitutional statutes of the Dominions, but in the two Imperial Acts controlling merchant shipping and the colonial courts of admiralty, which extended to the Dominions and overrode Dominion legislation by virtue of the Colonial Laws Validity Act. By the decision of the Conference of 1930, on the basis of the *O.D.L. Report*, the removal of this legal inequality was placed within the scope of the Statute of Westminster, and a clause was drawn up for insertion in the proposed Statute.[2] This is then the first element in the resolutions of the Conferences of 1926 and 1930 which is later to be given effect in the Statute of Westminster.

So much for the inequalities which arose from the existence and exercise of a power in the hands of the Governor-General to reserve Dominion Bills. But reservation included a further power—the power of the Sovereign to assent or refuse assent to a Bill so reserved. This power, which was exercised on the advice of United Kingdom ministers, constituted a further inequality. How should this be removed? It was decided in 1930, in accordance with the convention laid down in 1926, that it would not be in accordance with constitutional practice for advice to be tendered to His Majesty by His Majesty's Government in the United Kingdom in respect of any reserved Bill whatsoever contrary to the views of the Government of the Dominion concerned.[3] Thus the inequality involved in

[1] *O.D.L. Report*, para. 36. [2] *Ibid.*, paras. 120–3.
[3] *Ibid.*, paras. 32–4.

the power of the United Kingdom Government, for so long as the power of reservation existed, to advise the refusal of assent to a reserved Bill, was abolished.

There was next the legal inequality arising from the existence of the appeal to the Judicial Committee of the Privy Council. The Conference of 1926 alone made a declaration upon this question. It was stated that, as a result of their discussions, 'it became clear that it was no part of the policy of His Majesty's Government in Great Britain that questions affecting judicial appeals should be determined otherwise than in accordance with the wishes of the part of the Empire primarily affected.'[1] This was a recognition of the principle enunciated by Lord Haldane in *Hull* v. *McKenna*.[2] But the Conference went further and qualified their statement by the sentence:

It was, however, generally recognized that, where changes in the existing system were proposed which, while primarily affecting one part, raised issues in which other parts were also concerned, such changes ought only to be carried out after consultation and discussion.[3]

Here the United Kingdom obviously wished to safeguard its position in relation to the Irish Free State. The Free State, for its part, was not satisfied with this general statement and no more.[4] But though the problem was discussed in 1930, there the matter was allowed to rest. No specific proposals for legislative action to facilitate the restriction or abolition of the appeal were made by the Conferences of 1926 and 1930.

[1] Cmd. 2768, p. 19.   [2] *Supra*, p. 97.   [3] Cmd. 2768, pp. 19–20.
[4] *Ibid.* See also speech of Mr. McGilligan in the Dáil, July 17, 1931. Printed in Keith, *Speeches and Documents on the British Dominions*, pp. 249–50.

Perhaps the most important conventional rules agreed upon in 1926 concerned the regulation of British Commonwealth foreign relations. A technique of consultative negotiation, based upon consent, and executed through a system of distinct, direct, and co-ordinate representation for each member of the Commonwealth concerned, was elaborated. In this sphere, as has already been mentioned, the changes that were considered necessary found expression for the most part in the elaboration of new constitutional conventions, and did not require legislative action through the Statute of Westminster. It is not intended therefore to discuss this portion of the Report of 1926 in this book.[1]

2

It is interesting to notice that, with the small exception of the power of reservation as required by certain sections of the Merchant Shipping Act, 1894, and the Colonial Courts of Admiralty Act, 1890, the Conferences of 1926 and 1930 regarded it as expedient and sufficient to deal with the six inequalities of status so far considered by a series of resolutions which, though they envisaged changes by the method of statutory enactment as well as changes by the alteration of conventional rules, did not specifically and explicitly recommend action within the scope of the Statute of Westminster. In the view of these Conferences it is clear that the Statute of Westminster was not regarded as the sole instrument through which principle might be reconciled with practice, and constitutional equality of status most satisfactorily achieved. The Statute was a part of the process of

[1] See P. J. Noel Baker, *The Present Juridical Status of the British Dominions in International Law* for a study of the rules elaborated in 1923 and 1926.

readjustment and redefinition; its terms did not cover the whole of the subject. There was no rigid acceptance or assertion of the doctrine that through statutory enactment alone and, in particular, through the Statute of Westminster alone, could equality of status be made effective.

It has seemed justifiable to devote some space to the resolutions of the Conferences of 1926 and 1930 which were *not* given effect in the Statute of Westminster, in order that, from this negative standpoint, the scope and function of the Statute might be more clearly appreciated. At the same time it is important to stress the fact that the resolutions which were passed to deal with the six inequalities so far discussed were passed in the knowledge and upon the condition that certain other resolutions in respect of the remaining legal inequalities would be carried into effect in the terms of the Statute of Westminster. These changes through the method of statutory enactment would interact upon and supplement the changes recommended outside the terms of the Statute, and would by implication and by consequence have an important effect upon them.

When the Conference of 1929 came to consider the legal inequalities which arose from the Dominions' lack of power to legislate with extra-territorial effect, and from the existence of the legislative supremacy of the United Kingdom Parliament as expressed through the Colonial Laws Validity Act, it came to the conclusion that the adoption of a constitutional convention would not be sufficient to remove the inconvenience caused by these particular cases of a want of conformity between principle and practice. The Conference of 1926 had indeed adopted a convention in general principle on these points when it declared 'that legislation by the Parliament at Westminster applying to a Dominion would only be passed with the consent of the Dominion concerned'.[1] This was no more than a recognition of the rule which, as has already been shown, had become established before 1926 by the operation of usage and convention.[2] But the adoption of a convention did not alter the law. The Conference of 1929 concluded that the confusion and inconvenience resulting from the uncertainty of the law in the matter of extra-territoriality could be most satisfactorily dealt with only by a declaratory enactment of the United Kingdom Parliament, passed with the consent of the Dominions, stating, in terms which the Conference advised, that the Dominions did possess power to legislate with extra-territorial effect.[3] Similarly the Conference of 1929 decided that

effect can only be given to the principles laid down in the Report of 1926 by repealing the Colonial Laws Validity Act, 1865, in its application to laws made by the Parliament of a Dominion,

and they recommended that legislation be enacted declaring in terms that the Act should no longer apply to the laws passed by any Dominion.[4] These recommendations were adopted by the Conference of 1930.

A full consideration of all the recommendations adopted by the Conference of 1930 and carried into effect in the Statute of Westminster is not necessary at this point. They will be discussed in succeeding chapters when the precise terms of the Statute come to

[1] Cmd. 2768, p. 18.
[2] See above, pp. 80–3.
[3] *O.D.L. Report*, paras. 40–4.
[4] *Ibid.*, para. 50.

be examined. It is sufficient to say here that the Conference of 1930, in adopting the recommendations of the *O.D.L. Report*, passed resolutions designed to remove so far as possible the legislative inequality of the Dominion Parliaments by the enactment of the Statute of Westminster, and that this aspect of legal inequality in Dominion Status as it existed in 1926 was brought within the scope of the Statute. But, just as in 1926 the legal elements which formed a part of the constitutional status of a Dominion differed considerably from one Dominion to another, so also in 1929 when the passing of the Statute of Westminster was envisaged, there was a considerable difference of view, as between one Dominion and another, about the extent to which they desired to take advantage of the legal equality which the Statute was intended to confer. The Conference of 1929 found therefore that part of its task was not only to frame resolutions and clauses which should give effect to legal equality of status for those Dominions which desired it, but also to frame resolutions and clauses which should qualify the operation of the Statute in so far as certain Dominions desired such qualification. A consideration of these qualifications must be postponed until the application of the Statute to each of the Dominions comes to be treated in later chapters.

The Conferences of 1926 and 1930 (adopting the Report of 1929) passed, then, many important and comprehensive resolutions designed to remove legal inequalities, which were *not* intended to receive effect in the Statute of Westminster. At the same time, the Conference of 1929, carrying on the work of the Conference of 1926, did recommend that certain legal inequalities should be removed by the enactment of a Statute, and their Report contained proposed clauses for inclusion in such a Statute. The Conference of 1930 substantially adopted this Report,[1] and drew up a Schedule containing, with a small amendment,[2] the clauses which the 1929 Conference had proposed.[3] It recommended that the proposed Statute of the United Kingdom Parliament should contain the provisions set out in this Schedule, along with such further provisions as to its application to any particular Dominion as were requested by that Dominion; it fixed December 1, 1931, as the date as from which the proposed Statute should become operative; and it recommended that resolutions by both Houses of the Dominion Parliaments approving and requesting this legislation should be forwarded to the United Kingdom, if possible by July 1, 1931, and in any case not later than August 1.

The Dominion Parliaments discussed the clauses of the proposed Statute, and, after making such amendments, additions, and reservations as they thought fit in each particular case, passed Resolutions requesting legislation by the Imperial Parliament along the lines laid down. On November 10, 1931, the Speech of King George V, opening the Parliament at Westminster, foreshadowed the introduction of the proposed Bill, and accurately described its origin, scope, and purpose in the words:

In conformity with the undertaking given to the representatives of My Dominions in 1930, a measure will be laid before you to give statutory effect to certain of the declarations and resolutions of the Imperial Conferences of 1926 and 1930. This measure is designed to make clear the

[1] Cmd. 3717, p. 18.   [2] *Ibid.* See below, pp. 144–5.
[3] *Ibid.*, pp. 19–21.

powers of Dominion Parliaments and to promote the spirit
of free co-operation amongst Members of the British Commonwealth of Nations.[1]

The Statute of Westminster Bill was accordingly
introduced into the House of Commons by the Secretary
of State for Dominion Affairs on November 12, 1931.[2]
The Bill was given a second reading on November 20,[3]
and was considered by a Committee of the whole House
and was passed through its remaining stages on November 24.[4] It was introduced into the House of Lords on
November 25,[5] and given a second reading next day.[6]
December 1 had been fixed, it will be remembered, as
the date upon which the proposed Statute should come
into operation, but when that day arrived the Bill had,
owing to pressure of parliamentary business, reached
the Committee stage only in the House of Lords. The
clause of the Bill, therefore, which provided for its
coming into operation on December 1 was deleted in
Committee in the Lords,[7] and the Bill, thus amended,
passed its remaining stages in the House of Lords on
December 3.[8] On its return to the House of Commons
the amended Bill was agreed to,[9] and it received the
Royal Assent on December 11, 1931.[10]

[1] 83 *H.L. Deb.*, 5 s., 6.
[2] 259 *H.C. Deb.*, 5 s., 273.
[3] *Ibid.* 1173–1254.
[4] 260 *H.C. Deb.*, 5s., 245–368.
[5] 83 *H.L. Deb.*, 5 s., 153.
[6] *Ibid.* 176–228.
[7] *Ibid.* 245.
[8] *Ibid.* 297.
[9] 260 *H.C. Deb.*, 5 s., 1823.
[10] 83 *H.L. Deb.*, 5 s., 510.

VI

THE STATUTE AND THE UNITED KINGDOM PARLIAMENT

I

THE examination of the terms of the Statute of Westminster and the discussion of the sense in which and of the extent to which they give effect to the resolutions of the Conferences of 1926 and 1930, may begin most conveniently with a consideration of the definitions which the Statute enacted. The term 'Dominion', as has been seen, had had a conventional and a legal existence before 1926, but by the definition in the Interpretation Act, 1889, the Dominions were included in the term 'colony'. The Conference of 1929 recommended[1] the enactment in the proposed Statute of a clause to provide that 'in this Act and in every Act passed after the commencement of this Act the expression "Dominion" means the Dominion of Canada, the Commonwealth of Australia, the Dominion of New Zealand, the Union of South Africa, and the Irish Free State or any of them, and the expression "Colony" shall, notwithstanding anything in the Interpretation Act, 1889, not include a Dominion or any Province or State forming part of a Dominion'.[2] Curiously enough the Conference of 1930 recommended the enactment of a clause which gave effect to the latter part only of this proposed clause,[3] and its recommendation was carried out in section 11 of the Statute. None the less, in spite of the fact that the Conference of 1930 made no recommendation for the

[1] *Report*, para. 81.   [2] Newfoundland was omitted.
[3] Cmd. 3717, p. 20.

enactment of the former part of the clause proposed in 1929, that part was enacted in the Statute, in slightly different wording,[1] as section 1. It ran:

'In this Act the expression "Dominion" means any of the following Dominions, that is to say, the Dominion of Canada, the Commonwealth of Australia, the Dominion of New Zealand, the Union of South Africa, the Irish Free State and Newfoundland.'

This definition of 'Dominion' by enumeration gives no information about the criteria which determine the status of a Dominion. And, it may be added, the fact that a community is described in section 1 of the Statute as a Dominion does not necessarily mean that that community possesses Dominion Status, as that term has been defined; nor, on the other hand, does the fact that a community is not enumerated in section 1 prove that that community is not a Dominion. In 1933 Newfoundland, for example, ceased to possess Dominion Status, but it continued to enjoy legal enumeration as a Dominion in section 1 of the Statute.[2]

2

With these definitions in mind, it is proposed to consider first those portions of the Statute which deal with the relations of the United Kingdom Parliament and the Dominion Parliaments. The portions concerned are paragraphs 2 and 3 of the Preamble, and sections 2–6 of the main body of the Act.

The most surprising feature of these portions of the Statute was that they contained side by side the declaration of constitutional conventions and the positive enact-

[1] No reference was made to 'in every Act passed after the commencement of this Act', and Newfoundland was included.　　[2] See below, c. ix.

ment of statutory provisions; non-legal rules that is to say found a place within the very confines of the Statute of Westminster itself. On the one hand the Conferences of 1926, 1929, and 1930, when they had addressed themselves to the problem of the method by which first the legislative supremacy of the United Kingdom Parliament, and in particular its expression in the Colonial Laws Validity Act, and secondly the Dominions' lack of power to legislate with extra-territorial effect, should be brought into line with the declaration of equality of status, had recommended that it was essential, if these legal inequalities were to be removed, that specific clauses to this effect should be enacted in a statute of the United Kingdom Parliament. None the less they had recommended at the same time that this alteration in the rules of strict law should be confirmed and supplemented by the declaration in the preamble of the Statute of two constitutional conventions. Nowhere may a more striking illustration be found of the essential inter-action of law and convention in the development of the British Commonwealth.

The Preamble to the Statute was not wholly composed of constitutional conventions. Its remaining paragraphs narrated in a general way the series of steps which led up to the passing of the Statute. In paragraph 1 it was recited that the delegates of the different Members of the British Commonwealth at Imperial Conferences in 1926 and 1930 concurred in making the declarations and resolutions set out in the Reports of these Conferences; in paragraph 4 it was recited that it was necessary 'for the ratifying, confirming, and establishing of certain of the said declarations and resolutions' of these Conferences that a law be made and enacted in due form by the

Parliament of the United Kingdom; and in paragraph 5 it was recited that the Dominions had 'severally requested and consented to the submission of a measure to the Parliament of the United Kingdom for making such provision with regard to the matter aforesaid as is hereafter in this Act contained'. It is clear that these paragraphs of the Preamble were of a wholly different kind from paragraphs 2 and 3. They merely explained why the Statute came to be passed. Paragraphs 2 and 3, on the other hand, were not inserted for explanatory or narrative reasons. The motive which inspired their insertion

bore no resemblance to the reasons which are supposed to justify the use of a preamble. The purpose was simply to commit the British Parliament to making a formal record of Constitutional Conventions which it was thought would be thus firmly established.[1]

Consider first the method by which the sovereignty of the United Kingdom Parliament has been dealt with. The Conferences accepted 'the existence of a legal power in the Parliament of the United Kingdom to legislate for the Dominions'. They did not attempt to abolish that legal power, and the Statute of Westminster nowhere purports to do so. What they did attempt to do, and what the Preamble and operative clauses of the Statute purported to do, was to reconcile 'the existence of this power with the established constitutional position. . . '.[2] The Conference of 1926 took the first step by declaring

[1] See article by Mr. Justice Owen Dixon, of the High Court of Australia, *Australian Law Journal*, vol. x, supplement, p. 98.
[2] *O.D.L. Report*, para. 54. Cf. Mr. Bennett, Prime Minister of Canada, *Canadian Debates (House of Commons)*, June 30, 1931, vol. iii 1931, p. 3196.

the convention that 'legislation by the Parliament at Westminster applying to a Dominion would only be passed with the consent of the Dominion concerned'.[1] The Conference of 1929 elaborated the wording of the convention, and recommended that the Conference of 1930 should place the following statement on record:

It would be in accord with the established constitutional position of all members of the Commonwealth in relation to one another that no law hereafter made by the Parliament of the United Kingdom shall extend to any Dominion otherwise than at the request and with the consent of that Dominion.[2]

The Conference of 1929 recommended further that this constitutional convention itself should appear as a formal recital or preamble in the proposed Act of the United Kingdom Parliament. But this was not enough. The declaration of a constitutional convention did not alter the law. By the rule of construction contained in the Colonial Laws Validity Act,[3] an Act of the United Kingdom Parliament extended to a Dominion when it was made applicable to that Dominion by 'express words or necessary intendment'. The Courts were guided by this rule of construction in applying United Kingdom Acts. If the new principle stated in the above convention was to be effective, a new rule of construction would be necessary, in order to guide the Courts in applying United Kingdom Acts passed in the future. The Conference of 1929 considered that these 'practical considerations affecting both the drafting of Bills and the interpretation of Statutes' made it desirable that the principle enunciated in the constitutional convention and recited in the Preamble, should be expressed also

[1] Cmd. 2768, p. 18.   [2] *O.D.L. Report*, para. 54.   [3] s. 1.

in the enacting part of the Act. The intention of this enactment was, clearly, not to attempt to abolish the power of the United Kingdom Parliament to make laws for the Dominions. Its intention was to declare in what circumstances that power should be deemed to have been exercised. They proposed therefore a declaration and enactment in the following terms:

Be it therefore declared and enacted that no Act of Parliament hereafter made shall extend or be deemed to extend to a Dominion unless it is expressly declared therein that that Dominion has requested and consented to the enactment thereof.[1]

At the 1930 Conference, the United Kingdom delegates were afraid that the clause as so drafted might prevent a future Act of the United Kingdom Parliament having in the Dominions that measure of force which the legislation of one state normally has in another state.[2] They therefore proposed the insertion of the words 'as part of the law in force in that Dominion', so that the clause should read:

No Act of Parliament of the United Kingdom passed after the commencement of this Act shall extend, or be deemed to extend, to a Dominion *as part of the law in force in that Dominion*, unless it is expressly declared in that Act that that Dominion has requested, and consented to, the enactment thereof.

Of this proposed amendment, we are told, some Dominion delegations were somewhat afraid, feeling that it might imply the recognition of a right of the Parliament of the United Kingdom to legislate in relation to a Dominion (otherwise than at the request and with the consent of the Dominion) in a manner which, if the legislation had been

[1] *O.D.L. Report*, para. 55.　　　　[2] Cmd. 3717, p. 18.

enacted in relation to a foreign state, would be inconsistent with the principles of international comity.[1]

It was made clear that this was not the intention of the amendment, and, on the proposal of the United Kingdom delegates, a statement to this effect was placed on record.[2] It was then agreed that the constitutional convention of 1929, the declaration in the Preamble to the proposed Statute, and the enacted clause in the proposed Statute should be amended accordingly.[3]

But the paragraph in the Preamble and the clause as finally enacted in the Statute differ once more from the wording agreed upon in 1930. The words 'in force in' have been omitted, and the word 'of' substituted. Thus paragraph 3 of the Preamble reads:

And whereas it is in accord with the established constitutional position that no law hereafter made by the Parliament of the United Kingdom shall extend to any of the said Dominions as part of the law of that Dominion otherwise than at the request and with the consent of that Dominion.

And section 4 of the Statute enacts:

No Act of Parliament of the United Kingdom passed after the commencement of this Act shall extend, or be deemed to extend, to a Dominion as part of the law of that Dominion, unless it is expressly declared in that Act that that Dominion has requested, and consented to, the enactment thereof.

The reason for the substitution of the word 'of' for the words 'in force in' was that after the publication of the Report of 1930 it was discovered that the words 'in force in' were, from a drafting point of view, an error. The

[1] Cmd. 3717, p. 18.   [2] *Ibid.*   [3] *Ibid.*, pp. 18–21.

word 'of' was preferred because, in the first place, the phrase 'part of the law of' also occurs in section 2 of the Statute, and, secondly, it might be possible to give precisely the wrong interpretation to the phrase 'in force in'. For example the Army Act might be said to be *in force in* a foreign country though it is certainly not part of the law of that foreign country.

It is interesting to notice then that the Statute contains a few words which do not give effect directly to the resolution of the Imperial Conference of 1930 but depart from that resolution, though this departure was made by agreement with all the Dominions severally.

There was a further difficulty in connexion with the enactment of section 4. What was meant by the words 'that Dominion has requested, and consented to, the enactment thereof'? How could a Dominion consent? Was it the Government, the Parliament, the people, or some combination of all three who requested and consented? The point was taken up in the Australian Commonwealth Parliament in 1931 when the proposed clauses of the Statute were being discussed. On the motion of Mr. Latham, Leader of the Opposition,[1] the Commonwealth Parliament requested that a specific clause should be inserted in the Bill providing that in the application of the Statute to the Commonwealth of Australia the request and consent referred to in section 4 should mean the request and consent of the Parliament and Government of the Commonwealth.[2] This provi-

[1] Now Sir John G. Latham, Chief Justice of the High Court of Australia.

[2] The reasons for Mr. Latham's amendment are given in his speech, July 17, 1931, *Australian Commonwealth Parliamentary Debates*, vol. 131, pp. 4061–70, espec. pp. 4067–8. Mr. Latham also criticized the phrase 'request and consent'. *Ibid.*, p. 4066. Extracts from Mr. Latham's speech

sion was inserted in the Bill and enacted as section 9, subsection (3) of the Statute.[1] None of the other Dominions asked for such a provision, apparently, and for them the request and consent of the Government of the Dominion was sufficient.[2] It may be mentioned that the possibility of a difference of opinion between the Government of a Dominion and the Upper House of a Dominion Parliament is not remote,[3] and it could not therefore be assumed that the request and consent of the Government of a Dominion would necessarily have the support of both Houses of a Dominion Parliament. It was to meet these possibilities that the Australian amendment was drafted and inserted.

The first step that was taken, therefore, to reconcile the existence of the legislative supremacy of the United Kingdom Parliament throughout the Empire with the constitutional equality of the Dominions and the United Kingdom, was to attempt to make rules confining the exercise of that supreme legislative power in respect of the Dominions to those occasions when the Dominions requested and consented to such legislation. This was done first by the declaration of a constitutional convention in 1926 and in 1930; secondly by the recital and affirmation of this constitutional convention by the United Kingdom Parliament in the third paragraph of

are printed in Keith, *Speeches and Documents on the British Dominions*, pp. 263–74.

[1] The insertion of additional clauses of this kind after the Conference of 1930 had been especially provided for by that Conference when it resolved (Cmd. 3717, p. 19) 'that the Statute should contain such further provisions as to its application to any particular Dominion as are requested by that Dominion'.

[2] 260 *H.C. Deb.*, 5 s., 279. But for South Africa, see below, p. 157.

[3] Such a situation did exist in Australia at that time. See below, p. 209.

the Preamble to the Statute of Westminster—a sort of voluntary self-denying pledge by the Parliament the exercise of whose powers was being curtailed; and thirdly, the declaration and enactment in section 4 of the Statute itself of a rule of construction to supplement this convention.

So much for the power of the United Kingdom Parliament to make laws which would have effect as part of the law of the Dominions. There remained, however, the power of the United Kingdom Parliament to make a law which did not extend and was not intended to extend to a Dominion but which might affect the interests of a Dominion indirectly. How were these interests to be safeguarded in matters of common concern? This question was dealt with in general terms by the Conference of 1926 which declared that

the appropriate procedure with regard to projected legislation in one of the self-governing parts of the Empire which may affect the interests of other self-governing parts is previous consultation between His Majesty's Ministers in the several parts concerned.[1]

This convention was not specifically repeated by the Conference of 1930, though it proceeded to deal with questions of common concern, such as merchant shipping, upon this basis. Nor was the convention inserted in the Preamble to the Statute of Westminster. But it is clear that the United Kingdom Government in asking the United Kingdom Parliament to exercise its legislative power, apart from its power to legislate for the Dominions, is bound by the constitutional convention that any legislation affecting the interests of a Dominion

[1] Cmd. 2768, pp. 17–18.

shall be introduced only after consultation with the Government of the Dominion concerned.

That is the general rule. But there exists, in addition to this general rule, a rule dealing with one particular subject of common interest to Great Britain and the Dominions. The Conference of 1930, on the recommendation of the Conference of 1929,[1] placed on record a constitutional convention designed to regulate the exercise of legislative power by the Dominions or by the United Kingdom in respect of the Succession to the Throne and the Royal Style and Titles. The convention was adopted in these terms:

In as much as the Crown is the symbol of the free association of the members of the British Commonwealth of Nations, and as they are united by a common allegiance to the Crown, it would be in accord with the established constitutional position of all the members of the Commonwealth in relation to one another that any alteration in the law touching the Succession to the Throne or the Royal Style and Titles shall hereafter require the assent as well of the Parliaments of all the Dominions as of the Parliament of the United Kingdom.

Further, the Conference of 1930, adopting the recommendation of the 1929 Conference, decided that this convention should be recited in the Preamble to the Statute of Westminster, and it appears accordingly in paragraph 2.[2] It was agreed, however, that the convention should not be enacted in the main body of the Statute itself.[3] It appears, therefore, in the Preamble as

[1] *O.D.L. Report*, para. 60.   [2] *Ibid.*, para. 61.
[3] An attempt was made in the United Kingdom House of Commons to amend the Bill so as to enact this part of the Preamble, but the Government resisted the amendment strongly and it was withdrawn. 260 *H.C. Deb.*, 5 s., 355–62. South Africa was absolutely opposed to such

a supplementary conventional rule, regulating the Parliaments of the Dominions as well as of the United Kingdom. Nor is it irrelevant to and unconnected with the operative clauses of the Statute, for it is constitutionally an integral part of the body of rules which regulate the exercise of legislative power by the parliaments of all the Members of the Commonwealth.

The Statute of Westminster, it will be seen, did not give effect, nor was it intended by the Conferences of 1929 and 1930 to give effect, to all the resolutions of the Conferences of 1926 and 1930 which bear upon the exercise by the United Kingdom Parliament of its legislative power. Moreover, in those cases where it does give effect to certain resolutions—as in paragraphs 2 and 3 of the Preamble and section 4 of the Statute—it does so in such a way that one of these resolutions, viz. that dealing with the law touching the succession to the Throne and the Royal Style and Titles, is given not the effect of strict law, but merely the effect of a constitutional convention; while the other resolution, viz. that dealing with the exercise by the United Kingdom Parliament of its power to legislate for the Dominions, is given the effect not only of a constitutional convention in the Preamble but also of a rule of strict law in section 4.

It may be convenient to state shortly the rules which, as a result of the Conferences of 1926 and 1930 and of the Statute of Westminster, 1931, regulate the constitutional status of the United Kingdom Parliament in relation to the Dominions. First, the United Kingdom Parliament, in exercising its legal power to legislate either for the

an enactment. See Debate in House of Assembly on *O.D.L. Report*, May 20 and 22, 1930. *House of Assembly Debates*, vol. 15, cols. 4420–80; 4571–81.

United Kingdom itself or for some other part of the British Empire exclusive of the Dominions, is obliged by constitutional convention (but by constitutional convention alone) not to pass laws which may affect the interests of a Dominion except after consultation between the United Kingdom Government and the Government of the Dominion concerned. In the second place, should this legislation be legislation affecting the Succession to the Throne or the Royal Style and Titles, the United Kingdom Parliament is obliged, by a constitutional convention, which it affirmed in paragraph 2 of the Preamble to the Statute (but by constitutional convention alone), not to pass such legislation (although it will not have effect as part of the law of a Dominion) except with the assent of the Parliaments of all the Dominions. In the third place, the United Kingdom Parliament, in exercising its legal power to legislate for the Dominions, is obliged by a constitutional convention, which it affirmed in paragraph 3 of the Preamble to the Statute (but by constitutional convention alone), not to pass laws extending to a Dominion as part of the law of that Dominion otherwise than with the request and consent of the Dominion. But this convention was supplemented by the rule of construction enacted in section 4 of the Statute, whereby no Act of the United Kingdom Parliament should be deemed to extend to a Dominion as part of its law unless it was expressly declared in that Act that the Dominion had requested and consented to the enactment thereof, such request and consent meaning, in the case of the Commonwealth of Australia, the request and consent of the Parliament and Government of the Commonwealth, and in the cases of all the other Dominions, the request and consent of the Governments of those

Dominions. And fourthly, should this legislation, passed by the United Kingdom Parliament so as to extend to a Dominion as part of the law of that Dominion, be legislation touching the Succession to the Throne or the Royal Style and Titles, the United Kingdom Parliament is obliged by constitutional convention, which it affirmed also in paragraphs 2 and 3 of the Preamble to the Statute, (but by constitutional convention alone), not to pass such legislation except, first, at the request and with the consent of the Dominion or Dominions concerned, and except, secondly, with the assent of the Parliaments of all the Dominions. And further, by the rule of construction enacted in section 4, no such legislation should be deemed to extend to a Dominion as part of the law of that Dominion unless it was declared in the Act that that Dominion had requested and consented to the enactment thereof (with the qualification repeated in the case of Australia).

It may be added that in 1931 while all four rules had the force of constitutional conventions and applied to all the Dominions without exception, rules three and four had the additional force of strict law, in so far as they embodied the rule of construction enacted in section 4 of the Statute. But these rules applied with this additional force of strict law only to those Dominions to which sections 2–6 of the Statute extended, viz. Canada, South Africa, and the Irish Free State. Australia, New Zealand, and Newfoundland by a section of the Statute,[1] as will be seen, contracted out of sections 2–6 until such time as each saw fit to adopt them. The four rules will apply to all the Dominions in the form in which they were stated above only if and when Australia, New

[1] s. 10 (1), (2), and (3). See below cc. viii and ix.

Zealand, and Newfoundland adopt section 4 of the Statute.

3

There seems little doubt that this combination of statutory and conventional rules is sufficient to ensure in practice that the legislative sovereignty of the United Kingdom Parliament will for the future be exercised so far as the Dominions are concerned in accordance with the request and consent of the Dominions.[1] But it is necessary to emphasize that, in enacting section 4, the United Kingdom Parliament has not attempted in strict law to diminish or abolish its power to legislate for the Dominions. Section 4, as has been emphasized, is not a rule restricting power; it is a rule of construction. It is not directed to the United Kingdom Parliament; it is directed to the Courts. And, so long as it remains unrepealed, it is effective for that purpose. But it does not render it legally impossible for the United Kingdom Parliament to legislate for a Dominion without the request and consent of the Dominion. On the basis of the theory of sovereignty which was accepted by the Courts of the United Kingdom and of all the Dominions except the Irish Free State in 1931, there seems no doubt that section 4 of the Statute is ineffective in law to restrict the United Kingdom Parliament to the sphere of legislating for a Dominion only with the request and consent of that Dominion. If, at any time since the passing of the Statute, the United Kingdom Parliament were to pass

---

[1] Some members of Dáil Eireann doubted this. See, e.g., Mr. S. Lemass, July 17, 1931, *Dáil Debates*, vol. 39. Extracts quoted in Keith, *Speeches and Documents on the British Dominions*, pp. 242–5. Mr. McGilligan's reply is the only possible one, though it is doubtful if it convinced the Opposition. See Keith, *ibid.*, p. 246.

an Act which contained no express declaration that it had been passed with the request and consent of a Dominion but which contained some sufficient expression of intention, in terms, to indicate that it should apply to a Dominion, notwithstanding any law of the Dominion to the contrary, then that Act must be accepted by the Courts as prevailing over the Acts of the Dominion Parliament, even if subsequently enacted, and as amounting to a repeal *pro tanto* of section 4 of the Statute of Westminster.[1] The rule of construction is impliedly amended or repealed. On this accepted theory of the sovereignty of the United Kingdom Parliament, 'no law it makes can deprive it of supremacy over that law. The last expression of its legislative will repeals all prior inconsistent laws.'[2] It is not necessary for the United Kingdom Parliament to repeal section 4 of the Statute explicitly. It has merely to legislate for a Dominion, and that legislation frees it from the restriction voluntarily accepted and expressed in section 4. The position was recognized and stated by Lord Sankey in the *British Coal Corporation Case*[3] in the words:

It is doubtless true that the power of the Imperial Parliament to pass on its own initiative any legislation that it thought fit extending to Canada remains unimpaired; indeed, the Imperial Parliament could, as a matter of abstract law, repeal or disregard section 4 of the Statute. But that is theory and has no relation to realities.

Lord Sankey's words indicate that the reconciliation of the accepted theory of legal sovereignty with the

[1] Keith, *Constitutional Law of the British Dominions*, pp. 38–9; Mr. Justice Owen Dixon, *op. cit.*, p. 99; Jennings, *The Law and the Constitution*, p. 128.　　　　　[2] Mr. Justice Owen Dixon, *ibid.*, p. 98.
[3] [1935] A.C. 500 at p. 520.

UNITED KINGDOM PARLIAMENT

accepted fact of constitutional equality is not easy. For
law is law in the Courts, whether it be abstract or con-
crete, theoretical or real. And so long as the theory is
accepted by the Courts, for so long will it be impossible
to dismiss the difficulties which arise in strict law by a
reference to 'abstract law' or to a theory which 'has no
relation to realities'. A more consistent view was expressed by Mr. Justice Owen Dixon when he wrote:

... Probably it is legitimate for Courts to take into account
the now familiar definition of the position of the Dominions
in relation to the United Kingdom. For it explains the
reason of the Statute. But it is one thing to examine such a
description or definition in order to obtain a grasp of the
significance of what is enacted. It is another thing to
improve upon the Statute by developing from the con-
ceptions expressed in the definition rules which Courts may
recognise and even enforce.[1]

But at the same time it is well to examine what is meant
by the 'indestructible sovereignty of the King in Parliament over the law throughout the King's Dominions'.[2]
This sovereignty is indestructible by Parliament.
And the Courts have accepted this. Sovereignty may
belong to the United Kingdom Parliament by nature
but it is effective only in so far as and for so long as the
Courts recognize Parliament to be sovereign. Parliamentary sovereignty is a result of the law declared by
the Courts; it is an expression of the legal relation
between Parliament and the Courts. If it is asked why
the Courts did and do recognize Parliament as sovereign,
the answer is that they did and do so as a result of a particular political situation. And if the particular political

[1] *Loc. cit.*, p. 98. [2] *Ibid.*, at p. 99.

situation should warrant it in the future, there is no doubt that the Courts could qualify or reject the legal sovereignty of the United Kingdom Parliament. In other words that sovereignty. is indestructible by Parliament but not by the Courts. Applying this analysis to section 4 of the Statute, it may be conceived that, should the United Kingdom Parliament attempt to repeal section 4, explicitly or by implication, without the request and consent of a Dominion, the Dominion Courts might reject the accepted theory of sovereignty and might interpret section 4 not merely as a rule of construction but as a restriction upon power. They might declare that the United Kingdom Parliament, by the enactment of section 4, renounced all power to make laws for the Dominions otherwise than at the request and consent of the Dominions. This is the view in South Africa.[1]

It is clear, however, that a Dominion Court, without adopting any such revolutionary view of the legal effect of section 4, and merely by treating the section as no more than a rule of construction, can go to great lengths in refusing to apply, as part of the law of a Dominion, an Act of the United Kingdom Parliament which does not comply with the requirements of section 4, and in refusing to regard such an Act as impliedly repealing that section.

Doubts of the legal effectiveness and permanence of section 4 as a rule of construction appear to have prompted the Parliament of the Union of South Africa to devise an additional rule of construction to govern the extension to the Union of Acts passed by the United Kingdom Parliament. The Status of the Union Act, 1934, after declaring that 'the Parliament of the Union'

[1] Ndlwana v. Hofmeyr, [1937] A.D. 229, at 237.

shall be 'the sovereign legislative power in and over the Union', goes on to enact:

No Act of the Parliament of the United Kingdom and Northern Ireland passed after the eleventh day of December, 1931, shall extend, or be deemed to extend, to the Union as part of the law of the Union, unless extended thereto by an Act of the Parliament of the Union.[1]

The intention of this provision is that no Act of the United Kingdom Parliament, whether or not it is declared to be passed with the request and consent of the Union of South Africa, shall be accepted in the Courts of South Africa as part of the law of South Africa, unless and until it is declared by the Union Parliament[2] to extend to South Africa as part of the law of South Africa. It is designed to meet all legal contingencies envisaged under section 4.[3]

4

The first step that was taken to nullify the legal inequalities of status which existed as a result of the relations of the United Kingdom and Dominion Parliaments, was, then, to attempt to make the exercise of the acknowledged legislative supremacy of the United Kingdom Parliament over the Dominions conditional upon the request and consent of the Dominions. But a further legal inequality still remained since Dominion

[1] s. 2. Dec. 11, 1931, was the date upon which the Statute of Westminster received the royal assent. For Act, see Appendix III.

[2] It will be noted that the consent of the *Parliament* of the Union, as well as of the Government of the Union, thus becomes necessary, if a United Kingdom Act is to extend to the Union. The position is thus made to approximate closely to that envisaged in the case of the Commonwealth of Australia by s. 9 (3) of the Statute of Westminster.

[3] A fuller discussion is undertaken in Chapter X, below.

legislatures still possessed no general power to repeal or amend any past or future Act of the United Kingdom Parliament extending to a Dominion as part of the law of that Dominion. The doctrine of repugnancy as expressed in the Colonial Laws Validity Act subordinated Dominion legislation to legislation by the United Kingdom Parliament and rendered it void and inoperative to the extent of its repugnancy. The Conference of 1930, acting upon the recommendations of the Conference of 1929, addressed itself therefore to the task of attempting to give Dominion legislatures a supremacy over United Kingdom Acts in so far as such Acts formed part of the law of the Dominion. Its recommendations[1] are carried out in section 2 of the Statute.

First of all, it is enacted in section 2, subsection (1), that 'The Colonial Laws Validity Act, 1865, shall not apply to any law made after the commencement of this Act by the Parliament of a Dominion'. In this way it was intended that no Dominion Act passed after December 11, 1931, should be rendered void and inoperative upon the ground of repugnancy to an Act of the United Kingdom Parliament extending to a Dominion by express words or necessary intendment, whether that United Kingdom Act had been passed before or after December 11, 1931. This removed one criterion of repugnancy, viz. repugnancy to an Act of the United Kingdom Parliament extending to a Dominion by express words or necessary intendment. But it might have been argued that the removal of this criterion of repugnancy brought back into force, or at any rate did not explicitly deny, the old and vague common-law criteria of repugnancy which the Colonial Laws Validity Act had been expressly

[1] Cmd. 3717, p. 19.

passed to clarify. It was therefore considered wise[1] to enact section 2, subsection (2) in these words:

No law and no provision of any law made after the commencement of this Act by the Parliament of a Dominion shall be void or inoperative on the ground that it is repugnant to the law of England, or to the provisions of any existing or future Act of Parliament of the United Kingdom, or to any order, rule or regulation made under any such Act, . . .[2]

In these two provisions as so far disclosed it was intended that a Dominion legislature should be free to make laws upon all those matters within its competence before the passing of the Statute, and that the repugnance of these laws to United Kingdom legislation touching the same matters and extending to the Dominions, should not render Dominion laws void and inoperative. But section 2, subsection (2), went on to say:

. . . and the powers of the Parliament of a Dominion shall include the power to repeal or amend any such Act, order, rule or regulation in so far as the same is part of the law of the Dominion.

There was room for argument upon the meaning of this additional clause and upon the total effect of the powers conferred in section 2. On the one hand it might be said, in the words which Mr. Justice Owen Dixon has used, that the latter portion of section 2 (2) must be read as 'no more than explanatory and epexegetical' of what has gone before in section 2.

[1] *O.D.L. Report*, para. 51.

[2] It is to be noted that the section does not give retrospective validity to Dominion legislation passed before the enactment of the Statute and repugnant to the provisions of an Imperial Act extending to the Dominion. The freedom from the fetter of the Colonial Laws Validity Act extends only to Dominion laws '*made after the commencement of this Act*'.

It does not necessarily mean that the Parliaments of the Dominions shall have an independent power of repealing or amending Imperial statutes operating in the Dominion simply because they are Imperial statutes. It would be more natural to regard it as doing no more than removing from the legislative power of the Dominion the restriction on its exercise which the existence of an Imperial statute might impose. So regarded it would not enlarge the ambit of the powers of a Dominion Parliament. It would leave them no more and no less extensive than it found them. But it would increase the strength of the power operating within the same limits so that all the law relating to the subject matter of the power, including provisions of Imperial statute, would be liable to amendment by the exercise of the power.[1]

On this view of section 2, the *area* of Dominion legislative competence is the same after the passing of the Statute as it was before; but within that area the restriction arising from repugnance to an Act of the United Kingdom Parliament is removed. Thus it could be argued that by the Irish Free State Constitution Act, the Oireachtas, before the passing of the Statute of Westminster, was confined in the *area* of its legislative power to making laws and to amending the Constitution itself within the terms of the Scheduled Treaty.[2] Laws transgressing this area were void, because repugnant to this United Kingdom Act. Within this area, moreover, the Oireachtas was restricted in the exercise of its legislative power by the fact that in the matter of, say, merchant shipping legislation, it was unable to make effective laws repugnant to the Merchant Shipping Act, 1894. What is the new position, after the passing of the Statute of Westminster?

[1] *Loc. cit.*, p. 101.   [2] See p. 121 above.

On the view stated above in the words of Mr. Justice Owen Dixon, all that section 2 of the Statute does is to make it possible for the Oireachtas to legislate upon, say, merchant shipping in a manner repugnant to the Merchant Shipping Act, 1894, and to repeal or amend that Act, or any other Act of the United Kingdom Parliament which regulates a class of subject-matter falling within the ambit of the powers of the Oireachtas before the passing of the Statute. It confers no power upon the Oireachtas, however, to amend the Irish Free State Constitution Act in such a way as to extend the area of its legislative powers beyond the terms of the Scheduled Treaty.[1]

On the other hand, section 2 might be interpreted more liberally. It might be argued that the power conferred upon a Dominion Parliament was the power to amend or repeal any Act of the United Kingdom Parliament whatsoever, in so far as that Act was part of the law of the Dominion. This view appears, on one line of argument, to be the more tenable. The O.D.L. Conference evidently considered that the enactment of section 2 in the form which they recommended would lead to 'the acquisition by the Parliaments of the Dominions of full legislative-powers',[2] and that these powers would extend to the amendment and repeal by the Dominion Parliaments of their Constitution Acts. This would have meant in the Dominions of Canada and Australia, at any rate, that the federal parliaments of these Dominions had acquired an increase in the area of their powers as laid down in the Constitutions and would

[1] This argument was advanced by Mr. Wilfrid Greene (as he then was) in *Moore* v. *the Att.-Gen. for the Irish Free State.* See *The Times* newspaper, Dec. 4, 1934.   [2] *O.D.L. Report,* para. 57.

thus upset the entire federal structure. The acquisition of these full powers was not desired by these federal Dominions, nor did New Zealand desire to receive increased powers for the amendment of its Constitution Act. Accordingly the O.D.L. Conference recommended the insertion in the Statute of clauses providing that nothing in the Statute should be deemed to confer any power to repeal or alter the Constitution Acts of Canada, Australia, and New Zealand otherwise than in accordance with the law and constitutional usage and practice existing before the passing of the Statute; and providing further that nothing in the Statute should be deemed to authorize the Parliaments of the Dominion of Canada and the Commonwealth of Australia to make laws on any matter at that time within the authority of the Provinces of Canada or the States of Australia, as the case may be, not being a matter within the authority of the Parliaments or Governments of the Dominion or of the Commonwealth respectively.[1] Provisions to this effect were subsequently enacted in the Statute, with certain modifications consequent upon the extension of section 2 to the Provinces of Canada.[2] The assumption appears to have been, therefore, that in the absence of these express provisions to the contrary, the powers conferred by section 2 would have authorized the Parliaments of these Dominions to repeal any Imperial Act whatever in so far as it was part of the law of the Dominion, and thus would have extended the area of their powers laid down in their Constitutions.

On the whole, the above view of section 2 seems the more tenable. It is submitted that the exceptions made for the Constitution Acts of Canada, Australia, and

[1] *O.D.L. Report*, paras. 62–6.   [2] ss. 7, 8, 9. See below, cc. vii–ix.

New Zealand in the Statute confirm this view. But there has been no judicial decision on this point. The judgment of the Judicial Committee in *Moore's Case* where it was decided that the Free State legislature had power, as a result of the passing of the Statute of Westminster, to amend or repeal the Irish Free State Constitution Act, to any degree it thought fit, did not deal directly with this point.[1]

It is interesting to notice, in conclusion, that, whatever the extent of the powers conferred on Dominion Parliaments by section 2 of the Statute, that power may be exercised by them to repeal or amend an Act of the United Kingdom Parliament passed *after* the commencement of the Statute and it includes therefore Acts passed in accordance with section 4 of the Statute. This insures a great degree of practical equality between Dominion and United Kingdom Parliaments.

Is there any power to amend the Statute itself? The words 'existing or future Act of Parliament' in s. 2 (2) seem to exclude the Statute from the amending power of a Dominion Parliament. But the unrestricted repeal of the Colonial Laws Validity Act in s. 2 (1) seems to justify the view that in this sub-section at any rate a power to amend the Statute is conceded.

5

The intention of the Statute so far was to ensure first, that legislation by the United Kingdom Parliament for a Dominion should occur only at such times and in such terms as a Dominion requested and consented to, and secondly, that where legislation by the United Kingdom

[1] [1935] A.C. 484 at p. 498. The wording was ambiguous, and the question of area was not explicitly considered. See below, c. xi.

Parliament had occurred or might occur, the Dominion Parliament should have power to amend or repeal any such Act. Each of these two intentions had been realized in terms which left it open to doubt whether the United Kingdom Parliament had in strict law surrendered or the Dominion Parliament in strict law acquired the fullest powers necessary for the realization of equality of status between the United Kingdom and the Dominions. So long as the theory of the sovereignty of the United Kingdom Parliament was accepted, for so long might that Parliament legislate for the Dominions, and repeal section 4 *pro tanto*. So long as there was doubt whether the Dominion Parliaments had acquired powers under section 2 of the Statute extending the area of their legislative competence, for so long was there doubt whether they were authorized to legislate for all those spheres which formerly had been regulated by the United Kingdom Parliament. It was one thing to exclude the United Kingdom Parliament, by law or convention, from legislating upon certain matters of interest to a Dominion; it was quite another, at least upon the restrictive interpretation of section 2, to claim that the Dominion Parliament had powers to regulate those matters. And in the cases of those Dominions which had expressly excluded their Constitution Acts from the operation of the Statute—Australia, Canada, and New Zealand—the same restrictions in respect of the area over which Dominion legislative competence extended remained, and the same doubts of the precise limits of that area remained. The question of the lack of power to legislate with extra-territorial effect, for example, was not solved beyond all reasonable doubt by the enactment of sections 2 and 4 of the Statute, as modified by the exceptions in the cases of Australia, Canada, and New Zealand in sections 7, 8, and 9. In so far as that restriction was imposed by the terms of the Constitution Act, to that extent it was not more easily removed after the passing of the Statute by those three Dominions than before; and upon a restricted interpretation of section 2 the same could be said of South Africa and the Irish Free State.

The Conference of 1930, acting upon the recommendations of the Conference of 1929, advised a specific enactment in the Statute to deal with the question of extra-territoriality. The Statute accordingly provides in section 3:

It is hereby declared and enacted that the Parliament of a Dominion has full power to make laws having extra-territorial operation.[1]

The wording adopted here is interesting. The Imperial Conference of 1926, in referring the question of the territorial limitation on Dominion legislation to the proposed expert committee, asked them to consider:

(ii) (a) The present position as to the competence of Dominion Parliaments to give their legislation extra-territorial operation.

(b) The practicability and most convenient method of giving effect to the principle that each Dominion Parliament should have power to give extra-territorial operation to its legislation in all cases where such operation is ancillary to provision for the peace, order, and good government of the Dominion.[2]

[1] It was argued for the appellants in *Croft* v. *Dunphy*, [1933] A.C. 156, that this section was retrospective in effect. The Judicial Committee decided the case on other grounds and found it unnecessary therefore to pronounce upon the point.   [2] Cmd. 2768, p. 18.

When the 1929 Conference came to consider the matter, it seemed to them that any limitation upon the grant of extra-territorial power to a Dominion by reference either to a class of persons (e.g. the citizens of the Dominion) or to laws 'ancillary to provision for the peace, order and good government of the Dominion' would be unwise. The first limitation they regarded as undesirable in principle; the second as likely to introduce further confusion and possible unintentional limitation.[1] They therefore recommended a full grant of power,[2] remarking at the same time that the customary extra-territorial immunities, enjoyed by the forces of one government in the territory of another, ought to be provided for.[3] Their recommendation was adopted by the Imperial Conference of 1930, while the method of securing the customary immunities for the forces was discussed.[4] The principle of reciprocal legislation has been accepted, and legislation in substantially identical terms has been passed in the Union of South Africa, in the United Kingdom, and in Canada.[5]

There was considerable criticism of this wide grant of extra-territorial power,[6] but, in the opinion of the writer, most of it was based upon a misconception of what extra-

[1] O.D.L. Report, paras. 41 and 42.
[2] Ibid., para. 43.   [3] Ibid., para. 44.   [4] Cmd. 3717, p. 26.
[5] The need for similar legislation in Australia, New Zealand, and Newfoundland does not arise unless and until they exercise their power, already referred to, of adopting the relevant section of the Statute of Westminster.
[6] See, e.g., debate in Committee in the House of Commons on the Clause, 260 H.C. Deb., 5 s., 245–79, notably speeches of Sir Gerald Hurst and Mr. Marjoribanks. An explanation and defence of the clause was made by the Solicitor-General (ibid. 260–6) and by Mr. Amery (ibid. 270–3). In the Australian Parliament, Mr. Latham criticized the wording of the clause as too wide, but thought it would work. Australian Commonwealth Parliamentary Debates, vol. 131, p. 4063.

territorial powers are. These powers are possessed and exercised by most modern States. Extra-territorial legislation simply means legislation which attaches significance for courts within the jurisdiction to facts and events occurring outside the jurisdiction. This does not imply that one State can pass laws for another State or that several systems of law will be in operation regulating a particular sphere within any given State. It is true that the law governing activities in which extra-territorial powers are exercised may be different in different States and not uniform as is the case when one State legislates for a group of States. But the lack of uniformity does not necessarily result in gross injustice to and unfair discrimination against the citizens of other States. In the case of the British Commonwealth, it was not intended by the grant of extra-territorial power in the Statute of Westminster that New Zealand laws, for example, having extra-territorial operation should form part of the law of Australia and be enforceable there, whether the matters arose in Australia or elsewhere. The purpose of the clause was that the extra-territorial laws of a Dominion should be valid in its own courts. To construe the Statute as giving to each member of the Commonwealth power to make laws extending to all the other members without their consent seems hardly reasonable when one reflects that the chief object of the Statute was to restrict this very power in the case of one particular member, the United Kingdom. The exercise of extra-territorial power by any State and its grant to the Dominions simply means, in the words used by the Solicitor-General in defending the clause in the House of Commons,

that each nation has the capacity to legislate outside the

three-miles limit of its own territory, in respect of its own subjects, in such a way as to make them amenable to the law, as administered in its own courts, when they come within its jurisdiction.[1]

The only answer to those who fear the consequences of this grant of power to the Dominions is simply *abusus non tollit usum*. As the Prime Minister of Canada said:

I am not one of those who does not realize that the exercise of that power is fraught with very many possibilities of danger, but the fact that the possibility exists does not militate against the conferring of that power . . . we must trust the common sense and good judgement of our own parliament not to exercise that power in such a way as will cause either irritation or difficulty to others or evil consequences to ourselves.[2]

The extent and the implications of this wide grant of legal powers to the Dominion parliaments which the Statute confers in general terms in sections 2 and 3, is well illustrated when one considers the sphere of merchant shipping legislation, which was a matter which received special attention from the Conference of 1929. As a result of the powers conferred by section 2 it is clear that the Dominions to which the section applies have power to repeal in whole or in part the merchant shipping legislation which, up to 1911, the United Kingdom Parliament passed to regulate shipping throughout the Empire. As a result of the powers conferred by sections 2 and 3 the Dominions to which the sections apply may replace Imperial legislation with legislation of their own, or, without repealing Imperial legislation, may pass laws dealing with matters already regulated by Imperial

[1] 260 *H.C. Deb.*, 5 s., 263.
[2] *Canadian Debates* (*House of Commons*), vol. iii, 1931, p. 3195.

Acts, and these Dominion laws will no longer be void on the ground of repugnancy, and they will have extra-territorial effect. The new position is, therefore, in the words of the *O.D.L. Report*, that:

each Dominion will, amongst its other powers, have full and complete legislative authority over all ships while within its territorial waters or engaged in its coasting trade; and also over its own registered ships both intra-territorially and extra-territorially. Such extra-territorial legislation will, of course, operate subject to local laws while the ship is within another jurisdiction.[1]

From this it followed that the Dominions had power to repeal those provisions of the Imperial Acts to which reference was made in a previous chapter—sections 735 and 736 of the Merchant Shipping Act, 1894, and sections 4 and 7 of the Colonial Courts of Admiralty Act, 1890—which greatly limited the powers of a Dominion parliament to repeal or amend Imperial legislation on merchant shipping. The precise powers of the Dominion and Imperial parliaments on this matter and the procedure required for amendment had been a topic of considerable controversy,[2] and in order to make the new powers of the Dominions under the Statute quite clear and to remove any existing doubts, the 1929 Conference recommended the insertion in the Statute of a clause expressly declaring the position in this particular matter.[3] The Conference of 1930 accepted this recommendation and sections 5 and 6 of the Statute, therefore, provide as follows:

5. Without prejudice to the generality of the foregoing provisions of this Act, sections 735 and 736 of the Merchant

[1] *O.D.L. Report*, para. 93.   [2] *Ibid.*, paras. 83–90; 110–14.
[3] *Ibid.*, para. 123.

Shipping Act, 1894, shall be construed as though reference therein to the Legislature of a British possession did not include reference to the Parliament of a Dominion.

6. Without prejudice to the generality of the foregoing provisions of this Act, section four of the Colonial Courts of Admiralty Act, 1890 (which requires certain laws to be reserved for the signification of His Majesty's pleasure or to contain a suspending clause), and so much of section seven of that Act as requires the approval of His Majesty in Council to any rules of Court for regulating the practice and procedure of a Colonial Court of Admiralty, shall cease to have effect in any Dominion as from the commencement of this Act.

6

It will be noticed that whereas the Conference of 1930 attempted to reconcile the legal sovereignty of the United Kingdom Parliament with equality of Dominion Status not merely by the enactment of a rule of strict law in section 4 of the Statute, but also by the adoption of a constitutional convention in terms substantially identical with section 4 and by the declaration and affirmation of this constitutional convention by the United Kingdom Parliament in paragraph 3 of the Preamble to the Statute, on the other hand the Conference attempted to increase the powers of Dominion Parliaments merely by the enactment of rules of strict law in sections 2, 3, 5, and 6. No constitutional conventions in substantially identical terms with these sections were adopted by the Conference of 1930 or declared and affirmed by the United Kingdom Parliament in the Preamble to the Statute. The reason is apparent. The United Kingdom Parliament clearly possessed power to increase the legal competence of the Dominion Parliaments; that legal power could not be increased by any other method than by the enactment of rules of strict law. The declaration of a constitutional convention in the same terms as sections 2, 3, 5, and 6 of the Statute would have made no alteration either in the legal or in the constitutional position. With section 4 it was otherwise. That section did not attempt to remove legal inequality; it merely recognized it and provided for it. The declaration of the constitutional convention and the acceptance of that convention by the United Kingdom Parliament was a constitutional safeguard of greater value than the legal safeguard of section 4. Indeed, on the accepted theory of the legal supremacy of the United Kingdom Parliament, a constitutional rule in the form of a convention was the only effective constitutional rule.

But while it is true that the increases in the powers of Dominion Parliaments, which the Conference of 1930 proposed and which sections 2, 3, 5, and 6 of the Statute authorize, were carried into effect solely by an alteration in the rules of strict law, it is necessary to emphasize that the exercise of these increased powers is made subject to certain constitutional conventions. The Dominions are required to exercise these 'full legislative powers' which the passing of the Statute was intended to confer upon them, in accordance with the same two constitutional conventions as bind the United Kingdom Parliament in the exercise of its power to legislate for any part of the Empire other than the Dominions.

First of all, that is to say, the Dominion Parliaments are bound by the constitutional convention agreed upon in 1926 that:

the appropriate procedure with regard to projected legisla-

tion in one of the self-governing parts of the Empire which
may affect the interests of other self-governing parts is
previous consultation between His Majesty's Ministers in
the several parts concerned.   ·

In strict law, then, a Dominion may legislate upon a
matter, such as trade regulation, merchant shipping or
nationality, which obviously affects the interests of the
United Kingdom or of some other Dominion, without
submitting itself in any way to the control of those other
affected members of the Commonwealth. But by constitutional convention the Dominion Parliaments are
bound, as is also the United Kingdom Parliament, not
to pass such legislation unless the Governments concerned have engaged in prior consultation. In matters
of common interest, therefore, legislation should result
from consultation, and if possible, be carried out upon an
agreed basis. The Conference of 1930 carried the matter
further.

There are—they said—a number of subjects in which
uniformity has hitherto been secured through the medium
of Acts of the Parliament of the United Kingdom of general
application. Where uniformity is desirable on the ground of
common concern or practical convenience we think that
this end should in the future be sought by means of con-
current or reciprocal action based upon agreement.[1]

In particular they addressed themselves to two subjects
—nationality and merchant shipping. In respect of
nationality they agreed that:

no member of the Commonwealth either could or would
contemplate seeking to confer on any person a status to be
operative throughout the Commonwealth save in pursuance
of legislation based upon common agreement. . . .[2]

[1] Adopting *O.D.L. Report*, para. 80.   [2] *Ibid.*, para. 78.

In respect of merchant shipping the 1930 Conference went into more detail. Merchant shipping indeed not only illustrates the very wide powers which the Statute confers on Dominion Parliaments; it also indicates how these wide powers may be best used to further the common interests of all members of the Commonwealth and provides an answer to those critics who have already prophesied a chaos of jurisdictions and a conflict of powers. For the Conference of 1929, after outlining the existing position in regard to merchant shipping legislation throughout the Empire,[1] and the new position which would be created by the passage of the proposed Statute,[2] recommended the framing of an agreement between the members of the British Commonwealth to regulate certain matters of common interest and importance which they enumerated in a general way in their Report and concerning which they offered certain general recommendations.[3] A draft of an agreement covering these points was drawn up in the United Kingdom in 1930 and circulated to the Dominions. It was discussed at the Imperial Conference of 1930, and, after certain alterations had been made, was approved.[4] Upon the passing of the Statute of Westminster it came into force throughout the Commonwealth;[5] and in merchant shipping, at least, we have uniformity by voluntary agreement taking the place of uniformity imposed by

---

[1] *O.D.L. Report*, paras. 83-90.   [2] *Ibid.*, paras. 91-4.

[3] *Ibid.*, paras. 95-109.

[4] Cmd. 3717, p. 25. The draft agreement, as approved, appears in the Annex to Section VI (pp. 32-7).

[5] The agreement is dated Dec. 10, 1931. An amendment to the Statute of Westminster Bill to make the signature of the agreement a condition of clause 5 of the Statute's coming into operation, was negatived in the House of Commons. 260 *H.C. Deb.* 5 s., 285-90.

a single, overruling parliament upon subordinate legislatures.

Indeed, in summing up one's view of the significance for the future of the British Commonwealth of the wide extension of powers which the Statute of Westminster confers upon Dominion Parliaments, it is hardly possible to do better than to adopt the words of the 1929 Conference in regard to merchant shipping:

The ground is thus cleared for co-operation amongst the members of the British Commonwealth of Nations on an equal basis in those matters in which practical considerations call for concerted action. . . . But this concerted action must from its nature result from voluntary agreements by the members of the Commonwealth; it should be confined to matters in which concerted action is necessary or desirable in the common interest; it should be sufficiently elastic to permit of alterations being made from time to time as experience is gained; and it must not prevent local matters being dealt with in accordance with local conditions.[1]

That is the general rule. But there is a particular convention also regulating the exercise by the Dominion Parliaments of their extended legislative powers under sections 2, 3, 5, and 6 of the Statute. They also, like the United Kingdom Parliament, are bound by the constitutional convention adopted in 1930 and declared and affirmed by the United Kingdom Parliament in paragraph 2 of the Preamble to the Statute, that:

any alteration in the law touching the Succession to the Throne or the Royal Style and Titles shall hereafter require the assent as well of the Parliaments of all the Dominions as of the Parliament of the United Kingdom.

[1] *O.D.L. Report*, paras. 94–5.

The wording of this convention makes it clear, indeed, that it is intended to supplement and regulate the powers conferred on the Dominion Parliaments by section 2 of the Statute. For it is so phrased that it envisages the power of any Dominion Parliament to legislate for the Succession to the Throne and the Royal Style and Titles, and it goes on to say that that power ought to be exercised with the assent, not only of the Parliaments of all the Dominions but also of the Parliament of the United Kingdom.

It is well to stress that the scope of this convention is limited. It requires the consents of the Parliaments of all the members of the Commonwealth only for alterations in the laws touching the succession to the Throne or the Royal Style and Titles. These are two specific and relatively restricted topics. They are not coterminous with, for example, the concept of 'common allegiance to the Crown', though they may form an element in it. They do not include, I would submit, the topic of regency, nor should it be lightly assumed that they have any necessary connexion with the topic of secession from the Commonwealth. Regency and secession may well be topics which must be included in the concept of common allegiance to the Crown; they are matters of common concern to all the members of the Commonwealth, and are therefore matters, legislation upon which by any member of the Commonwealth should be preceded by consultation with other members.[1] But they are not matters upon which the consent of the Parliaments of other members is required.

[1] Such consultation was undertaken by the United Kingdom, for example, before it introduced legislation upon regency in 1937 and in 1943. See 319 *H.C. Deb.*, 5 s., 1452-3 and 392 *H.C. Deb.*, 5 s., 1251.

VII
THE STATUTE AND THE LEGAL STATUS OF CANADA

I

THE powers which the Statute of Westminster conferred upon the Parliaments of the Dominions were stated in the last chapter at their possible maximum. But, as has already been hinted, the Dominions were not unanimous in desiring an extension of the powers of their legislatures to this possible maximum. No sooner had legal inequalities been removed by sections 2–6 of the Statute than qualifications began to be inserted in order to safeguard or to exclude certain classes of subject-matter from the operation of these sections of the Statute in so far as certain of the Dominions were concerned. Thus Dominion Status, after the passing of the Statute of Westminster, as before, though its predominant characteristic is conventional equality of status, contains legal ingredients which are different and are unequal from one Dominion to another. Apart from this common ingredient of conventional equality, the recipe differs in each case to a greater or less degree. Dominion Status to-day, it should be emphasized, means equality of conventional status, but it does not necessarily mean equality of legal status or identity in the legal rules which define that status for each Dominion.

It is proposed, therefore, to examine the legal status of each of the Dominions in order to discover what change has been effected in that status as a result of the passing of the Statute of Westminster, and in particular, to what extent the Statute has brought about legal equality of status as between each of the Dominions and the United Kingdom. The main object of the inquiry is, it will be realized, rather restricted. No attempt will be made to expound in detail the consequences which flow from the passing of the Statute for the constitutional structures of each Dominion, though it is realized that these consequences are as important as, in many cases, they are unexpected and paradoxical. Such a study, however, requires a knowledge of the constitutional law of each of the Dominions which the present writer does not possess. He confines himself, therefore, to the narrower inquiry, upon which attention has been concentrated heretofore in this book, viz. the extent to which the passing of the Statute removed or made possible the removal of those legal inequalities of status which formed part of the concept of Dominion Status as it existed before 1931. A start may be made with the legal status of the Dominion of Canada.

2

The fundamental fact in the case of the Dominion of Canada was that it was a federation. The powers and functions of the federal and provincial parliaments and governments were demarcated and their existing distribution was guaranteed by an act of the United Kingdom Parliament, the British North America Act, 1867. This Act was unalterable in essentials by the federal or provincial legislatures in Canada; it was completely alterable by the United Kingdom Parliament only.[1] From 1867

---

[1] The history and nature of the amending process in Canada up to 1950 is discussed with great authority by P. Gérin-Lajoie in *Constitutional Amendment in Canada*, University of Toronto Press, 1950. See also R. Mac G. Dawson, *The Government of Canada*, chap. vii.

to 1930 inclusive, it had been amended seven times by that Parliament. No clear rules regulated the procedure by which amendments of the British North America Act, desired by the provincial or federal parliaments in Canada, should be transmitted to and executed by the United Kingdom Parliament. There was a convention that no amendment should be made by the United Kingdom Parliament otherwise than at the request and with the consent of the federal government of Canada. Beyond this it was difficult to say that the rules which existed amounted to anything more than usages. There appeared[1] to be a usage that a request to the United Kingdom Parliament to amend the Act from the Dominion Government alone, without action of any sort by the Dominion Parliament, would not be adequate. Actually, in passing the second of the seven amendments, viz. the Parliament of Canada Act, 1875, the United Kingdom Parliament acted on the request of the Dominion Government alone, without the passing of addresses by both Houses of the Dominion Parliament; but in this case action had already been taken by the Dominion Parliament which showed that it approved of the proposed amendment. In passing the remaining six amendments, viz. the British North America Acts of 1871,[2] 1886, 1907, 1915, 1916, and 1930, the United Kingdom Parliament acted upon addresses from both Houses of the Dominion Parliament.

[1] The discussion which follows is based upon the evidence of Dr. O. D. Skelton, Under-Secretary of State for External Affairs in the Dominion of Canada, given before the Special Committee of the Canadian House of Commons on the British North America Act, which was set up in 1935. (*Proceedings and Evidence and Report*, pp. 31–8.)

[2] The Act of 1871 was erroneously described by Skelton as requested by the Canadian Government alone. See Gérin-Lajoie, *op. cit.*, pp. 50–8.

But there was not only the question whether amendments should require the request and consent of the Dominion Parliament as well as of the Dominion Government. There was the further and more important question whether amendments should require the request and consent of all or of a majority of the provincial parliaments and/or governments. The usage here was that in six out of the seven amendments, action was taken by the United Kingdom Parliament as a result of requests from the Dominion Government or Parliament without consulting or seeking the consent of the provinces generally. The amendments of 1871, 1886, and 1915 affected either all or some of the provinces, but none of them was consulted. The amendment of 1930 affected certain provinces and these alone were consulted and their consent obtained. The Dominion Government and Parliament evidently did not consider themselves bound by a convention to consult all the provinces or to obtain their consent. And the one case, that of 1907, where consultation of all occurred and consent of all was sought does not support a usage or convention of unanimous consent, for the province primarily concerned, British Columbia, did not consent to the proposed amendment, which nevertheless was requested by the Dominion Parliament and passed by the United Kingdom Parliament. The example of 1907 'while indicating some measure of British adherence . . . to the view that provincial consent was necessary, left the question of degree undetermined and uncertain—as to how many provinces were to consent'.[1] And finally, it should be

[1] Dr. O. D. Skelton, *loc. cit.*, p. 38. Professor Kennedy and Professor F. R. Scott concurred with Dr. Skelton that no convention of provincial consent had been established by the seven amendments. See *Proceedings*

emphasized that the seven amendments which had been made up to 1931 'include no major alteration of the distribution of federal and provincial powers and do not touch, in that sense, the heart of the matter. They throw no certain light on the attitude the United Kingdom parliament would take on a request from the Dominion parliament for a change in powers if opposed by, say, three or five provinces.'[1] It is clear then that the most important safeguard which the provinces of Canada had before 1931 that their powers under the British North America Act would not be altered in opposition to what they considered their rights and interests, was that the Act was alterable by the United Kingdom Parliament alone, and that although the United Kingdom Parliament was bound by convention not to alter the Act except with the request and consent of the Dominion Government and (usually) Parliament, it was not bound by convention to alter the Act if and when the Dominion Government and Parliament requested it to do so. It is clear, too, that the whole process of constitutional amendment in Canada was vague and ill-defined, and that it was only because no fundamental alteration in the federal system had been attempted that this process had not proved unsatisfactory or even unworkable.

The consequences of an unqualified application of section 2 of the Statute of Westminster to the Dominion Parliament of Canada may now be indicated. On the liberal interpretation of the affirmative portion of section 2 (2), the Dominion Parliament would have been

and Evidence and Report, p. 70 and p. 80, respectively. It may be mentioned here that for the eighth amendment, in 1940, the consent of all the provinces was sought and obtained.

[1] Dr. O. D. Skelton, *loc. cit.*, p. 38.

empowered to amend any United Kingdom Act whatsoever, in so far as it was part of the law of the Dominion.
In consequence it would be able to amend the British
North America Act, 1867, and the seven subsequent
amending acts, as it thought fit, altering the federal
structure as therein defined, without reference to the
wishes of the federated provinces, the powers and status
of which could be reduced to those of the provinces
of South Africa, or indeed abolished altogether. The
guarantee which the provinces had previously enjoyed
from the fact that the United Kingdom Parliament
alone could alter the British North America Act would
be destroyed; thereafter the Dominion Parliament would
share that power in strict law with the United Kingdom Parliament, and by convention would exercise it
alone.

Further, on this view of section 2 (2), the Dominion
Parliament could invade the provincial sphere not only
by a direct amendment of the Act of 1867 and subsequent amending Acts, but also, on the assumption that
'the law of the Dominion' included the law of the Provinces, by an amendment or repeal of any other United
Kingdom Acts, such as the Judicial Committee Acts,
1833 and 1844, which formed part of the law of the
Provinces.

It has been mentioned already that the words of
section 2 (2) may not require so wide an interpretation.
All that it did, it might be submitted, was to empower a
Dominion Parliament to repeal or amend any Act to
which a Dominion law, passed on a subject within the
area of its powers under its Constitution, was repugnant.
In the case of Canada, no law of the Dominion Parliament would be within this area if it invaded the Pro-

vincial sphere, for section 91 of the Act of 1867 empowered the Dominion Parliament 'to make laws for
the peace, order, and good government of Canada in
relation to all matters not coming within the classes of
subjects by this Act assigned exclusively to the Legislatures of the Provinces'. At the same time it is probable
that, even on this view of the effect of section 2 (2), the
Dominion Parliament would have acquired some power
to amend the Act of 1867, provided that no encroachment was made upon the Provincial sphere. The
authority of the Constitution was involved either way.

These possible consequences were taken into consideration by the O.D.L. Conference of 1929. It was realized
that the question of alternative methods of amending
the British North America Act was a matter for future
consideration by the appropriate Canadian authorities,
and that, pending some agreed change in the process,
the existing system should remain unaltered by the
Statute of Westminster. It was thought necessary also
to make an express declaration that the passing of the
Statute in no way increased the area of the powers
possessed by the Dominion Parliament in such a way as
to authorize that Parliament 'to make laws on any
matter at present within the authority of the Provinces,
not being a matter within the authority of the Dominion'.[1]

Similar restrictions were considered necessary in the
case of Australia, and in addition the Dominion of New
Zealand expressed a wish to make no alteration in the
status quo in so far as the amendment of its Constitution
Act was concerned. The O.D.L. Conference proposed,
therefore, that the position of the Constitutions of Canada

[1] *O.D.L. Report*, para. 63.

and of these other two Dominions should be safeguarded by the insertion of a clause in the Statute in the following terms:

(1) Nothing in this Act shall be deemed to confer any power to repeal or alter the Constitution Acts of the Dominion of Canada, the Commonwealth of Australia, and the Dominion of New Zealand, otherwise than in accordance with the law and constitutional usage and practice heretofore existing.

(2) Nothing in this Act shall be deemed to authorize the Parliaments of the Dominion of Canada and the Commonwealth of Australia to make laws on any matter at present within the authority of the Provinces of Canada or the States of Australia, as the case may be, not being a matter within the authority of the Parliaments or Governments of the Dominion of Canada and of the Commonwealth of Australia respectively.[1]

The Report of the O.D.L. Conference was unanimously approved by the Canadian House of Commons in May 1930, after some criticism by members of the Conservative Party, then in opposition. At the General Election of July 1930, the Conservative Party, under the leadership of Mr. R. B. Bennett, was returned to power.[2] Before Mr. Bennett left for the Imperial Conference of 1930 he received from the Premier of Ontario, Mr. Howard Ferguson, also a Conservative, a memorandum in which the terms of the proposed Statute were severely examined. In particular the two clauses quoted above

[1] *O.D.L. Report*, para. 66.
[2] The following statement of the course of events is based upon Mr. Bennett's survey of the negotiations in his speech, introducing the resolution requesting the passing of the Statute, in the Canadian House of Commons in 1931. (See *Canadian Debates (House of Commons)*, vol. iii, 1931, pp. 3191 ff.)

were criticized as vague and inconclusive, and it was asserted 'that no restatement of the procedure for amending the Constitution of Canada can be accepted by the Province of Ontario that does not fully and frankly acknowledge the right of all the Provinces to be consulted and to become parties to the decision arrived at'. Quebec and all the other Provinces proved to be in agreement with these views. In consequence it was necessary for the Canadian delegation at the Imperial Conference of 1930 to ask that, in effect, the whole question of the repeal of the Colonial Laws Validity Act, in its application to Canada, should be left in suspense until the views of the Provinces on the matter could be obtained. The reference to the Dominion of Canada and to the Provinces of Canada was therefore deleted from the proposed clause, and it appeared in the Schedule drawn up by the Conference with a specific reference to Australia and New Zealand only. It was stated that 'a section dealing exclusively with the Canadian position will be inserted after the representations of the Provinces have received consideration'.[1] At the same time the Conference deemed it advisable to place on record

that the sections of the Statute relating to the Colonial Laws Validity Act should be so drafted as not to extend to Canada unless the Statute was enacted in response to such requests as are appropriate to an amendment of the British North America Act. It also seemed desirable to place on record the view that the sections should not subsequently be extended to Canada except by an Act of the Parliament of the United Kingdom enacted in response to such requests as are appropriate to an amendment of the British North America Act.[2]

[1] Cmd. 3717, p. 20.   [2] Cmd. 3717, pp. 17-18.

A Conference of Federal and Provincial Governments was held in Canada in April 1931. It appears that the provincial governments had two main demands to make. First of all they wished to have the wording of the section proposed by the Conference of 1929 revised so as to make quite certain that the passing of the Statute would not alter the method by which the British North America Act was amended. In the second place they wished to have the fetter imposed by the Colonial Laws Validity Act upon provincial legislation removed. In other words they wished the provisions which came to be enacted as section 2 of the Statute to apply to the provincial legislatures as well as to the Dominion legislature. Agreement upon these two questions was unanimously obtained at the Conference and appropriate clauses were drawn up. These were adopted by the Senate and House of Commons in June 1931, and, as a result of an address from both these Houses, were included, in the identical form in which they were proposed, in section 7 of the Statute.

The extension to the provincial legislatures of Canada of the powers granted to the legislatures of the Dominion by section 2 of the Statute was carried out in sub-section 2 of section 7. The sub-section enacted: 'The provisions of section 2 of this Act shall extend to laws made by any of the Provinces of Canada and to the powers of the legislatures of such Provinces.' This is the most startling innovation inserted in the terms of the Statute between the drawing up of the Schedule by the Imperial Conference of 1930 and the enactment of the Statute in 1931. The proposal had not been discussed at the Conferences of 1926, 1929, and 1930. The Provinces had not been represented at these Conferences, any more than had the States of Australia. But it is probably not true to say that

4303

O

the extension of the terms of section 2 to the Canadian Provinces at the last minute, so to speak, was unauthorized by the Conference of 1930. For it had been agreed by that Conference that 'the Statute should contain such further provisions as to its application to any particular Dominion as are requested by that Dominion'.[1] As the demand of the Canadian Provinces was accepted by the Dominion Parliament and Government, and the enactment of a provision in the terms of section 7 (2) was requested and consented to by the Dominion Parliament, the United Kingdom Government was evidently bound to ask Parliament to pass such a provision. On the same argument it would seem that had the Parliament of the Commonwealth of Australia made a similar request on behalf of the States of Australia, as a result of an agreement between the States and the Commonwealth, the United Kingdom Government would have been obliged by the resolution of the Conference of 1930, to ask Parliament to extend the powers of section 2 to the States of Australia. In fact no such request was made. In consequence of section 7 (2) of the Statute the legislatures of the Provinces of Canada came to occupy, therefore, a different status in their relation with the United Kingdom Parliament from that enjoyed by the legislatures of the States of Australia.

The fetter imposed by the Colonial Laws Validity Act upon the Parliament of Canada had thus been removed by section 2 of the Statute, and the same fetter imposed upon the legislatures of the Provinces of Canada had been removed by section 7 (2) of the Statute. On the liberal interpretation of the powers which section 2 conferred, it followed that Dominion and provincial legis-

[1] Cmd. 3717, p. 19.

latures were empowered to repeal or amend any existing
or future Act of the United Kingdom Parliament in so far
as it formed part of the law of Canada, and in particular
they were empowered to amend or repeal the British
North America Act. It was necessary therefore to safeguard that Act, not only against the exercise of these
increased powers by the Parliament of Canada, but also
against their exercise by the provincial legislatures of
Canada. This was carried out in subsection (1) of
section 7. The terms of the subsection were much more
rigid and much more sweeping than those suggested
by the O.D.L. Conference of 1929. The subsection
enacted:

Nothing in this Act shall be deemed to apply to the
repeal, amendment or alteration of the British North
America Acts, 1867 to 1930, or any order, rule or regulation made thereunder.

Two points deserve notice. First of all, instead of the
vaguer reference to the Constitution Act of the Dominion
of Canada, proposed by the O.D.L. Conference, there
was a specific and inclusive reference to the British North
America Acts, 1867 to 1930. Not only was the original
Act of 1867 excluded from the operation of the Statute,
but also certain subsequent amending Acts. At the same
time it is worth mentioning that the sub-section was not
as comprehensive as it might have been, for, as thus
worded, it did not exclude from the operation of the
Statute either all the amending Acts up to and including
the Act of 1930, or any amending Act subsequent to the
Act of 1930. The expression 'British North America
Acts, 1867 to 1930', is a statutory expression which has
been defined in certain of these amending Acts up

to and including the British North America Act, 1930. But the expression as so defined does not include either the Parliament of Canada Act, 1875 or the British North America Act, 1907.[1] The expression covers, therefore, the British North America Acts of 1867, 1871, 1886, 1915, 1916, and 1930. The point is one to which attention does not appear to have been directed at the time the subsection was framed and enacted, and it seems to deserve mention in order that the precise significance of the expression 'British North America Acts, 1867 to 1930', should be appreciated.[2]

The second point which deserves notice is that the subsection expressly excluded the British North America Acts, 1867 to 1930, from the operation of the entire Statute, that is to say from its operative sections and from its Preamble. The repeal, amendment, or alteration of these Acts will be carried out by the United Kingdom Parliament. Such legislation, in order to extend to Canada, is not required to contain a declaration that it has been passed at the request and with the consent of Canada, for section 4 of the Statute is not applicable. On the other hand, although the terms of the Preamble do not apply to the enactment of such legislation, the two constitutional conventions contained in paragraphs

[1] See British North America Act, 1915, s. 3, where it is enacted that this Act of 1915 and the Acts of 1867, 1871, and 1886 may be cited as the British North America Acts, 1867–1915; also Acts of 1916 and 1930.

[2] Since the passing of the Statute there has been enacted the British North America Act, 1940, which places unemployment insurance under the exclusive control of the Dominion Parliament. This Act is not safeguarded by section 7 (1) of the Statute nor were subsequent amending acts, but it must not be concluded that, on this account alone, they might be repealed or amended by the Parliament of Canada. See P. Gérin-Lajoie, *op. cit.*, pp. 16–19.

2 and 3 of the Preamble are binding upon the United Kingdom Government, quite irrespective of their declaration and affirmation in the Preamble.

For, as has been pointed out in the previous chapter, these two constitutional conventions owe their existence and their obligatory force to the fact that they were declared and accepted by the Conference of 1930, in adopting the recommendations of the Conference of 1929. By constitutional convention, then, the United Kingdom Government is obliged not to ask Parliament to pass a law altering the British North America Acts, 1867 to 1930, otherwise than at the request and with the consent of the Dominion of Canada, and, should such law alter also the Succession to the Throne or the Royal Style and Titles, it would require the assent also of the Parliaments of Canada and of all the other Dominions.

But it was not considered enough merely to remove the British North America Acts, 1867 to 1930, from the operation of the Statute of Westminster. To do this ensured that neither the Dominion Parliament nor the provincial legislatures might exercise their increased powers under the Statute in such a way as to amend, alter, or repeal these Acts. But section 7 (1) did not exclude the remaining possibility that the affirmative portion of section 2 (2) had brought within the ambit of the powers of Dominion and provincial legislatures the power to repeal or amend any Acts of the United Kingdom Parliament other than the British North America Acts, 1867–1930, in so far as such Acts were part of the law of the Dominion. In this way Dominion and Provincial legislatures might be able in particular to invade the spheres of the Provinces and the Dominion respectively, by repealing or amending such Acts in so far as they regulated matters within the spheres of the Provinces and the Dominion respectively. It was considered necessary therefore to enact subsection (3) to section 7 of the Statute in these terms:

The powers conferred by this Act upon the Parliament of Canada or upon the legislatures of the Provinces shall be restricted to the enactment of laws in relation to matters within the competence of the Parliament of Canada or of any of the legislatures of the Provinces respectively.

The subsection was in much the same terms as that originally proposed by the O.D.L. Conference, but it had required amendment as a result of the extension of section 2 to the Provinces of Canada. Not only was it necessary now to protect the provincial sphere from encroachment by the Dominion Parliament; it was necessary also to protect the Dominion sphere from encroachment by the provincial legislatures.

The position thus was that the problem of the proper method of amending the Canadian Constitution remained, after the passing of the Statute, as the *O.D.L. Report* said, 'for future consideration by the appropriate Canadian authorities'. While that consideration proceeded, the United Kingdom parliament passed amendments to the Constitution by the British North America Acts of 1940, 1943, 1946, and 1949 (No. 1). In 1949 action began to be taken to discuss alternatives to the amending process and at the end of 1949 the United Kingdom parliament passed, at the request of the Canadian parliament, the British North America (No. 2) Act, 1949. By this Act the parliament of Canada was empowered to amend the Constitution of Canada, except as regards matters coming within the classes of subjects by this Act [of 1867] assigned exclusively to the Legislatures of the provinces, or as regards rights or privileges by this or any other Constitutional Act granted or secured to the Legislature or the government of a province, or to any class of persons with respect to schools or as regards the use of the English or the French language or as regards the requirements that there shall be a session of the Parliament of Canada at least once each year, and that no House of Commons shall continue for more than five years from the day of the return of the Writs for choosing the House; provided, however, that a House of Commons may in time of real or apprehended war, invasion or insurrection be continued by the Parliament of Canada if such continuation is not opposed by the votes of more than one third of the members of such House.

This Act clearly modifies the position which section 7 (1) of the Statute safeguarded; equally clearly it does not alter it entirely. Within the important area exempted from the operation of the amending power conferred by the Act upon the parliament of Canada, the position guaranteed by the Statute still stands. Thus in 1951 the United Kingdom parliament amended the Act of 1867 by the British North America Act, 1951 (14 & 15 Geo. 6, c. 32). Meanwhile the old uncertainties remain.

3

To what extent did the Statute of Westminster remove those legal inequalities of status to which the Dominion of Canada was subject before the passing of the Statute?

Take first the legal inequality of status which arose from the existence of a legal power in the Parliament of the United Kingdom to legislate for the Dominion of Canada. Before the passing of the Statute this legal inequality had been nullified by the establishment of a convention that the United Kingdom Parliament should not exercise this power in respect of the Dominion otherwise than at the request and with the consent of the Dominion. This convention had been declared at the Imperial Conferences of 1926 and 1930. But the legal inequality, though nullified, was not abolished. What was the effect of the Statute? In the first place, in paragraph 3 of the Preamble, it declared and affirmed this convention. This strengthened the convention, but it had no legal effect. Next, in virtue of section 4 of the Statute, no Act of the United Kingdom Parliament passed after the commencement of the Statute should extend or be deemed to extend to the Dominion of Canada as part of the law of the Dominion, unless it was expressly declared in that Act that the Dominion of Canada had requested and consented to it. Section 4, as has been seen, did not attempt to remove the legal inequality. It was no more than a rule of construction. Moreover, in virtue of section 7 (1) of the Statute, nothing in section 4 shall be deemed to apply to laws passed by the United Kingdom Parliament for the repeal, amendment, or alteration of the British North America Acts, 1867 to 1930, or of any order, rule, or regulation made thereunder. The new rule of construction, therefore, did not apply in this sphere. The old rule, declared in the Colonial Laws Validity Act, still obtained. On the other hand, as has been mentioned, the convention of request and consent, recognized at the 1930 Imperial Conference, does apply.

Take next the fact that, by the Colonial Laws Validity Act, laws passed by the Parliament of the Dominion which were repugnant to any provisions of an Act of the United Kingdom Parliament extending to the Dominion by express words or necessary intendment, or to any order or regulation made under the authority of such Act, were, to the extent of such repugnancy, void and inoperative. Section 2 of the Statute removed this legal inequality, subject to the provisos, first,[1] that the increased powers of the Parliament of the Dominion shall not be deemed to apply to the repeal, amendment, or alteration of the British North America Acts, 1867 to 1930, or any order, rule, or regulation made thereunder; and second,[2] that the powers conferred by the Statute on the Parliament of Canada shall be restricted to the enactment of laws in relation to matters within the competence of the Parliament of Canada. The area of legislative competence enjoyed by the Dominion Parliament was not extended; but within that area the legal inequality imposed by the Colonial Laws Validity Act was removed.

Consider next the legal inequality of status which was held to arise from the fact that the Parliament of the Dominion of Canada lacked power, to some ill-defined extent, to make laws with extra-territorial effect. Section 3 of the Statute removed this inequality, though here again it is necessary to state that any increased powers which the Parliament of the Dominion obtained as a result of this section were subject to the two provisos stated above.[3] In virtue of the powers conferred by

[1] In virtue of s. 7 (1) of the Statute.
[2] In virtue of s. 7 (3) of the Statute.
[3] See *British Columbia Electric Rly. Co.* v. *King*, [1946] A.C. 527.

section 3 of the Statute, the Parliament of the Dominion passed the Extra-territorial Act in 1933[1] providing that every act then in force and enacted before the passing of the Statute, which in terms or by necessary or reasonable implication was intended, as to the whole or any part thereof, to have extra-territorial operation, should be construed as if at the date of its enactment the Parliament of Canada then had full power to make laws having extra-territorial operation, as provided by the Statute of Westminster. This Act was passed to ensure that doubts of the kind which had arisen in the case of *Croft* v. *Dunphy*[2] should not arise in the future. In that case, decided in 1933, the Judicial Committee had to consider whether or not certain Canadian legislation passed before the commencement of the Statute of Westminster had extra-territorial effect. It was argued in support of this proposition that section 3 of the Statute was retrospective in effect. Their Lordships decided that the legislation in question did possess extra-territorial effect, but they based their judgment on the terms of the British North America Act, and did not find it necessary therefore to decide whether or not section 3 of the Statute was retrospective in effect.[3] It is clear, however, that whether or not section 3 is retrospective in effect, it gives a power to the Dominion Parliament which may be used with retrospective effect.

Consider next the inequalities which arose from the existence of the powers of disallowance and reservation. The power of the Sovereign to disallow legislation by the Dominion Parliament was found in section 56 of the British North America Act, 1867. Before the passing of

[1] Cap. 39 of 1932–3.   [2] [1933] A.C. 156.
[3] Lord Macmillan, [1933] A.C. 156 at p. 167.

the Statute that power had been nullified by the declaration of a constitutional convention in 1930,[1] but it had not been abolished. Nor had the Dominion Parliament power to abolish it. At the same time it had been agreed in 1930 that, if so requested by the Dominion, the Government of the United Kingdom would ask Parliament to pass the legislation necessary to abolish the legal power. What effect had the Statute? It made no alteration in the legal position, for the increased powers which it conferred on the Parliament of Canada did not extend to an alteration of the British North America Act, 1867. Nor did it alter the conventional position, for the terms of the Preamble similarly did not extend to the alteration of the British North America Act, 1867. The legal power of disallowance remained, therefore, as strong after the passing of the Statute as it was before. The position was governed by convention alone. By convention the power could not be exercised; and by convention the United Kingdom Government would ask Parliament to abolish the power, if the Dominion so requested.[2] To this it must be added that, when the power of disallowance was abolished, Canada could take advantage of the alternative arrangement in respect of Dominion securities made possible by the Colonial Stock Act, 1934.

The power of reservation, in so far as it was provided for in sections 55 and 57 of the British North America Act, 1867, may next be considered. Before the passing of the Statute the inequalities of the power in all its forms in respect of the Dominion of Canada had been nullified by convention, finally confirmed in 1930,[3] but it had

---

[1] Adopting para. 23 of *O.D.L. Report*. [3] Adopting para. 32 of *O.D.L. Report*.

[2] By the B.N.A. Act (No. 2) of 1949 the parliament of Canada acquired power to repeal disallowance itself. The same is true of reservation. See next page, note 1.

not been legally abolished. The Dominion Parliament lacked the power to abolish it, but the United Kingdom Government had agreed to ask Parliament to pass legislation to that end, if so requested by the Dominion.[1] The Statute made no alteration in either the legal or the conventional position, for nothing in the Statute applied to the alteration of the British North America Act, 1867. The exercise and continued existence of the power was governed therefore by convention, and by convention equality had replaced inequality.

On the other hand, in so far as the Dominion of Canada was subject to the power of reservation, or similar restrictions, by virtue of provisions in the Colonial Courts of Admiralty Act, 1890, and the Merchant Shipping Act, 1894, the Statute did make an alteration in the legal position. Sections 5 and 6 of the Statute abolished these legal inequalities in so far as the Dominion was concerned, though this abolition was subject to the proviso that the increased powers of the Dominion Parliament should not extend to the repeal, amendment, and alteration of the British North America Acts, 1867 to 1930, or to the making of laws on matters outside the competence of the Dominion Parliament.[2] In pursuance of the powers conferred by sections 2, 5, and 6 of the Statute, the Dominion Parliament has passed legislation dealing with courts of admiralty in the Dominion,[3] and with merchant shipping,[4] repealing and replacing

[1] *O.D.L. Report*, para. 36. See previous page, note 2.

[2] By virtue of section 7 (1) and (3) of the Statute.

[3] The Admiralty Act, 1934, cap. 31 of 1934, which came into operation on March 1, 1935.

[4] The Canada Shipping Act, 1934, cap. 44 of 1934, which came into operation on August 1, 1936.

and, to some extent, re-enacting United Kingdom legislation.

It is necessary to mention two additional rules which were to regulate the exercise by the Parliament of Canada of the powers it acquired at the passing of the Statute of Westminster. In the first place there was the general rule, agreed upon in 1926, in virtue of which the appropriate procedure in regard to projected legislation by the Parliament of Canada which might affect the interests of other self-governing parts of the Empire, was that previous consultation should take place between His Majesty's Government in Canada and His Majesty's Governments in the other affected self-governing parts.[1] This convention bound the Dominion of Canada, the other Dominions, and the United Kingdom. The Statute made no alteration in the position, for it contained no affirmation of the convention, and no translation of its terms into strict law.

In the second place there were the conventional rules agreed upon in 1930, and approved by the Parliament of Canada,[2] in virtue of which any alteration by the Parliament of Canada in the law touching the Succession to the Throne or the Royal Style and Titles should thereafter require the assent of the Parliaments of all the other Dominions and of the Parliament of the United Kingdom; while any such alteration by the Parliament of any other Dominion or of the United Kingdom should require the assent of the Parliament of Canada, along with that of the Parliaments of the remaining Members

[1] Cmd. 2768, pp. 17–18.
[2] In passing the Address requesting the enactment of the Statute; for the rules were contained in the Preamble to the Statute, and these parts of the Preamble were approved by the Dominion Parliament. The same is true of the Parliaments of all the other Dominions.

of the Commonwealth. Moreover, in the case of action by the Parliament of the United Kingdom, there was the further rule that if such legislation was intended to apply to the Dominion of Canada as part of the law of that Dominion, it was necessary to obtain not only the assent of the Parliament of Canada and of the Parliaments of all the other Dominions, but also the request and consent of the Dominion of Canada. The passing of the Statute affected these rules, in so far as their application to Canada was concerned, in two ways. In the first place it affirmed the rules, reciting them in paragraphs 2 and 3 of the Preamble. In the second place it supplemented the conventional rules by a rule of construction, in terms of strict law. For section 4 enacted that no law thereafter passed by the United Kingdom Parliament—and this includes laws altering the Succession to the Throne and the Royal Style and Titles—should extend to the Dominion of Canada as part of the law of the Dominion, unless it was declared in that Act that the Dominion had requested and consented to it. The passing of the Statute thus added an element of strict law to the conventional rules governing the enactment by the United Kingdom Parliament of laws, extending to Canada, altering the Succession to the Throne or the Royal Style and Titles.

There remained the legal inequality which arose from the existence of the appeal to the Judicial Committee by special leave. The Statute did not expressly deal with this subject. But it removed the two fetters which in *Nadan* v. *the King* had been held to prevent the abolition of the appeal in criminal cases by the Parliament of Canada, viz. the ground of repugnancy expressed in the Colonial Laws Validity Act, and the ground of lack of extra-territorial power. On the other hand, although these two fetters had been removed by sections 2 and 3 of the Statute respectively, it had been expressly stated in section 7 (3) of the Statute that these increased powers were restricted to the enactment by the Parliament of Canada of laws in relation to matters within the competence of that Parliament. It was necessary, therefore, to decide if the abolition of appeals, in criminal cases, by special leave to the Judicial Committee was a matter within the competence of the Parliament of Canada, a question which had not been directly considered in *Nadan* v. *the King*. The point was decided in *British Coal Corporation* v. *the King* in 1935.[1] It was held that the Parliament of Canada did possess power under the terms of the British North America Act, 1867, to regulate and abolish such appeals, and accordingly, in the absence of the two fetters referred to above, a provision of a Canadian Act of 1933,[2] purporting to abolish the appeal in criminal cases, was valid. Thus in consequence of the powers conferred by the Statute, the Parliament of Canada was enabled to abolish this legal inequality, and it did so in respect of appeals in criminal cases.

The powers of the Parliament of Canada in relation to appeals in civil cases were considered in 1947 when the Judicial Committee,[3] upholding a majority decision of the Supreme Court of Canada,[4] declared valid a Bill[5]

[1] [1935] A.C. 500. See p. 95 above.   [2] Cap. 53 of 1932–3, s. 17.
[3] *Attorney-General for Ontario* v. *Attorney-General for Canada*, [1947] A.C.
[4] *Re Privy Council Appeals*, [1940] S.C.R. 49.
[5] The Bill, No. 9 of 1939, received a first reading in 1939 and was referred thereafter to the Supreme Court. Leave to appeal from the Supreme Court's decision was granted by the Judicial Committee in 1940, but it was agreed between the parties to postpone the hearing of the appeal until after the war.

abolishing appeals whether in civil or criminal cases, not only from the Supreme Court of the Dominion but also from the superior courts of the Provinces. The Bill's validity was based on section 101 of the British North America Act, which empowered the Parliament 'to provide for the constitution, maintenance, and organization of a general court of appeal for Canada', 'notwithstanding anything in this Act'. It was true that section 92 (14) gave to the Provinces exclusive control over 'the administration of justice in the province' and that Lord Sankey had said in the *British Coal Corporation Case* that 'a most essential part of the administration of justice consists of the system of appeals'. But the grant of power in section 101 was made 'notwithstanding anything in this Act', and it must be held to prevail over section 92 (14) if there was any conflict between them. Sections 2 and 3 of the Statute of Westminster had removed any obstacle which arose from imperial legislation or from lack of power to legislate with extra-territorial effect. It remained only to decide, therefore, whether the powers granted in section 101 were wide enough to entitle the Dominion Parliament not only to deal with the prerogative but to deal with it in such a way that its exercise in relation to the Provinces as well as to the Dominion might be restricted. In other words, it was necessary to show that section 101 conferred a power on the Dominion Parliament to make recourse to the general court of appeal not only final but also exclusive. In the opinion of the Judicial Committee such a power had in fact been conferred.

VIII

THE STATUTE AND THE LEGAL STATUS
OF AUSTRALIA

I

SIMILAR problems were encountered in the application of the Statute to Australia[1] to those which had arisen in the case of Canada. Here again there was a federal system of government, with the difference that whereas in Canada the residual powers rested with the federal parliament and government, in Australia the residual powers rested with the parliaments and governments of the States. The latter were much more powerful units in the federal system than were the Canadian Provinces, and their complete autonomy within their own sphere as against the federal parliament was more rigidly guaranteed and safeguarded. The States retained direct relations with His Majesty and His Majesty's Government in the United Kingdom through their Governors, who were appointed by His Majesty, on the advice of the United Kingdom Government, though usually in consultation with the State Government concerned. No such independent relations existed between the Provinces of Canada and His Majesty or the United Kingdom Government, for the provincial

---

[1] The writer is indebted, for his exposition in this chapter, to an article by Professor K. H. Bailey, in *The Australian Law Journal*, vol. v (1931–2), at pp. 362 and 398, and to the same author's learned *Opinion* upon the application of the Statute to the States of Australia. This *Opinion* is the most authoritative study of the Statute in relation to any one Dominion yet printed. It was printed by the Government Printer, Melbourne, 1935, but, unfortunately, it was not placed on sale, nor is it available in libraries outside Australia.

P

Lieutenant-Governors were appointed by the Governor-General of Canada on the advice of the Dominion Government. Similarly, the powers to reserve Bills or to disallow acts passed by the State legislatures in Australia, were under the control of the United Kingdom Government, whereas the same powers in Canada were under the control of the Dominion Government. To the student of political institutions, the Australian system comes nearer to the perfect type of federation than does the Canadian. And it is not surprising that the safeguards inserted in the Statute of Westminster, in order to maintain the Australian federal system unimpaired after the passing of the Statute, should be even more elaborate and rigid than in the case of Canada.

The first precaution which it was thought necessary to insert in the case of Australia, as also of Canada, was directed against the possible consequences of the increased powers proposed to be conferred upon the federal Parliament by section 2 of the Statute. On a liberal interpretation of the affirmative part of section 2 (2) the Commonwealth Parliament would have been empowered to repeal or amend any Act of the United Kingdom Parliament in so far as it was part of the law of the Commonwealth. Now the Constitution of the Commonwealth was contained in an Act of the United Kingdom Parliament, the Commonwealth of Australia Constitution Act, 1900. The first eight sections of that Act, which establish the federal Commonwealth, were alterable by the United Kingdom Parliament alone. Section 9 contained the Constitution in 128 sections. This Constitution also was alterable, of course, by the United Kingdom Parliament, but in addition a power of amendment was conferred in section 128 upon the Parliament

of the Commonwealth and the Electorate acting together according to a prescribed manner and form. The
chief characteristic of that prescribed manner and form
was that great care was taken to ensure that no changes
in the Constitution should receive the royal assent unless
in a majority of the States a majority of the electors
voting approved the proposed law, and unless a majority
of all the electors voting also approved the proposed
law. Moreover, it was provided that

no alteration diminishing the proportionate representation
of any State in either House of the Parliament, or the
minimum number of representatives of a State in the House
of Representatives, or increasing, diminishing, or otherwise altering the limits of the State, or in any manner
affecting the provisions of the Constitution in relation
thereto, shall become law unless the majority of the electors
voting in that State approve the proposed law.

But, provided the procedure prescribed in section 128
was followed, there were no limits imposed upon the
power of the Parliament and the Electorate to alter the
Constitution, including section 128 itself. The federal
system itself could be modified or abolished, for example,
if the procedure in section 128 were followed, although
such an amendment would appear to contravene the
provisions of section 3 of the Constitution Act itself.[1]
The amending process provided in section 128, with its
safeguards for the rights of the States, could be modified
or abolished by following the procedure prescribed in
section 128. But while the constitutional structure of the
Commonwealth could be completely re-moulded by the
competent authorities in Australia, the Commonwealth

[1] See Opinion of Mr. Owen Dixon, K.C. (as he then was), in *Report
of the Royal Commission on the Australian Constitution*, 1929, Appendix F.

itself could not be dissolved, nor could any part of the
Commonwealth secede from or be ceded by the Commonwealth except through the medium of an Act of the
United Kingdom Parliament, for the Commonwealth
had been established in sections 1–8 of the Constitution
Act, and those sections of the Act were alterable only by
the United Kingdom Parliament.

The unqualified extension of section 2 of the Statute of
Westminster to the Commonwealth Parliament would
have conferred, it was feared, a power on that Parliament to amend the Constitution Act and the Constitution of the Commonwealth otherwise than in accordance
with the provisions of section 128. The position was discussed at the O.D.L. Conference of 1929, and it was
decided to recommend the inclusion of a clause in the
Statute by which the Constitution Act of Australia, as
also the Constitution Acts of Canada and New Zealand,
should be safeguarded.[1] By this clause, which has
already been quoted on p. 183, it was to be provided,
inter alia, that nothing in the Statute should be deemed
to confer any power to repeal or alter the Constitution
Act of the Commonwealth of Australia, otherwise than
in accordance with the law and constitutional usage and
practice theretofore existing. At the Conference of 1930,
the reference in the clause to the Dominion of Canada,
as has been mentioned, was deleted; the reference to the
'Constitution Act' of the Commonwealth was expanded
to 'the Constitution or the Constitution Act' of the Commonwealth; and the reference to 'constitutional usage
and practice' was deleted.[2] The clause, as thus amended
in 1930, was approved by the Commonwealth Parlia-

[1] *O.D.L. Report*, para. 66.
[2] Cmd. 3717, p. 20.

ment in 1931 and was enacted as section 8 of the Statute.
It ran:

Nothing in this Act shall be deemed to confer any power
to repeal or alter the Constitution or the Constitution Act of
the Commonwealth of Australia or the Constitution Act of
the Dominion of New Zealand otherwise than in accordance
with the law existing before the commencement of this Act.

It was considered necessary at the same time in the
case of Australia, as in the case of Canada, to go further
in order to ensure that nothing in section 2 of the Statute
should be deemed to extend the *area* of the powers conferred upon the Parliament of the Commonwealth by
the Constitution. For section 8 did not exclude the
remaining possibility that the affirmative part of section
2 (2) might be deemed to confer upon the Commonwealth Parliament a power to repeal or amend United
Kingdom Acts, other than the Constitution Act, in so
far as such Acts were part of the law of the Dominion,
and in particular—on the assumption that 'the law of
the Dominion' included the law of the States as well as
of the Commonwealth—to invade the sphere of the
States by repealing or amending United Kingdom Acts[1]
in so far as they formed part of the law of the States. A
clause had been drawn up by the O.D.L. Conference
designed to embody this additional safeguard both for
Canada and for Australia. It, too, has already been
quoted on p. 183. In 1930, as has been described, the
reference to Canada in this proposed clause was deleted,
and a new clause to meet Canadian requirements was
drawn up by the Dominion and Provincial Governments
in consultation, and was enacted as section 7 (3) of the

[1] The Australian States Constitution Act, 1907, and the Merchant
Shipping Act, 1894, were Acts of this kind.

Statute. The original clause, with its reference solely now to the case of Australia, was amended in a few small particulars at the Conference of 1930, and was recommended for enactment in the Statute.[1] It was approved by the Commonwealth Parliament in 1931 and was enacted in identical terms in section 9 (1) of the Statute. It ran:

Nothing in this Act shall be deemed to authorize the Parliament of the Commonwealth of Australia to make laws on any matter within the authority of the States of Australia, not being a matter within the authority of the Parliament or Government of the Commonwealth of Australia.

It was argued that the liberal interpretation of the affirmative part of section 2 (2) of the Statute, which gave rise, in the case of Canada, to section 7 (1) and (3), and, in the case of Australia to sections 8 and 9 (1), was of doubtful validity. And the case for this view seems rather more conclusive in respect of Australia than in respect of Canada. All that section 2 (2) did, it could be said, was to empower the Commonwealth Parliament to repeal or amend any United Kingdom Act to which a Commonwealth law, otherwise valid, was repugnant. A Commonwealth law, in order to be 'otherwise valid', must be *intra vires*, and to be *intra vires* it must deal with a class of subject-matter falling within the area of a list of topics specifically enumerated in the Constitution, and of these enumerated powers amendment of the Constitution Act was not one. The Commonwealth Parliament, therefore, remained confined, after the enactment of section 2 (2) as before, within the area of its powers enumerated in the Constitution, and was unable, in particular, to invade the sphere of the States. At the same time it could be held that

[1] Cmd. 3717, p. 20. The words 'at present' were omitted.

the provisions of sections 7 (1) and (3), 8, and 9 (1) were justified on the ground that they stabilized beyond doubt the existing constitutional arrangements of the two federal Dominions, and made it clear that the Statute made no alteration in this respect.

It will be seen that the proposals made by the 1929 Conference to safeguard the Australian constitutional system received only very slight modifications at the Conference of 1930. There appeared to be nothing comparable to the controversy which had arisen in Canada as a result of the protests of the Provinces, and which had made it necessary for the Canadian delegates, in 1930, to ask in effect that all proposals in respect of Canada should be suspended until the Provinces could be consulted and their wishes met. But this appearance of harmony between Commonwealth and States in Australia proved to be deceptive. When the proposed Statute came before the Commonwealth Parliament in July 1931 for approval, the extent of the opposition of the States became manifest, and it was found necessary to devise still further safeguards to meet their anxieties and suspicions. The story of the amendments and additions to which the proposed clauses were subjected before they were submitted to the United Kingdom Government cannot be entered upon in detail here, nor is it possible at this date to discover all the factors which were at work in determining the course of events. It must suffice to say that in the Commonwealth House of Representatives,[1] in the Senate,[2] where each State had

---

[1] See, e.g., *Australian Commonwealth Parliamentary Debates*, vol. 131, pp. 4061-82, 4478-93.

[2] See, e.g., Senator Johnston's amendment, *ibid.*, vol. 131, p. 4508, and debate, pp. 4509-28.

equal representation, and in the Parliaments of certain States,[1] considerable opposition was expressed on behalf of some States to the proposed clauses. Largely owing to the influence of Mr. Latham, the Deputy-Leader of the Opposition in the Commonwealth Parliament, and a former Attorney-General of the Commonwealth, substantial attempts were made to meet the wishes and to remove the doubts of the States. A series of amendments which he moved in July,[2] and which were supplemented by a further amendment in October 1931,[3] were adopted by the Parliament, and a set of clauses designed to safeguard the rights and powers of the States under the Constitution was arrived at and transmitted to the Imperial Government for insertion in the Statute.

The objections which were made by the Australian States to the clauses of the proposed Statute after the meeting of the Imperial Conference in 1930 were directed not so much at the clause which was to become section 2, but at the clause which was to become section 4. The objections to an unqualified extension of section 2 to the Commonwealth Parliament had been met by the two safeguarding clauses proposed by the O.D.L. Conference and adopted, with small amendments, by the Conference of 1930. These clauses, as has been said, were accepted by the Commonwealth Parliament and enacted in the Statute as sections 8 and 9 (1). But difficulties were now foreseen in the unqualified applica-

---

[1] See announcement in Commonwealth Parliament, *Australian Commonwealth Parliamentary Debates*, vol. 132, p. 1884.

[2] *Ibid.*, vol. 131, pp. 4061 ff.

[3] Oct. 22, 1931. *Ibid.*, vol. 132, p. 1083. New South Wales, Victoria, and Queensland accepted the clauses as finally drafted, but South Australia, Western Australia, and Tasmania were still dissatisfied. *Ibid.*, p. 1084.

tion to the Commonwealth Parliament of the proposed clause that

no Act of Parliament of the United Kingdom passed after the commencement of this Act shall extend or be deemed to extend to a Dominion as part of the law in force in that Dominion unless it is expressly declared in that Act that that Dominion has requested, and consented to, the enactment thereof.[1]

Three main objections were taken to the proposed clause, and three safeguarding amendments were put forward to meet these objections. Of these three proposed amendments, the first was not primarily directed to the safeguarding of States' rights, though the remaining two were.

First of all it was objected that the phrase 'that Dominion' was too vague. Did it mean the executive government, the parliament, or the electorate? On the whole it looked as if it meant the executive government. The Commonwealth Parliament was not prepared to confide this degree of authority to the executive government alone. In 1931 the Commonwealth Government was in a minority in the Senate, and it was natural that members of the Commonwealth Parliament and representatives of the States should feel that the phrase 'request and consent of the Government' was not necessarily equivalent, in Australia at any rate, to 'request and consent of the Parliament and Government' of the Dominion. On the motion of Mr. Latham it was agreed, therefore,

[1] Cmd. 3717, p. 20. The clause, as here proposed, differed from the original recommendation of the *O.D.L. Report*, para. 55, by the insertion of the words, 'as part of the law in force in that Dominion', and it differed from section 4, as finally enacted, for the words 'in force' were to be deleted, and the word 'of' substituted. See above, pp. 144–6.

that the proposed clause should be amended so as to read, 'that the Parliament and Government of that Dominion have requested'.[1] The other Dominions, as it turned out, did not desire a safeguard of this kind.[2] The amendment was inserted in the Statute with reference only to Australia. It appears as section 9 (3).

In the second place it was feared that an unqualified application of the clause to Australia would make it possible for the Commonwealth Parliament and Government to request and consent to the passage of legislation by the United Kingdom Parliament, amending or altering the Constitution Act or the Constitution of the Commonwealth, or regulating matters confided by the Constitution to the authority of the States, and thus directly or indirectly to modify the division of powers between Commonwealth and States otherwise than in accordance with section 128. It was thought, evidently, that such a request from the Parliament and Government of the Commonwealth would automatically be acceded to by the United Kingdom Parliament, and that the wording of the proposed clause made it impossible for the United Kingdom Parliament to exercise any discretion in the matter. There seems little doubt that these fears were exaggerated, for neither by paragraph 3 of the Preamble nor by the terms of the clause was the United Kingdom Parliament obliged to legislate for a Dominion whenever requested by the Dominion. However, it was decided to meet this possible interpretation by an amendment, agreed upon on July 28, 1931,

[1] *Australian Commonwealth Parliamentary Debates*, vol. 131, p. 4068. See also Keith, *Speeches and Documents on the British Dominions*, p. 274.

[2] A similar amendment was moved in the House of Commons by Sir J. Withers, and, when the attitude of the other Dominions was explained, was negatived. (260 *H.C. Deb.*, 5 s., 279.) But see below, p. 325, for New Zealand.

which was to provide that nothing in the Act should be deemed

to authorize the Parliament or the Government of the Commonwealth without the concurrence of the Parliament and Government of the States concerned, to request or consent to the enactment of any Act by the Parliament of the United Kingdom on any matter which is within the authority of the States of Australia, not being a matter within the authority of the Parliament or the Government of the Commonwealth of Australia.[1]

Actually this amendment did not appear in the Statute. The United Kingdom Government held that the purpose of the amendment was included in a third amendment proposed by the Commonwealth Parliament in October, 1931, with which we are about to deal. This view was not accepted by the Commonwealth Government, and it would seem that the United Kingdom Government did not clearly appreciate the two distinct federal problems involved.[2]

The third proposed amendment was put forward to meet the objection that the proposed clause, as framed, might be held to require the concurrence of the Commonwealth Parliament and Government in any request by a State of Australia for legislation by the United Kingdom Parliament in respect of some matter within the competence of that State. The States of Australia, unlike the Provinces of Canada, were largely responsible for the administration of criminal law. For the efficient conduct of this administration extra-territorial powers were necessary, and, as the State legislatures in general had lacked these powers, the United Kingdom Parlia-

---

[1] *Australian Commonwealth Parliamentary Debates*, vol. 131, p. 4490.
[2] *Ibid.*, vol. 132, p. 1927.

ment had passed laws, such as the Fugitive Offenders Act and the Jurisdiction in Territorial Waters Act, to assist in the regulation of these spheres. In matters within the competence of the States, therefore, it might conceivably be necessary for the United Kingdom Parliament to legislate, if requested to do so by the States. It was admitted in the Commonwealth Parliament in 1931 that it was difficult to imagine a subject upon which United Kingdom legislation for the States might prove necessary in the future,[1] but at the same time it was considered wise to propose an amendment to make it clear that nothing in section 4 should be held to require the request and consent of the Commonwealth Parliament and Government to such legislation, otherwise than in accordance with constitutional practice before the passing of the Statute. An additional amendment was agreed upon in October 1931, and it appears in the Statute as section 9 (2) in these words:

Nothing in this Act shall be deemed to require the concurrence of the Parliament or Government of the Commonwealth of Australia in any law made by the Parliament of the United Kingdom with respect to any matter within the authority of the States of Australia, not being a matter within the authority of the Parliament or Government of the Commonwealth of Australia, in any case where it would have been in accordance with the constitutional practice existing before the commencement of this Act that the Parliament of the United Kingdom should make that law without such concurrence.

A difficulty to which the clause may give rise is found in the phrase 'constitutional practice'. Who is to judge what is the constitutional practice? It would

[1] *Australian Commonwealth Parliamentary Debates*, vol. 132, p. 1085.

appear that the United Kingdom Parliament must do so. But a judgment on this question will involve a decision whether the matter upon which legislation is requested is a matter within the exclusive authority of the States of Australia. A question is raised, in effect, of the limits *inter se* of the powers of the Commonwealth and the States. But by section 74 of the Constitution of Australia a decision on this question is solely within the jurisdiction of the High Court of Australia. However, if United Kingdom legislation was passed at the request of the States and it did infringe the federal sphere, the Commonwealth Parliament could repeal it under the powers of section 2 (2) of the Statute, which to this extent was unqualified by section 9 (1).

After the Imperial Conference of 1930, therefore, two additional amendments explicitly designed to safeguard States' rights were proposed by the Australian Commonwealth Parliament, though one only was inserted in the Statute. It seems necessary to emphasize that each of these two proposed amendments was designed to deal with a separate problem. It is true that both amendments proceeded upon the assumption that the words 'the law in force in that Dominion' in the clause which was to become section 4 meant, in the case of Australia, the law of the States as well as the law of the Commonwealth, and that the section required, therefore, the request and consent of the Parliament and Government of the Commonwealth before any future Act of the United Kingdom Parliament could extend to Australia either as part of the law of the Commonwealth or as part of the law of the States. It is true, too, that both proposed amendments referred to legislation by the United Kingdom Parliament with respect to matters within the exclusive authority of the States. But the proposed amendment which was not finally enacted in the Statute dealt with a request by the Commonwealth for United Kingdom legislation upon exclusively State matters, and it proposed that nothing in the Statute should be deemed to authorize the Commonwealth to make such a request without the concurrence of the States concerned. On the other hand, the amendment which was enacted in the Statute, as section 9 (2), dealt with a request by the States for United Kingdom legislation upon exclusively State matters, and proposed that nothing in the Statute should be deemed to require the concurrence of the Commonwealth in any such request, where such concurrence was not required by existing constitutional practice. It is probable that the first of the two amendments was unnecessary. It assumed that the United Kingdom Parliament would give effect automatically to any request by the Commonwealth for legislation upon exclusively State matters without considering the wishes of the States concerned. This assumption, it is submitted, cannot be justified. The second of the two amendments was probably necessary, for the assumption upon which it proceeded, viz. that section 4 would require the request and consent of the Commonwealth for any future United Kingdom legislation which was to extend to Australia as part of the law either of the Commonwealth or of the States, may well be justified.

But there was another amendment also which owed something to the anxieties about States' rights, but which was not directly designed to safeguard these rights. By this fourth amendment it was proposed that the Commonwealth Parliament should follow the example of the

Dominion of New Zealand,[1] and retain in its own hands
the right to decide when, and to what extent, the powers
conferred by the Statute should extend to the Commonwealth. Accordingly clauses were proposed,[2] and were
later amalgamated with similar clauses applying to
New Zealand and Newfoundland, to provide that none
of the sections 2–6 of the Statute should extend to the
Commonwealth unless adopted by the Commonwealth
Parliament, that such adoption should have effect either
from the commencement of the Statute or from such
later date as was specified in the adopting Act, and that
finally the Commonwealth Parliament should have
power to revoke its adoption of any of these sections.
These clauses appeared in the Statute as section 10 (1),
(2), and (3).[3] At the same time the Commonwealth
Government gave an undertaking to the States that no

[1] Cmd. 3717, p. 21.
[2] *Australian Commonwealth Parliamentary Debates*, vol. 131, pp. 4068–9.
[3] Clause 10 (3), as it originally appeared in the Bill presented to the
House of Commons, gave power to the Parliament of any Dominion to
which it applied to 'revoke the adoption of any section of this Act'. It
was suggested in the debate in the House that this might be construed
to mean that the Commonwealth Parliament had power to revoke ss. 8
and 9 of the Statute which had been inserted to safeguard the States.
An amendment was therefore moved to make the subsection read,
'revoke the adoption of any section referred to in subsection (1) of this
section', i.e. ss. 2–6. Although it was not admitted by the Government
that the original wording was open to the interpretation placed upon it,
since 'revoke the adoption of any section' could only be held to refer to
those sections which could be 'adopted', viz. ss. 2–6, none the less the
amendment was accepted in order to place the matter beyond all possible
shadow of doubt. (See 260 *H.C. Deb.*, 5 s., 294.) This amendment, and
the amendment moved in the House of Lords to delete the clause providing that the Statute should come into operation on December 1,
1931 (see 83 *H.L. Deb.*, 5 s., 245, and *supra*, p. 138), were the only
amendments made to the Bill during its passage through the United
Kingdom Parliament.

action would be taken towards the adoption of any of sections 2–6 without prior consultation with them.[1]

2

More than a decade was to pass before the Commonwealth Parliament adopted the sections. The Labour Government of Mr. Scullin which had been in office in the years in which the Statute had been framed and passed was defeated at elections in December 1931 and a government under Mr. Lyons, supported by the United Australia Party and the Country Party, had succeeded it. The opposition pressed for the adoption of the sections and Mr. Brennan, Attorney-General in the Scullin Government and responsible, when in office, for piloting the resolutions for the Statute through the House of Representatives, was particularly persistent in his reminders[2] on one occasion moving the adjournment of the House in order to discuss the question.[3] It was not until the end of 1936 that Mr. Menzies, Attorney-General in the Lyons Government, introduced a Bill to adopt the sections. The Bill went no further than the formal first reading, however, and it lapsed upon the prorogation of Parliament in May of 1937.[4] In the new session, which began on June 17, 1937, it was announced in the Governor-General's speech that the government proposed to reintroduce the Adopting Bill.[5] Accordingly the Bill was brought in again and was explained in a

[1] *Australian Commonwealth Parliamentary Debates*, vol. 132, p. 1083.
[2] See, for example, *Australian Commonwealth Parliamentary Debates*, vol. 146, p. 514 (Mar. 29, 1935); *ibid.*, pp. 992–5 (Apr. 8, 1935); vol. 147, p. 986 (Oct. 23, 1935); *ibid.*, p. 1366 (Nov. 7, 1935); vol. 150, p. 1042 (Apr. 30, 1936); vol. 151, p. 25 (Sept. 10, 1936); *ibid.*, p. 1027 (Oct. 13, 1936).   [3] *Ibid.*, vol. 148, pp. 2031–6 (Nov. 28, 1935).
[4] *Ibid.*, vol. 152, pp. 2170, 2733.   [5] *Ibid.*, vol. 153, p. 9.

second reading speech by Mr. Menzies on August 25, 1937.[1] But the debate was adjourned immediately upon Mr. Menzies's speech; the House of Representatives was dissolved in the following month and the Bill once more lapsed. The elections confirmed the Lyons Government in office and once more the Governor-General's speech foreshadowed the reintroduction of the Bill.[2] But, in spite of persistent reminders,[3] no action was taken in that parliament. It was not until October 1942 that a Bill was finally introduced, this time by a Labour government, with Mr. Curtin as Prime Minister and Dr. Evatt as Attorney-General. There was a debate both on the motion for leave to bring in the Bill on October 1, 1942[4] and again on the second reading,[5] where an amendment, moved by Mr. Hughes, Prime Minister from 1915 to 1923, that the Bill be referred to a select committee, was lost. The Bill was passed and received the royal assent on October 9, 1942. It is printed in Appendix V.

In the years between 1931 and 1942 the Commonwealth had remained subject to those restrictions upon its legislative competence which have already been enumerated, except in so far as the United Kingdom Parliament modified these restrictions from time to time by *ad hoc* legislation. Thus the limitation upon its powers of extra-territorial legislation was modified by

[1] *Ibid.*, vol. 153, pp. 192, 251; vol. 154, pp. 83–95. The Bill is printed in Appendix IV.

[2] *Ibid.*, vol. 155, p. 8 (Nov. 30, 1937).

[3] See, e.g., *ibid.*, vol. 155, p. 1068 (Mr. Ward, May 11, 1938); vol. 157, p. 998 (Mr. Brennan, Oct. 20, 1938) and p. 1339 (Mr. Brennan, Nov. 8, 1938).

[4] *Ibid.*, vol. 172, pp. 1321–38.

[5] *Ibid.*, pp. 1387–1400; 1424–78, for debate in House of Representatives. The Senate debate is on pp. 1492–1514; 1551–69.

the Whaling Industry Act of 1934,[1] which provided that the provisions of any Act of the Commonwealth Parliament for the regulation of the whaling industry which purported to have extra-territorial operation should be deemed to have such operation as respects ships registered in the Commonwealth or in any territory administered by the Government of the Commonwealth.[2] The Geneva Convention Act, of 1937,[3] gave powers to the Commonwealth Parliament to legislate for the purpose of carrying out the terms of Article 28 of the Convention. The outbreak of war in 1939 made necessary a further extension or clarification of the Commonwealth's powers of extra-territorial legislation, and section 5 of the Emergency Powers (Defence) Act, 1939,[4] and section 3 of the Army and Air Force (Annual) Act, 1940,[5] of the United Kingdom Parliament both confer such powers, limited in each case to the purposes of the Acts. In this way the inconveniences resulting from Australia's unwillingness to adopt section 3 of the Statute were overcome piecemeal.

The United Kingdom Acts themselves applied· to Australia as part of the law of the Commonwealth by virtue of the Colonial Laws Validity Act, 1865, for they referred to the Commonwealth by express words, and so long as sections 2 and 4 of the Statute had not been adopted the rule of construction in the Colonial Laws Validity Act still held. Nor were these Acts extending the powers of the Commonwealth Parliament the only

[1] 24 & 25 Geo. 5, c. 49.
[2] S. 15. The section applied to New Zealand also.
[3] 1 Ed. 8 and 1 Geo. 6, c. 15, section 2. The Commonwealth legislated in pursuance of these powers by No. 14 of 1938.
[4] 2 & 3 Geo. 6, c. 62.
[5] 3 & 4 Geo. 6, c. 18.

ones to become part of the law of the Commonwealth, under the provisions of the Colonial Laws Validity Act, in this period. Certain other Acts were passed by the United Kingdom Parliament which clearly also applied. The Prize Act of 1939,[1] which extended the law of prize to aircraft, was made applicable to Australia by express words;[2] while the Regency Act, 1937,[3] might well be held to apply by necessary intendment.

By the constitutional convention agreed upon in 1930 and recited in paragraph 3 of the Preamble to the Statute, these Acts, in so far as they were intended to extend to Australia, should have done so only at the request and with the consent of the Commonwealth, although, since section 4 of the Statute had not been adopted, there was no legal requirement that this request and consent should be obtained, nor that it should be recited in the Acts themselves, nor that it should be the request and consent of the Parliament and Government of the Commonwealth. In fact it would seem that the constitutional convention was respected and the Commonwealth's request and consent were obtained in the case of the Whaling Industry Regulation Act, 1934, the Geneva Convention Act, 1937, the Emergency Powers (Defence) Act, 1939, the Prize Act, 1939, and the Army and Air Force (Annual) Act, 1940, so far as these Acts applied to Australia. It would appear, however, that request and consent was not sought for the Regency Act, 1937, although there had been consultation between the United Kingdom and the Dominions before the Act was passed.[4]

---

[1] 2 & 3 Geo. 6, c. 65.   [2] S. 4.
[3] 1 Ed. 8 and 1 Geo. 6, c. 16.
[4] This Act was deliberately stated by Sir John Simon (as he then was),

But in spite of extensions of power by *ad hoc* legislation from the United Kingdom Parliament, particularly at the outbreak of war in 1939, the Australian Government found itself handicapped by the uncertainty of its legislative competence, and also by the actual legal restrictions themselves. Some examples may be mentioned. For the prosecution of the war it was necessary for the Commonwealth to institute extensive control over shipping. Its powers were confined, however, under the Merchant Shipping Act of 1894, to ships registered in the Commonwealth or ships engaged in the coasting trade. Obviously this proved a great handicap at a time when allied shipping, for example, from all over the world was using Australian ports. Yet the restriction existed and it meant that section 6 of the National Security Act passed by the Commonwealth Parliament in 1939, and several national security regulations made under the Act, together with parts of the Navigation Act, were probably to some degree invalid.[1] This brought an element of frustration and uncertainty into the administration of the war, which could be avoided by the adoption of section 2 of the Statute of Westminster. But repugnancy was not the only obstacle. The Commonwealth was obliged, under the Merchant Shipping Act of 1894, to reserve its Bills deal-

319 *H.C. Deb.*, 5 s, 1452–3, not to be intended to extend to the Dominions; they were free to make their own arrangements about regency. Yet the Act contains no express territorial limitation in its terms, and would appear to extend to Australia and New Zealand by necessary intendment. It clearly does not purport to extend to South Africa and Eire because their request and consent is not recited in the Act. There is some doubt whether it extends to Canada; it might be held that it involves a modification of the British North America Act, and is thus excluded from the operation of s. 4 of the Statute.

[1] See Memorandum by Dr. Evatt, referred to below, paras. 28 and 29.

ing with shipping, and this meant, in war-time, a delay in bringing legislation into effect. Dr. Evatt reported in 1942 that delays of up to four months had occurred in receiving the royal assent to reserved Bills.[1] This difficulty could have been removed by adopting section 5 of the Statute. And finally there remained still some uncertainties about extra-territorial legislation which could only be set at rest finally by the adoption of section 3.

It was for reasons of this kind that the Commonwealth Government proposed in 1942 to introduce a Bill to adopt sections 2–6. Dr. Evatt prepared a memorandum setting out the matters in which uncertainty and restriction were encountered and this was circulated to members of Parliament with the text of the Bill.

The case for adopting the sections of the Statute was based, therefore, on the need to remove difficulties which hampered the successful prosecution of the war. This attitude was reflected in the Preamble to the Bill, which declared:

Whereas certain legal difficulties exist which have created doubts and caused delays in relation to certain Commonwealth legislation, and to certain regulations made thereunder, particularly in relation to the legislation enacted and regulations made for securing the public safety and defence of the Commonwealth of Australia, and for the more effectual prosecution of the war in which His Majesty the King is engaged.

This purpose was reflected also in the title of the Act:

An Act to remove doubts as to the validity of certain

---

[1] *Australian Commonwealth Parliamentary Debates*, vol. 172, p. 1397. See also Senator Ashley, *ibid.*, p. 1497.

Commonwealth legislation, to obviate delays occurring in its passage, and to effect certain related purposes . . .

It is interesting to compare it with the Bill which Mr. Menzies had introduced in 1937 where the title had simply run: 'To provide for the adoption of Sections 2, 3, 4, 5 and 6 of the Statute of Westminster, 1931, and for other purposes', and where the Preamble had recited in a series of paragraphs the steps by which the Statute had come to be passed and the fact that sections 2–6 would not apply to Australia unless adopted by the Commonwealth, and had then gone on to assert, without giving reasons, that it was desirable for these sections to be adopted. The first two paragraphs of the Preamble in Mr. Menzies's Bill resemble closely paragraphs 2 and 3 of the Preamble to the Status of the Union Act, 1934, of South Africa,[1] and may well have been based upon them. They are notable in that they incorporate the declaration of equality of status from the Balfour Report of 1926, a device which is valuable in that it places the principal constitutional convention defining or describing Dominion Status alongside the principal legal document relating to the subject. This was not done in framing the Preamble to the Statute of Westminster itself, and it is interesting to notice that it was embodied in the Status of the Union Act and in Mr. Menzies's Bill, but that it finds no place in Dr. Evatt's Act.

One further point of contrast between the two measures may be noticed. Mr. Menzies's Bill, introduced in August 1937, intended that the adoption of sections 2–6 should have effect from January 1, 1938. Dr. Evatt's Bill and subsequent Act provided that adoption should

[1] See below, pp. 242 ff., and Appendix III.

have effect from the commencement of the war with Germany, and in section 3 of the Act the date is given as September 3, 1939. This adoption with retrospective effect may be justified by the fact that the legislation of which the validity was uncertain dated from the commencement of the war. And it will be remembered that the Commonwealth was empowered, under section 10 of the Statute, to adopt sections 2–6 with effect either from the commencement of the Statute itself or from such later date as was specified in the Adopting Act.[1]

Apart from these points of difference, Mr. Menzies's Bill and Dr. Evatt's Act resemble each other in that each provides quite simply for the adoption of all the relevant sections of the Statute without qualification. They resemble each other, too, in that each provoked criticism in parliament and aroused uneasiness among sections of political opinion in the Commonwealth. Indeed it would appear that uneasiness among the supporters of the Lyons Government led to the dropping of the Bill before even the second reading stage had been concluded in 1937 and to the failure to reintroduce it in 1938 in spite of the Government's intentions expressed in the Governor-General's speech. On the Labour side there was virtual unanimity in support of the adoption of the Statute in 1936 and thereafter, and when Dr. Evatt introduced his Bill in 1942 it was again on the side of the Country Party and the United Australia Party, then in opposition, that criticism was expressed. But the Opposition were not unanimous. Some spoke in the debate in favour of adoption, some against. Thus Mr. Hughes reiterated his view that it was wrong to set down the Constitution of the British Empire in

[1] See p. 215 *supra.*

black and white,[1] while Mr. Menzies, without enthusiasm, advised adoption.[2]

Misgivings and opposition were expressed on the same two main grounds which had been brought forward in 1931. Firstly, it was feared that the adoption of sections 2–6 would weaken Australia's links with the United Kingdom, or at any rate that it would appear to do so, and that this was most undesirable at a time when the two nations were engaged side by side in a desperate struggle, and when it could provide ammunition for enemy propagandists. This point of view is understandable if we remember that in 1942 Australia's dependence upon the United States for assistance against Japan was almost complete. The Labour Government's frank recognition of this fact and in particular Mr. Curtin's statement in a broadcast on December 28, 1941, that 'without any inhibitions of any kind, I make it clear that Australia looks to America, free of any pangs as to our traditional links or kinship with the United Kingdom',[3] had disturbed some people, who said that the opportunity was being taken to 'cut the painter', and who saw in the adoption of sections 2–6 of the Statute one more step in the process. To such critics the only answer that could be given was that expressed by Mr. Menzies: '. . . the big battle which might have been waged in 1930 or 1926 as to whether these great principles should be expressed, and as to how they should be expressed, has been fought, and won, or lost, according to the point of view of the contenders. . . . We might just as well say that that is past; and

[1] *Australian Commonwealth Parliamentary Debates*, vol. 172, pp. 1424–30. Mr. Hughes had said the same in 1931 and in 1921. See p. 5, n. 1, *supra*.
[2] *Ibid.*, pp. 1434–8. [3] *Sydney Morning Herald*, Dec. 29, 1941.

turn to the future. And turning to the future, we find that we have a small set of legislative propositions, ancillary and minor propositions, to put the final touch on the technical powers of Australia.'[1]

The second ground of misgiving was that the adoption of the sections would disturb the federal system and in particular weaken the position of the States. And, as in 1931,[2] it was towards section 4 of the Statute, not section 2, that criticism was directed. In particular there was revived, in 1937 and in 1942, the proposal which the Commonwealth Parliament had accepted in a particular form in 1931,[3] that some safeguard should be provided to prevent the Parliament and Government of the Commonwealth from requesting and consenting to legislation by the United Kingdom Parliament upon matters within the authority of the States of Australia. This safeguard, in the form adopted in 1931, had not been inserted in the Statute because the United Kingdom Government, erroneously it would seem, had thought it unnecessary.[4]

In 1937 three of the States—New South Wales, Victoria, and Queensland—had asked that a safeguard should be inserted in the form of a recital and a declaratory clause in the Adopting Act asserting that the constitutional position was that it would not be proper for the Commonwealth, without the concurrence of a State, to request or consent to any amendment of the Statute of Westminster affecting the legislative powers of the States.[5]

[1] *Australian Commonwealth Parliamentary Debates*, vol. 172, p. 1438.
[2] See p. 208, *supra*.
[3] See pp. 210–11, *supra*.
[4] See pp. 211, 213–14, *supra*.
[5] *Australian Commonwealth Parliamentary Debates*, vol. 154, p. 1152.

In 1942 the State of Victoria asked that there should be inserted in the Preamble to the Adopting Act a declaration that it would not be in accordance with constitutional practice for the request and consent of the Commonwealth to be required except for matters within the exclusive jurisdiction of the Parliament of the Commonwealth.[1] This was asking for a greater restriction in some ways than that adopted in 1931, for on that occasion it was intended that the Commonwealth should be free to request and consent to legislation both upon matters within its exclusive jurisdiction and also upon matters it shared concurrently with the States. Only for legislation upon matters within the *exclusive* jurisdiction of the States,[2] was its request and consent to be unnecessary. On the other hand the safeguard requested in 1942 was to take the form of a declaration in the Preamble to the Adopting Act, not of a section in the Act itself. In 1942, however, the Government would not accept any restriction, whether expressed in the Preamble or in a section of the Adopting Act, upon its power to request and consent to legislation.

Dr. Evatt's defence of this position was that, first of all, since the request and consent needed in the case of Australia was the request and consent of the Parliament and Government, and that since the Parliament represented the States, there was no likelihood of a request for legislation being put forward upon matters within the exclusive jurisdiction of the States.[3] The balance of power between States and Commonwealth would be altered, if at all, by the normal process of constitutional

[1] *Australian Commonwealth Parliamentary Debates*, vol. 172, pp. 1396–7.
[2] See p. 211 *supra*.
[3] *Australian Commonwealth Parliamentary Debates*, vol. 172, p. 1396.

amendment. In the second place Dr. Evatt argued that, even if some such request and consent were put forward by the Parliament and Government of the Commonwealth, the United Kingdom Parliament would not grant the request contrary to the wishes of the States. He asserted that the United Kingdom Parliament was not to be thought of as acting automatically upon such requests.[1]

With this answer the States had to be content. And perhaps, since the original safeguard of 1931 had been rejected, this was the best that they could expect. Any safeguard inserted as a Preamble in a Commonwealth Act could have little more force than an assurance from the Government in the terms which Dr. Evatt gave. None the less the misgivings of the States had justification.[2] Their point was as substantial in 1942 as it was in 1931 when the Commonwealth Parliament had been prepared to meet it.

It may be added that, so far as can be seen, there was no prior consultation with the States before the introduction of Dr. Evatt's Bill, and that the promise given in 1931 by a previous Labour government does not appear to have been fulfilled.[3] On the other hand it would seem that adoption was generally favoured throughout the Commonwealth, although where opposition and misgivings were expressed they were expressed keenly and sometimes violently.

It remains to ask: What is the effect of the adoption of the sections of the Statute as from September 3, 1939,

[1] *Ibid.* And see p. 210 *supra.*
[2] See p. 214 *supra.*
[3] See pp. 215–16 *supra.* There was such consultation in 1936 and 1937 before Mr. Menzies introduced his Bill. *Australian Commonwealth Parliamentary Debates*, vol. 150, p. 1042; vol. 151, p. 25; vol. 154, p. 1152.

upon legislation of the United Kingdom Parliament passed after that date and referring to Australia by express words or necessary intendment—Acts like the Army and Air Force (Annual) Act of 1940? It has already been pointed out that until the adoption of the sections of the Statute in 1942 these Acts were part of the law of Australia by virtue of the Colonial Laws Validity Act. The position on the adoption of the sections must be that these Acts, inasmuch as they contain no recital that they have been passed at the request and with the consent of the Parliament and Government of the Commonwealth, are no longer part of the law of the Commonwealth. No law passed by the United Kingdom Parliament after September 3, 1939, can be a part of the law of the Commonwealth unless it contains a recital of such request and consent—unless of course it be adopted by the Commonwealth Parliament. No inconvenience arises from the fact that such an Act as the Army and Air Force (Annual) Act of 1940 ceases to apply because the extra-territorial powers it conferred in a limited sphere upon the Parliament of the Commonwealth are now acquired without qualification by the adoption of section 3 of the Statute.

It is interesting to notice that the Emergency Powers (Defence) Act, 1939, does not automatically cease to be part of the law of the Commonwealth by the adoption of the sections of the Statute, because it was passed before September 3, 1939,[1] but it is now superfluous, since the adoption of section 3 of the Statute grants the powers which the Act had conferred. The Prize Act, 1939,[2] similarly continues to apply to the Common-

---

[1] It received the royal assent on Aug. 24, 1939.
[2] It received the royal assent on Sept. 1, 1939.

wealth as part of the law of the Commonwealth. But it is, of course, open to the Commonwealth Parliament by virtue of section 2 (2) of the Statute to repeal these Acts and such earlier Acts as the Whaling Industry (Regulation) Act, 1934, the Geneva Convention Act, 1937, and the Regency Act, 1937,[1] in so far as they are part of the law of the Commonwealth.

[1] It is interesting to notice that while the Regency Act, 1937, may be held to extend to the Commonwealth by necessary intendment, the amendment of it contained in the Regency Act, 1943, certainly cannot extend to the Commonwealth because it contains no declaration of request and consent. It would appear, however, that the Commonwealth has no power itself to legislate upon regency; it must rely upon United Kingdom legislation.

3

To what extent did the Statute remove or make possible the removal of those legal inequalities of status to which the Commonwealth of Australia was subject theretofore? In view of the extensive qualifications with which the application of the Statute to Australia was surrounded, it is difficult to give a short answer to this question.

Before the passing of the Statute the United Kingdom Parliament was obliged, by the convention declared in 1930, not to legislate for the Commonwealth of Australia otherwise than at the request and with the consent of the Commonwealth. There was no requirement that this request and consent should come either from the Parliament or from the Government of the Commonwealth or from both. This convention was approved by the Commonwealth Parliament and it remained unimpaired by the passing of the Statute. It was, however, affirmed by the United Kingdom Parliament in paragraph 3 of the Preamble, it could be supplemented by the rule of construction in section 4 of the Statute, and, as thus affirmed and supplemented, it was qualified by section 9 (2) and (3) of the Statute. By virtue of section 9 (2) nothing in the convention as stated in the Preamble nor in section 4, when adopted, was to be deemed to require the concurrence of the Parliament or Government of the Commonwealth in any law made by the United Kingdom Parliament with respect to any matter within the exclusive authority of the States of Australia in any

[1] *Australian Commonwealth Parliamentary Debates*, vol. 132, p. 1083.

case where such concurrence was not required by the constitutional practice existing before the passing of the Statute; and, by virtue of section 9 (3), the 'request and consent' referred to in section 4[1] shall mean the request and consent of the Parliament and Government of the Commonwealth.

In the result the legal power of the United Kingdom Parliament to amend the Constitution Act and the Constitution of the Commonwealth was to be exercised, both before and after the adoption of section 4, according to the same rules of construction as were in force before the passing of the Statute. The rule laid down in the Colonial Laws Validity Act still prevailed. On the other hand, according to the convention declared in 1930, and affirmed in the Preamble, no law of the United Kingdom Parliament to amend the Constitution Act or the Constitution would be passed except at the request and with the consent of the Commonwealth. But it was still undecided how the request and consent of the Commonwealth, under this convention, was to be conveyed, and to what extent the dissent of portions of the Commonwealth should be taken into consideration by the United Kingdom Parliament. Nor was the position completely clarified by the Report, in 1935, of the Joint Select Committee of Lords and Commons, appointed to consider the receivability of the petition from the State of Western Australia, praying that the Constitution Act should be amended by the United Kingdom Parliament in order to provide for the secession of that State from the Commonwealth.[2] The most that can be said, from a study of that Report, is that no request

---

[1] But not necessarily the 'request and consent' referred to in paragraph 3 of the Preamble.   [2] H.L. 52, 75; H.C. 88.

for an amendment of the Constitution Act or the Constitution from a State or States only will be considered by the United Kingdom Parliament. The request must come through the Parliament or Government of the Commonwealth. 'The State of Western Australia', said the Report, 'has no *locus standi* in asking for legislation from the Parliament of the United Kingdom in regard to the constitution of the Commonwealth, any more than it would have in asking for legislation to alter the constitution of another Australian State, or than the Commonwealth would have in asking for an amendment of the constitution of the State of Western Australia.'[1]

On the other hand, certain passages in the Report appear to indicate that action by the United Kingdom Parliament upon a request by the Parliament and Government of the Commonwealth would not necessarily be automatic. It speaks of a request 'conveying the clearly expressed wish of the Australian people as a whole',[2] or 'a general demand by the citizens of the Commonwealth constitutionally expressed in the Commonwealth Parliament and transmitted by the Commonwealth Government'.[3] This is vague language. But at least it suggests that the United Kingdom Parliament must be regarded as constitutionally competent to look behind a request from the Commonwealth Parliament to see whether it is generally supported by the people of a majority of the States, even if the Parliaments and Governments of these States have no *locus standi*. But it is apparent that in the case of Australia, as in the case of Canada, there is room for uncertainty about the appropriate action which the United Kingdom Parliament should take in response to a request from the federal authorities in

[1] *Report*, p. ix.   [2] *Ibid.*, p. x.   [3] *Ibid.*, p. viii.

the Dominion which is not supported by a substantial majority of the federated units.

Before the passing of the Statute the Commonwealth Parliament was subject to the limitations imposed by the Colonial Laws Validity Act and by the lack of a general power to legislate with extra-territorial effect. By the adoption of sections 2 and 3 of the Statute these limitations are now removed, but subject to the proviso, first, that nothing in those sections shall be deemed to confer upon the Commonwealth Parliament any power to repeal or alter the Constitution or the Constitution Act of the Commonwealth otherwise than in accordance with the law existing before the passing of the Statute;[1] and second, that nothing in those sections shall be deemed to confer a power on the Commonwealth Parliament to make laws upon matters within the exclusive competence of the States.[2] By the adoption of sections 5 and 6, the legal inequalities of reservation or similar restrictions imposed upon the Commonwealth by the Merchant Shipping Act, 1894, and the Colonial Courts of Admiralty Act, 1890, are also removed, subject to the two provisos mentioned above. But the legal basis, and the amending process in law and in convention, of the Australian Constitution Act and Constitution remain unaltered by the passing of the Statute, both before and after the adoption of sections 2–6.

Before the passing of the Statute, Australia was subject to the power of disallowance as provided in the Constitution. That power was nullified by constitutional convention in 1930,[3] and its abolition could be carried out by Australia through the ordinary process of constitu-

---

[1] By s. 8. [2] By s. 9 (1).
[3] *O.D.L. Report*, para. 23.

tional amendment prescribed by section 128. The position remained the same after the passing of the Statute, whether or not sections 2–6 were adopted. In the event of abolition, some alternative form of undertaking in respect of Australian trustee securities would be necessary, and the alternative provided by the Colonial Stock Act, 1934, could be adopted. Again, before the passing of the Statute, Australia possessed authority, by the process prescribed in section 128, to abolish the powers of discretionary and obligatory reservation provided in the Constitution. The position remained unaltered by the passing of the Statute, whether or not sections 2–6 were adopted.

In exercising its increased powers obtained or obtainable under the Statute, the Parliament of the Commonwealth, like the Parliament of Canada, was bound by certain rules, in virtue of conventions agreed upon in 1930 before the passing of the Statute. In the first place, projected legislation by the Parliament of the Commonwealth which might affect the interests of some other Dominion or of the United Kingdom, must be preceded by consultation between the Commonwealth Government and the other Governments concerned. The passing of the Statute made no alteration in the terms or force of this convention. In the second place there were rules regulating legislation to alter the law touching the Succession to the Throne or the Royal Style and Titles. The first of these rules was that any such legislation passed by the Parliament of the Commonwealth[1] must

[1] The Commonwealth Parliament possesses no power under the Constitution to make laws on these subjects, and, in view of the restrictions imposed in section 8 of the Statute, the Parliament obtains no extension of the area of its power when it adopts section 2. See K. H. Bailey, *Politica*, June 1938, p. 156.

obtain the assent of the Parliaments of all the other
Dominions and of the United Kingdom. This rule was
approved by the Commonwealth Parliament. It was
affirmed by the United Kingdom Parliament in paragraph 2 of the Preamble to the Statute, but it remained
a convention. The second of the rules was, by virtue of
the same convention of 1930, that any such legislation
passed by the Parliament of any other Dominion, or of
the United Kingdom, must obtain the assent of the
Parliament of the Commonwealth and the Parliaments
of all the other Members of the British Commonwealth.
This rule also had been approved by the Commonwealth Parliament. It was affirmed by the United Kingdom Parliament in paragraph 2 of the Preamble to the
Statute, but it remained a convention. The third rule
was that any such legislation passed by the United Kingdom Parliament, which was intended to extend to the
Commonwealth as part of the law of the Commonwealth,
should require not only the assent of the Parliaments of
the Commonwealth and of all the other Dominions, as
in the first rule, but should require also the request and
consent of the Commonwealth. This rule had been
approved by the Commonwealth Parliament. It was
affirmed by the United Kingdom Parliament in paragraphs 2 and 3 of the Preamble to the Statute, and to that
extent amounted to no more than a convention. But, in
so far as request and consent of the Commonwealth was
required, the rule was supplemented by a rule of construction in terms of strict law in section 4, and, further,
the request and consent referred to in that section were
to be request and consent of the Parliament and Government of the Commonwealth.[1] But the rule, as thus

[1] By s. 9 (3) of the Statute.

supplemented, did not apply to the Commonwealth until the adoption of section 4. Any such legislation by the United Kingdom Parliament before such adoption was regulated solely by the conventions declared in 1930 and confirmed in paragraphs 2 and 3 of the Preamble to the Statute.

In so far as the Commonwealth of Australia was subject by the terms of its Constitution to the legal inequality of the appeal to the Judicial Committee by special leave, the Statute, both before and after the adoption of sections 2–6, made no alteration in the position. Before the passing of the Statute the appeal could have been dealt with in one of three ways. First, legislation limiting the appeal might have been passed by the Commonwealth Parliament,[1] and this legislation, when reserved by the Governor-General, would have received the Royal Assent in virtue of the convention agreed upon in 1930;[2] secondly, it might have been abolished completely by ordinary process of constitutional amendment; or, finally, the requirement in the constitution[1] that legislation by the Commonwealth Parliament limiting the appeal must be reserved, might have been abolished by ordinary process of constitutional amendment, and the appeal thereafter limited by the Commonwealth Parliament. The same three possible courses remained open after the passing of the Statute. The only difference which the Statute made in respect of judicial appeals was that, in so far as it might be contended that, even if Australia abolished the appeal from its Constitution, none the less the Judicial Committee Acts of 1833 and 1844 still applied to Australia, the Commonwealth Parliament was empowered, on adopting sections 2 and

[1] Under s. 74 of the Constitution.   [2] *O.D.L. Report*, paras. 33–4.

3 of the Statute, to repeal those Acts in so far as they applied to the Commonwealth.

It remains to be noted that the Statute makes no extension to the States of Australia of the powers conferred in ss. 2, 3, 4, and 5 upon the Commonwealth. There is little doubt that the extension of these powers is in many ways desirable, and it is difficult to accept arguments put forward to demonstrate that the States of Australia or the Provinces of Canada are, or ought to be, placed upon a status of constitutional inequality in relation to the United Kingdom. A Dominion is not a government or a parliament; it is a territorial community. It has been declared that these territorial communities are equal in status to the territorial community of the United Kingdom. The people of Australia or Canada, that is to say, are in no way subordinate in constitutional status to the people of the United Kingdom, and that proposition is unaffected by the fact that the people of Australia or Canada are for some purposes governed from Canberra or Ottawa and for other purposes from the State or provincial capitals. 'Both in theory and practice there is much to be said for treating Dominion powers of self-government as a whole, irrespective of the particular authority by which, in a federal Dominion, they may come to be exercised.'[1] The O.D.L. Conference in 1929 did not make proposals for the removal of the inequalities to which the Canadian Provinces and the Australian States were subject. It regarded the matter as one for consideration by the competent authorities in those Dominions,[2] and, as has

[1] Bailey, *Australian Law Journal*, vol. v, at p. 402. See also Evatt, *The King and his Dominion Governors*, c. xxii.
[2] *O.D.L. Report*, paras. 68–71.

been seen, the fetter of the Colonial Laws Validity Act was removed by the Statute from the Canadian Provinces as a result of agreement between the competent authorities in Canada. The Australian States, however, though their status should be one of constitutional equality—if the Declaration of 1926 is rightly interpreted—continued to possess a status of legal and conventional inequality to the United Kingdom after the passing of the Statute. They were subject to disallowance, reservation, the Colonial Laws Validity Act, the lack of complete power to legislate with extra-territorial effect, and the appeal to the Judicial Committee by special leave. In addition no convention has been adopted, as in the case of the Governors-General of the Dominions, to define the status of the State Governors, in relation both to ministers in the State and to ministers in the United Kingdom.

The continued application of the Colonial Laws Validity Act to the States, and its repeal in respect of the Canadian Provinces, had consequences which went beyond the mere question of repugnancy dealt with in sections 2 and 3 of the Colonial Laws Validity Act. For it was decided by the Judicial Committee in 1932[1] that the power conferred upon colonial legislatures, in section 5 of the Act, to pass laws amending the constitution, powers, and procedure of such legislatures 'provided that such laws shall have been passed in such manner and form as may from time to time be required by any act of parliament, letters-patent, order in council, or colonial law for the time being in force in the said colony', authorized a colonial legislature to impose limitations upon the powers of its successors to amend the Constitu-

[1] *Att.-Gen. for New South Wales* v. *Trethowan* [1932] A.C. 526.

tion of the colony. In this way effective legal safeguards could be devised for the whole or a part of the constitutional structure of the colony. This provision in section 5 had obviously important consequences for the domestic politics of an Australian State or a Canadian Province.

By section 7 (2) of the Statute, section 5 ceased to apply to the Canadian Provinces, but it remained in force in respect of the Australian States. At the same time it cannot be assumed that the limitation which found expression in the terms of section 5 has necessarily been abolished entirely in so far as the Canadian Provinces are concerned, or that it would be so abolished for the Australian States, if the provisions of section 2 of the Statute were extended to them. It may be that it is inherent in the nature of a legislature, the powers of which are derived from a Constitution, that it may be bound by its predecessors, and that it may bind its successors. That is to say, it may lack, by nature, the powers of a completely sovereign legislature, such as the United Kingdom Parliament, which cannot bind its successors, nor is itself bound by its predecessors.[1] This is a question which the Judicial Committee did not attempt to decide in *Trethowan's Case*. It confined itself to the terms of section 5. It may be argued that section 5 was no more than declaratory, and that its abolition leaves untouched the inherent limitation upon the powers of a derivative legislature. In that case the legislatures of the Canadian Provinces remain subject, in this matter, to similar limitations to those which apply in the case of the Australian States.

It is interesting to notice, in conclusion, that although

---

[1] Cf. Owen Dixon, J. in *Attorney-General for New South Wales* v. *Trethowan*, 44 C.L.R. 394 at pp. 428–9.

there was no extension to the Australian States of the powers conferred on the Commonwealth Parliament by sections 2, 3, and 5 of the Statute, the wording of section 6 of the Statute appears to justify the view that the powers which that section confers extend to the States as well as to the Commonwealth. For whereas the powers of sections 2, 3, and 5 are conferred upon the Parliament of a Dominion, the powers of section 6 are conferred upon the Dominion. The section, it will be recalled, enacted that s. 4 of the Colonial Courts of Admiralty Act, 1890, and so much of s. 7 of that Act as required the approval of His Majesty in Council to any rules of court regulating the practice and procedure of a Colonial Court of Admiralty, 'shall cease to have effect in any Dominion as from the commencement of this Act'. If 'Dominion' is taken to mean the Commonwealth and the States, and not the Commonwealth exclusive of the States, then the restriction which section 6 removes will be removed from the parliaments and the courts of the States as well as from the parliament and courts of the Commonwealth when section 6 is adopted by the Commonwealth Parliament. The use of 'Dominion' in section 6, instead of 'Parliament of a Dominion' as in section 5, was necessitated by the fact that the relevant parts of section 7 of the Act of 1890 referred not to a Dominion Parliament but to the rules of court made by a Colonial Court of Admiralty, and therefore a reference to the 'Parliament of a Dominion' alone would not have been sufficient.

IX

THE STATUTE AND THE LEGAL STATUS OF NEW ZEALAND AND NEWFOUNDLAND

I

THE Dominion of New Zealand had maintained from the outset a lukewarm attitude to proposals at the Conference of 1926 that the legal status of the Dominions should be brought into line with their conventional status.[1] In its view the legal inequalities which persisted in spite of conventional developments did no harm, and indeed did some good. In the proceedings of the Conferences of 1929 and 1930, therefore, it is not surprising to find that the New Zealand delegates, while recognizing that other Dominions were fully entitled to claim increased legal powers for their legislatures, were anxious to ensure that no alteration should be made in the legal position of New Zealand for the time being.

At the Conference of 1929, New Zealand associated itself with the federal Dominions of Canada and Australia in requesting that a clause should be inserted in the proposed Statute to provide that nothing in the Statute should be deemed to confer any power to repeal or alter the Constitution Acts of the Dominion of Canada, the Commonwealth of Australia, and the Dominion of New Zealand, otherwise than in accordance with the law and constitutional usage and practice theretofore existing.[2] The Constitution Act of New Zealand was an

---

[1] This attitude is well illustrated in the speech of the New Zealand Prime Minister, in the House of Representatives in 1931, when moving the resolution requesting the passage of the Statute by the United Kingdom Parliament. (*New Zealand Parliamentary Debates*, vol. 228, p. 549.)

[2] *O.D.L. Report*, para. 66.

Act of the United Kingdom Parliament, passed in 1852.[1] By a further Act of that Parliament, passed in 1857,[2] power was conferred upon the New Zealand Parliament[3] to amend all of the Constitution Act except certain specified sections. Of these it may be convenient to mention the section establishing the Parliament itself (s. 32); the sections regulating the time or place of its meeting, and regulating its prorogation and dissolution, the taking of an oath or the making of an affirmation by its members (ss. 44, 46, 47); the section endowing the Parliament with power to make laws and defining that power (s. 53); the section regulating the appropriation and issue of public monies (s. 54); the sections providing for the Governor's power to assent, refuse assent, or reserve Bills duly passed by the two Houses of the Parliament, and for the disallowance of Acts duly passed by the two Houses and assented to by the Governor (ss. 56–9); and finally, the section defining the terms 'Governor' and 'New Zealand'—the latter including a definition of the boundaries of the colony (s. 80). With the passing of the Colonial Laws Validity Act, 1865, the New Zealand Parliament obtained, by virtue of section 5 of that Act, 'full power to make laws respecting the constitution, powers, and procedure of such legislature', but it was doubtful whether this endowment of power was sufficient to remove completely the restrictions imposed by the Act of 1857.[4]

In 1929, then, the Act of 1857 and the Colonial Laws Validity Act, 1865, formed the principal elements in the

[1] 15 & 16 Vict., c. 72. [2] 20 & 21 Vict., c. 53, s. 2.
[3] It is styled 'General Assembly' in the Constitution.
[4] R. O. McGechan, in *New Zealand and the Statute of Westminster* (ed. J. C. Beaglehole), pp. 100–3, favours the view that a wider power was conferred.

law regulating the power of the New Zealand legislature to repeal or alter the Constitution Act. At the same time the United Kingdom Parliament had power to alter any part of the Constitution Act, but, according to the constitutional usage and practice then existing, it would not exercise that power except at the request of New Zealand expressed through the Government or the Parliament. It was this position in law and in constitutional usage and practice which the Conference of 1929 intended to preserve. It would be 'for the appropriate authorities in New Zealand to consider whether, and, if so, in what form, the full power of alteration should be given'.[1]

It seems clear that, on the liberal interpretation of section 2 (2) of the Statute, the unqualified extension of section 2 to New Zealand would have empowered the New Zealand Parliament to repeal or amend any United Kingdom Acts whatsoever, including the Constitution Act, in so far as they were part of the law of New Zealand. But it is probable also that the same result would have followed for New Zealand, unlike Canada and Australia, even on the more restricted view of the effect of section 2 (2) which some writers adopted. For, it might be argued, the New Zealand Parliament, unlike the federal parliaments of Canada and Australia, was empowered to make laws for the peace, order, and good government of New Zealand without any restriction of area in respect of subject matter; and it was prevented from repealing such United Kingdom Acts, therefore, on the ground only that they were United Kingdom Acts. Section 2 of the Statute removed the obstacle of repugnancy, and the Parliament would be free therefore to amend the Constitution Act as it thought

[1] *O.D.L. Report*, para. 65.

fit, unless some safeguarding clause had been inserted in the Statute.

At the Conference of 1930 the reference to Canada in the proposed safeguarding clause was omitted, as has been seen, but New Zealand and Australia were included in a clause, based upon the proposed clause of 1929, but with the reference to 'constitutional usage and practice' omitted.[1] The clause recommended in 1930 was approved by the New Zealand legislature, and it appears as section 8 of the Statute. It was provided in that section, in so far as New Zealand was concerned, that nothing in the Statute 'shall be deemed to confer any power to repeal or alter . . . the Constitution Act of New Zealand otherwise than in accordance with the law existing before the commencement of this Act'. The Colonial Laws Validity Act, therefore, continued to apply to New Zealand in so far as the repeal or alteration of the Constitution Act was concerned, in spite of the provisions of section 2 of the Statute.

But a further restriction upon the application of the Statute to New Zealand was proposed at the Conference of 1930. After consideration of the report and recommendations of the O.D.L. Conference, the New Zealand Government decided to request the insertion of a clause in the Statute to provide that no provision of the Statute should extend to New Zealand, as part of the law thereof, unless that provision was adopted by the Parliament of New Zealand, and that any such adopting Act might provide that the adoption should have effect, either as from the commencement of the Statute, or as from such later date as might be specified by the adopting Act.[2] This proposed clause was approved by the New Zealand

[1] Cmd. 3717, p. 20.   [2] *Ibid.*, p. 21.

parliament in 1931 and included in the resolution passed
requesting the enactment of the Statute.[1] Meanwhile,
the Australian Commonwealth Parliament had decided
to follow the example of New Zealand, and to request the
enactment of a similar provision in respect of Australia.
Newfoundland also decided to be associated in the same
provision. In the clauses finally drafted for all three
Dominions and enacted as section 10 (1), (2), and (3) of
the Statute, the power of adoption was confined to
sections 2–6 of the Statute, and was not extended to the
whole Statute as the original New Zealand proposal had
intended; and, in addition, the Parliaments were empowered not only to adopt these sections, but also to
revoke the adoption—an amendment to the original
New Zealand proposal which was suggested by the
Australian Parliament.[2]

2

On November 25, 1947, the Parliament of New Zealand adopted sections 2–6 of the Statute[2] and thereupon,
in accordance with section 4, requested and consented
to the enactment by the Parliament at Westminster of
an act—duly passed on December 10, 1947, as the New
Zealand Constitution (Amendment) Act, 1947—to
remove all restrictions upon New Zealand's power to
amend its Constitution and thereby to alter the position which had been preserved by section 8 of the
Statute. The effects of this legislation may be briefly
stated.

[1] *New Zealand Parliamentary Debates*, vol. 228, pp. 549–50.
[2] The adopting Act is printed in Appendix VI with an explanatory note.

Before the passing of the Statute, the United Kingdom Parliament was bound—in virtue of the constitutional convention finally recognized in 1930—not to exercise its legal power to make laws for New Zealand otherwise than at the request and with the consent of New Zealand. This convention applied to all laws extending to New Zealand as part of the law of New Zealand, and regulated therefore the power of the United Kingdom Parliament to alter the Constitution Act of New Zealand. The convention was approved by the New Zealand Parliament. On the passing of the Statute, it was affirmed by the United Kingdom Parliament in paragraph 3 of the Preamble, and it was supplemented by the rule of construction in terms of strict law enacted in section 4 of the Statute. This rule now extends to New Zealand with the adoption of section 4 and was indeed immediately used. By section 3 (1) of the Adoption Act it was provided, too, that the request and consent required by section 4 of the Statute should be made and given by the Parliament of New Zealand and not otherwise.

Before the passing of the Statute the New Zealand Parliament was subject to the fetters imposed by the Colonial Laws Validity Act, the lack of power to pass laws with extra-territorial effect, and the provisions in the Merchant Shipping Act, 1894, and the Colonial Courts of Admiralty Act, 1890, requiring reservation or some similar process in respect of New Zealand legislation upon these subjects. The Statute removed those fetters by sections 2–6, and the increased powers therein conferred were obtained by New Zealand upon the adoption of these sections, subject to the proviso that nothing in those sections should be deemed to confer a power on the New Zealand Parliament to repeal or alter the Constitution Act otherwise than in accordance with the law theretofore existing. This last proviso was rendered of no effect by the passing of the New Zealand Constitution (Amendment) Act, 1947.

Before the passing of the Statute, New Zealand was subject, by the terms of its Constitution Act, to disallowance and to discretionary and obligatory reservation. Obligatory reservation under instructions had ceased in 1907, and in 1930 the inequalities involved in the exercise of the powers of disallowance and discretionary reservation were abolished by convention. But obligatory reservation under the Constitution Act continued in force, and must be exercised unless and until that Act was amended. The power of the New Zealand Parliament to abolish reservation and disallowance from the Act was doubtful, and the adoption of sections 2–6 of the Statute made no alteration in the position. But the United Kingdom Act of 1947 gave full power to New Zealand to remove these restrictions. If disallowance were abolished completely, the alternative provided in the Colonial Stock Act, 1934, could be utilized to ensure the continuance of New Zealand stocks as trustee securities.

In exercising its new powers, New Zealand is bound, as are the other Dominions and the United Kingdom, by the convention of 1926 that projected legislation by the New Zealand Parliament which might affect some other Member of the Commonwealth should be preceded by consultation between the New Zealand Government and the Governments of the other affected Members. The passing of the Statute made no alteration in this convention. Similarly, New Zealand was bound by

certain rules in respect of legislation altering the law
touching the Succession to the Throne or the Royal Style
and Titles. In the first place by virtue of a convention,
agreed upon in 1930, any such legislation by the Parliament of New Zealand must receive the assent of the
Parliaments of all the other Dominions and of the United
Kingdom. The New Zealand Parliament approved this
convention. The Statute affirmed it on behalf of the
United Kingdom Parliament in paragraph 2 of the
Preamble, and as thus affirmed it extended to New Zealand. In the second place, by virtue of the same convention of 1930, any such legislation by a Parliament of
any other Dominion or of the United Kingdom should
require the assent of the Parliament of New Zealand
and of the Parliaments of all the other Members of the
Commonwealth. This also was approved by the New
Zealand Parliament and was affirmed by the United
Kingdom Parliament in paragraph 2 of the Preamble
to the Statute, and as thus affirmed it extended to New
Zealand. In the third place, in virtue of the above
convention and of a further convention of 1930, any
such legislation by the Parliament of the United Kingdom which was intended to extend to New Zealand
as part of the law of New Zealand, should require not
only the assent of the Parliament of New Zealand and
of the Parliaments of all the other Dominions, but should
require also the request and consent of New Zealand.
This third rule was approved by the New Zealand
Parliament and was affirmed by the United Kingdom
Parliament in paragraphs 2 and 3 of the Preamble to
the Statute, and as thus affirmed extended to New Zealand. But in so far as the request and consent of New
Zealand was required, this rule was supplemented by

a rule of strict law enacted in section 4 of the Statute, so
that, now that New Zealand has adopted that section,
no such law passed by the United Kingdom Parliament
shall be deemed to extend to New Zealand unless it is
declared in that Act that New Zealand has requested
and consented to the enactment thereof.

Finally, before the passing of the Statute, New Zealand was subject to the legal inequality involved in the
existence of the appeal by special leave to the Judicial
Committee. That appeal, in respect of New Zealand,
was provided for not in the Constitution Act but in the
Judicial Committee Acts of 1833 and 1844. New Zealand was unable to restrict or abolish the appeal by
reason of the two fetters mentioned in *Nadan* v. *the King*,[1]
viz. the Colonial Laws Validity Act and the lack of
extra-territorial power. By the adoption of sections 2
and 3 of the Statute the New Zealand Parliament
removes these two fetters.

3

The Dominion of Newfoundland had, like New Zealand, shown no great eagerness that the declaration of
conventional equality of status in 1926 should be followed
by a corresponding and consequential alteration in the
rules of strict law. None the less, at the Conferences of
1929 and 1930, Newfoundland did not feel compelled,
evidently, to request, as did New Zealand, that clauses
should be inserted in the Statute to safeguard its Constitution or to postpone the application of the Statute
to the Dominion until its legislature adopted it. In the
Schedule drawn up by the Conference of 1930 there
appeared, therefore, no proposed clause intended to
restrict the application of the Statute with respect to

[1] [1926] A.C. 480.

Newfoundland. But it was provided in that Schedule that the Statute should contain such other provisions in respect of any Dominion as were requested by that Dominion. In the interval between the Conference of 1930 and the introduction of the Statute of Westminster Bill into the House of Commons, Newfoundland requested the insertion in the Statute of a clause postponing the application of sections 2–6 of the Statute to Newfoundland until its Parliament adopted any or all of these sections. Newfoundland was included, therefore, in section 10 (1), (2), and (3) of the Statute, along with Australia and New Zealand, and obtained, as did these Dominions, power not only to adopt the sections but also to revoke such adoption.

There is little to be said now of the effect of the Statute on the legal status of Newfoundland. It had been agreed in 1930, before the passing of the Statute, that no law should be passed by the United Kingdom Parliament to extend to a Dominion, as part of the law of the Dominion, otherwise than at the request and with the consent of the Dominion. That constitutional convention was approved by the Newfoundland Parliament and was affirmed by the United Kingdom Parliament in paragraph 3 of the Preamble to the Statute and, as thus affirmed, extended to Newfoundland. The convention was supplemented by the rule of construction enacted in section 4, which would apply to Newfoundland if and when adopted by the Newfoundland Parliament. In 1933, as the result of a financial crisis, a royal commission recommended[1] that the existing Constitution of Newfoundland, which was contained in letters patent, should be suspended, and that the government of the Island

[1] Cmd. 4480.

should be placed in the hands of a commission under the control of the United Kingdom Government. To achieve this and kindred objects, legislation by the United Kingdom Parliament was considered necessary. Section 4 of the Statute had not yet been adopted by the New-foundland Parliament, but the constitutional conventions declared in 1930 and affirmed in the Preamble were in operation. The Newfoundland Parliament therefore passed an address to the King requesting the passage of legislation by the United Kingdom Parliament, and in consequence the Newfoundland Act, 1933,[1] was passed. The Act recites in its Preamble that the Address had been passed by the Newfoundland Parliament, and the Address itself is attached as the First Schedule to the Act.

In the new Constitution, issued in letters patent under the authority of this Act,[2] the former bicameral Parliament of Newfoundland was abolished, and power to make laws for the peace, welfare, and good government of Newfoundland was transferred to the Governor acting with the advice and consent of the Commission of Government. In law Newfoundland appeared to be a Dominion still (though in name only), since section 1 of the Statute extended to Newfoundland and had not been amended to omit the name of Newfoundland, and section 11, which abolished the term 'Colony', as applied to the Dominions, still extended to Newfoundland. But constitutionally Newfoundland lacked the fundamental element in Dominion Status, viz. equality. It was in many ways subordinate to the United Kingdom in aspects of its external and domestic affairs, though still united by a common allegiance to the King, and freely

[1] 24 Geo. 5, c. 2.
[2] *Statutory Rules and Orders*, 1934, vol. ii, p. 774.

associated. It might almost be said that, whereas before the passing of the Statute there existed, in the British Empire, several examples of a community which was constitutionally a Dominion but by legal enumeration[1] a colony, after the passing of the Newfoundland Act, 1933, there existed an example of a community which was by legal enumeration[2] a Dominion but constitutionally a colony.

So the anomaly persisted until on March 31, 1949, Newfoundland became a province of Canada by virtue of the British North America (No. 1) Act, 1949.[3] It is not possible to discuss here the constitutional proprieties or improprieties associated with the passing of that Act.[4] Suffice it to say that thereafter the provisions of the Statute of Westminster applied to Newfoundland in the same way as to the other provinces of Canada. What was said of them in Chapter VIII can be said now of Newfoundland. It is interesting to notice also that the British North America (No. 1), Act, 1949, not being, like the British North America Acts of 1940, 1943, 1946, and 1949 (No. 2) an act solely to amend the British North America Acts, 1867 to 1930, but being also an act to give force of law to the terms of union apart from any amendment they involved, came within the purview of section 4 of the Statute of Westminster, and it was therefore declared in the preamble to the Act that Canada had requested and consented to it. No such declaration is found in the Acts of 1940, 1943, 1946, and 1949 (No. 2) by reason of section 7 (1) of the Statute.[5]

[1] In the Interpretation Act, 1889, s. 18 (3). See p. 139 above.
[2] In the Statute of Westminster, s. 11.
[3] 12 and 13 Geo. 6, c. 22.
[4] They were discussed by the Attorney-General in the House of Commons, 462 *H.C. Deb.*, 5 s., cols. 1260 ff.   [5] See p. 152 above.

X

THE STATUTE AND THE LEGAL STATUS
OF SOUTH AFRICA

I

THE application of the Statute of Westminster to the
Union of South Africa was, in many respects, a less
complicated matter than it had been in the case of the
Dominions so far discussed. Unlike Canada and Australia the Union was not troubled with the conflicting
authorities of a federal constitution, and the elaborate
provisions inserted in the Statute in the case of these
Dominions to safeguard the rights of the federated units
were not necessary in the case of South Africa. Further,
unlike the unitary Dominions of New Zealand and Newfoundland, the Union of South Africa felt no reluctance
in accepting the increased legal powers which the Statute
proposed to confer upon those Dominions which wished
to receive them. In consequence there appeared in the
Statute no qualifying clause to restrict its operation with
respect to the Union. The Government and Parliament
of the Union were prepared to accept the fullest powers
which the Statute was capable of bestowing.

But while the Union was not troubled with the conservative scruples of some other unitary Dominions nor
with the specific legal conflicts of the federal Dominions, it
possessed some of the political conflicts of a unified rather
than of a united state. In consequence the Constitution
of the Union[1] contained certain safeguards to protect the
rights of the original colonies which went to make up the

[1] See W. P. M. Kennedy and H. J. Schlosberg, *The Law and Custom of
the South African Constitution.*

Union. By section 152 of the South Africa Act, 1909, the Parliament of the Union was empowered to repeal or alter any of the provisions of the Act, subject to the proviso that no provision of the Act, for the operation of which a definite period of time was prescribed, should be repealed or altered during that period; and further that no repeal or alteration of section 152 itself, or of sections 33 and 34 (until the number of members of the House of Assembly had reached the limit therein prescribed or until a period of ten years had elapsed after the establishment of the Union, whichever was the longer period), or of sections 35 and 137, should be valid unless the Bill had been passed by both Houses of Parliament sitting together, and at the third reading had been agreed to by not less than two-thirds of the total number of members of both Houses. These sections thus safeguarded were referred to as the 'entrenched clauses' of the South Africa Act. The general effect of section 152 was that difficulties were placed in the way of an amendment of those portions of the Act which regulated the proportionate representation of the original four colonies in the House of Assembly (ss. 33 and 34); which safeguarded the continuance of the native franchise in Cape Province (s. 35); and which guaranteed the equality of the English and Dutch languages (s. 137). Section 152 was itself safeguarded also, in order that the requirements therein contained for a two-thirds majority in a joint session might not themselves be repealed by a simple majority in separate sessions. So long as the Colonial Laws Validity Act was in force in the Union, the requirements of section 152 were unalterable by the Union Parliament except in accordance with the procedure there laid down.[1]

[1] Kennedy and Schlosberg, *op. cit.*, pp. 99–100.

It was feared that the unqualified extension of section 2 of the Statute to the Union Parliament would destroy the legal safeguard provided in section 152, and that the Union Parliament would be empowered to repeal or alter any section of the South Africa Act, including section 152, by the process of ordinary legislation. A section of opinion in the Union, consequently, desired the insertion of some reservation in the Statute in so far as the 'entrenched clauses' were concerned. However, when in the South African Parliament during the debates in 1931 on the Resolution requesting the passage of the Statute by the United Kingdom Parliament, the question of a safeguard was raised, notably by General Smuts, the leader of the Opposition,[1] the Government were unwilling to accept this proposal. But, by agreement between General Hertzog, the Prime Minister, and General Smuts, the Resolution requesting the passage of the Statute was agreed to 'on the understanding that the proposed legislation will in no way derogate from the entrenched provisions of the South Africa Act', these words being an amendment by General Smuts. The view of the Government and its supporters might be stated in the words of Dr. Stals in the House of Assembly: '. . . I think that no one in the House, or in the Union, doubts the moral obligation of the Parliament and the people to respect the basic principle in our constitution, and therefore it appears to me to be unnecessary to include a provision for securing it.'[2]

This resolution had no legal force, but it could have

[1] See *House of Assembly Debates*, vol. 17, cols. 2397–2403, and 2736–2763; *Senate Debates*, 1931, cols. 479–487.

[2] *House of Assembly Debates*, vol. 17, col. 2739. Senator Malan expressed the same view, *Senate Debates*, 1931, col. 484.

become a constitutional convention. In this connexion it is interesting to notice that the Speaker of the House of Assembly gave it as his view in 1934 'for the guidance of honourable members' that 'if it is desired to amend or repeal any of the entrenched clauses, then the procedure laid down in the South Africa Act must be followed';[1] and that this procedure was followed by the Union Parliament when legislation abolishing the Cape native franchise, provided for in 'entrenched' clause 35 of the South Africa Act, was passed in 1936.

In the years that followed, however, the fears of those that doubted the efficacy of the entrenched clauses seemed justified. In 1937 the Supreme Court of South Africa in the case of *Ndlwana* v. *Hofmeyr* (1937 A.D. 229) appeared to have adopted the view that the Union Parliament was no longer bound to follow the special procedure laid down in section 152 of the South Africa Act. In 1950 the Government of the Union adopted the same view in introducing legislation to abolish the Cape coloured franchise and the Speaker of the House of Assembly reversed the ruling of his predecessor, basing his opinion on the decision of 1937. It was not until 1952 that the Supreme Court reversed its decision of 1937 and asserted the efficacy of the entrenched clauses.[2]

In considering the extent to which the Statute removed or made possible the removal of those legal inequalities of status to which South Africa was subject theretofore, it will be convenient to discuss along with the Statute two Acts of the Union Parliament which were passed in 1934. They are the Status of the Union Act, 1934,[3] and the Royal Executive Functions and

[1] Kennedy and Schlosberg, *op. cit.*, p. 103.   [2] See Appendix VIII.
[3] No. 69 of 1934. The Act is printed as Appendix III to this book.

Seals Act, 1934.[1] To the former Act there were scheduled, in English and in Afrikaans, the entire Preamble and sections 1–6, 11, and 12 of the Statute of Westminster, with certain slight verbal alterations.[2] The portions thus scheduled are, by section 3 of the Status Act, deemed to be an Act of the Parliament of the Union and are to be construed accordingly. The significance of these Acts[3] goes far beyond the mere removal of legal inequalities of status as between the Union and the United Kingdom. Their chief importance lies in the modifications they introduced in the domestic constitutional structure of the Union.[4] It is proposed, however, to concentrate attention here on the narrower and less important question of the extent to which these Acts, in conjunction with the Statute, remove certain of those legal inequalities in the status of South Africa whose nature and extent have already been discussed.

2

Consider first the relations of the Union Parliament and the United Kingdom Parliament. Before the passing of the Statute, the United Kingdom Parliament was obliged by the convention declared in 1930 not to exercise its legal power to make laws for the Union otherwise than at the request or with the consent of the Union. The Statute confirmed that convention in paragraph 3

[1] No. 70 of 1934. The Act is printed as Appendix VIII to Kennedy and Schlosberg, *op. cit.*

[2] e.g. the reference in s. 1 of the Statute to the Dominions other than South Africa is omitted, and also the reference to 'State' in s. 11.

[3] The main objects which the Union Government sought to achieve by the passing of the Acts were explained by the Minister introducing the Bills in *House of Assembly Debates*, vol. 23, cols. 1864–76.

[4] See H. J. Mandelbrote, 'The Royal Prerogative in the Union' in *South African Law Journal*, vol. 53, p. 426.

of the Preamble, and supplemented it with the rule of construction in terms of strict law in section 4. But this did not satisfy completely the South African desire for equality. For it was admitted that, in spite of the requirement in section 4 that no Act of the United Kingdom Parliament should be deemed to extend to a Dominion unless it was declared in that Act that that Dominion had requested and consented to the enactment thereof, none the less it could be held, on the hitherto accepted doctrine of sovereignty, that any subsequent Act of the United Kingdom Parliament which referred in terms to South Africa, must be deemed to extend to South Africa, and to constitute a repeal *pro tanto* of section 4, so far as South Africa was concerned. And, even assuming that section 4 remained unrepealed, was it not still possible for that Parliament to pass an Act containing a declaration, in accordance with the terms of section 4, that that Act was passed with the request and consent of South Africa, although no such request and consent had, in fact, been given? And would not such an Act extend to South Africa as part of the law thereof?

It appeared, therefore, that whether section 4 was respected by the United Kingdom Parliament or not, a legal inequality of status remained. To meet this and other difficulties, it was enacted in section 2 of the Status Act that:

the Parliament of the Union shall be the sovereign legislative power in and over the Union, and notwithstanding anything in any other law contained, no Act of the Parliament of the United Kingdom and Northern Ireland[1] passed

---

[1] The correct title of the United Kingdom Parliament, under the Royal and Parliamentary Titles Act, 1927, s. 2, was the 'Parliament of

after the eleventh day of December, 1931,[1] shall extend, or be deemed to extend, to the Union as part of the law of the Union, unless extended thereto by an Act of the Parliament of the Union.

It is doubtful whether section 2 of the Status Act succeeds or was intended to succeed in imposing a restriction upon the United Kingdom Parliament. If it should happen that section 4 of the Statute be explicitly or impliedly repealed by the United Kingdom Parliament, then it might be argued that section 2 of the Status Act alone would not be sufficient to prevent the extension to South Africa, as part of the law of South Africa, of Acts passed by the United Kingdom Parliament expressly referring to South Africa. If, on the other hand, section 4 of the Statute is observed in form by the United Kingdom Parliament, though, in fact, no request and consent has been obtained from the Union, then it might be argued that section 2 of the Status Act could only be effective if construed as an amendment of section 4; for section 2 purports to substitute the words 'unless extended thereto by an Act of the Parliament of the Union' for the words 'unless it is expressly declared in that Act that that Dominion has requested, and consented to, the enactment thereof', in section 4. This cannot be effective unless a Dominion parliament has power to amend the Statute of Westminster.[2] But it would seem possible to avoid these difficulties by the

the United Kingdom of Great Britain and Northern Ireland', but the words 'of Great Britain' were omitted in the Status Act.

[1] The day upon which the Statute of Westminster received the Royal Assent.

[2] See Mr. Latham's view in *Australian Commonwealth Parliamentary Debates*, vol. 131, p. 4069. Printed in Keith, *Speeches and Documents on the British Dominions*, p. 272. See also Keith's view, *ibid.*, Introduction, p. xxx.

following argument. Section 2 of the Statute gave power to a Dominion Parliament to repeal or amend 'any existing or future Act of Parliament of the United Kingdom', to which a Dominion law, passed after the enactment of the Statute, is repugnant. Section 2 of the Status Act might be described, therefore, as no more than the repeal in advance of hypothetical future Acts of the United Kingdom Parliament in so far as they purport to extend to the Union as part of the law of the Union, unless and until such Acts are extended to the Union by by the Union Parliament. This would be a perfectly valid exercise of the power given in section 2 of the Statute. It would be effective to prevent the operation in the Union, until extended thereto by the Union Parliament, of any United Kingdom Act whether passed in accordance with the provisions of section 4 of the Statute in fact as well as in form, or whether passed in accordance with the provisions of section 4 in form only, or whether amounting to a repeal or amendment, express or implied, of the provisions of section 4.

But quite apart from consideration of the respective powers of the Union Parliament and the United Kingdom Parliament, it has been argued that section 2 of the Status Act raises a further difficulty. For it might conflict with section 4 of the Statute in so far as section 4 has been enacted in the Schedule to the Status Act, and has been declared to be part of an Act of the Union. If the two sections cannot be reconciled in accordance with the above argument, then it would be necessary to decide which of the two provisions is to prevail.

It is true, of course, that the legal inequality of status of the Union Parliament in relation to the powers of the United Kingdom Parliament to make laws for the Union remains even after the passing of the Status Act, because the United Kingdom Parliament may, in law, repeal section 2 of the Statute.

The Statute removed by sections 2, 3, 5, and 6 the legal inequalities imposed upon South Africa by the existence of the Colonial Laws Validity Act, the lack of a general power to make laws with extra-territorial effect, and the requirements of reservation or similar restrictions imposed in the Merchant Shipping Act, 1894, and the Colonial Courts of Admiralty Act, 1890. No qualifications were imposed on this grant of power. In the words of the spokesman of the Union Government at the time of the introduction of the Status of the Union Bill: 'South Africa accepts to the fullest possible extent this offer of autonomy'.[1]

Since the Union Parliament, unlike the federal parliaments of Canada and Australia, was not restricted in the area of its subject-matter, but possessed, under section 59 of the South Africa Act, 'full power to make laws for the peace, order, and good government of the Union', it acquired by section 2 of the Statute—even on the conservative interpretation of section 2—a power to amend any United Kingdom Act whatsoever in so far as it was part of the law of the Union. And, as decided in *Ndlwana* v. *Hofmeyr*, it was not restricted as to manner and form in respect of its power to amend the South Africa Act in certain matters. Further, it is submitted, it obtained power to repeal or amend the Statute itself. In the result, therefore, the Union Parliament acquired, on the conservative interpretation of section 2, a power substantially identical with that which it would acquire on the liberal interpretation of section 2.[2]

[1] *House of Assembly Debates*, vol. 23, col. 1866.   [2] See Appendix VIII.

Before the passing of the Statute the Union was subject to disallowance,[1] to discretionary reservation, and to obligatory reservation under instructions and under the provisions of sections 64 and 106 of the South Africa Act and paragraph 25 of the Schedule to the Act. The inequalities involved in the exercise of the powers of disallowance, of discretionary reservation, and of obligatory reservation had been abolished by convention in 1930. The Union Parliament, moreover, had authority to abolish the power of disallowance and all forms of reservation from the South Africa Act, subject in certain specified cases to reservation of the Bills purporting to make these changes.[2] The effect of the Statute was, if anything, to strengthen this power, but it did not release the Union Parliament from the requirements that such legislation must itself be reserved. In fact disallowance and reservation were dealt with in the Status of the Union Act, and the procedure prescribed by the South Africa Act was followed.

The power of disallowance was repealed from the South Africa Act by section 11 (2) of the Status Act, but this repeal was not to have effect until proclaimed by the Governor-General. For, in the absence of the power of disallowance, South Africa would have been unable to comply with the third of the Treasury Rules under the Colonial Stock Act, 1900, with the result that its stocks would have been unable to enjoy the status of trustee securities. It was necessary therefore to postpone the coming into effect of the repeal of disallowance until an alternative arrangement for South African stocks could be made with the United Kingdom. This led to the passing of the Colonial Stock Act, 1934,[3] by the United

[1] s. 65 of South Africa Act.   [2] By s. 64.   [3] 24 & 25 Geo. 5, c. 47.

Kingdom Parliament and the provision therein of an
alternative form of undertaking in respect of Dominion
stocks whereby the exercise of disallowance was avoided.
South Africa, having passed the necessary legislation,
took advantage of this alternative, and the repeal of disallowance[1] came into effect.

In respect of reservation, the Governor-General's
power to reserve Bills limiting the matters in regard to
which special leave to appeal to the Judicial Committee
may be asked,[2] and his power to reserve Bills altering the
terms of the Schedule to the Act relating to the government of the native territories when transferred to the
Union,[3] were not repealed by the Status Act. But the
remaining powers of reservation—discretionary and
obligatory—were repealed by sections 8, 9, and 11 (1) of
the Status Act.[4] The Governor-General retained a discretion, and the power to issue instructions to him
remained, but this discretion must be exercised according
to his instructions. And since by section 4 of the Status
Act, the King was required to exercise his functions 'on
the advice of His Ministers of State for the Union', the
King's instructions to the Governor-General would be
issued on the advice of South African ministers.[5] Moreover this discretion was not a discretion to reserve, but
a discretion to assent or withhold assent to Bills. It was
explained that the power to withhold assent was retained

---

[1] Except from para. 20 of the Schedule. See above, p. 129.   [2] s. 106.
[3] ss. 150 and 151 of the Act, and paragraph 25 of Schedule.
[4] The repeal involved an amendment of s. 64 of the South Africa Act,
and by the terms of this section such amending legislation itself was
required to be reserved. Accordingly the Status of the Union Bill was
reserved by the Governor-General and assented to by the King on the
advice of the Prime Minister of the Union. See Kennedy and Schlosberg, *op. cit.*, p. 617.   [5] See below, p. 254.

for administrative convenience, in order that a Bill, duly passed by the two houses of the legislature but found for some reason to be unsuitable or unnecessary, might be prevented from acquiring force of law.[1]

The exercise of the powers and functions of the King and of the Governor-General in respect of the Union were, indeed, subjected to considerable regulation in rules of strict law by the terms of the Status Act and the Royal Executive Functions and Seals Act. For the present purpose, however, it is enough to mention that the latter Act authorized the setting up of a Great Seal of the Union, the custody of which was confided to the Prime Minister of the Union or his deputy. The existence and use of this Great Seal removed in particular the legal inequality which had persisted in the conduct of foreign affairs on behalf of the Union until 1934, from the necessity of making use of the Great Seal of the Realm, the release of which required the formal intervention of a Secretary of State of the United Kingdom.[2] Since the passing of the Royal Executive Functions and Seals Act the conduct of foreign relations by the Union is constitutionally under the complete control of Union ministers.

In exercising its powers under the Statute the Union Parliament was bound by similar rules to those which regulated the Parliaments of the other Dominions and the United Kingdom. First of all, in virtue of the convention agreed upon in 1926, projected legislation in the Union Parliament which might affect some other part of the Commonwealth should be preceded by

[1] *House of Assembly Debates*, vol. 23, col. 1868.
[2] The Irish Free State similarly had its own Great Seal since 1931, and Canada passed its Seals Act in 1939 with similar effect.

consultation between the Union Government and the Governments of the other Members of the Commonwealth affected. This convention remained unaffected by the passing of the Statute. It was stated in the Union House of Assembly that consultation had occurred between the Union Government and the United Kingdom Government before the Status Bill was introduced, but that such consultation had been confined to the question of the removal of disallowance and of the arrangements which should be made in consequence. It would appear that the convention was somewhat narrowly interpreted. On the other hand, it was stated that the Status Bill and the Royal Executive Functions and Seals Bill had been submitted to the King for his consideration, and that in so far as His Majesty's interest was affected by the Bill, the King had expressed his willingness to place the matter in the hands of the Union Parliament.[1]

Then there were the rules regulating legislation altering the law touching the Succession to the Throne or the Royal Style and Titles. In the first place, by virtue of the convention agreed upon in 1930, any such legislation passed by the Union Parliament required the assent of the Parliaments of all the other Dominions and of the United Kingdom. The Statute affirmed this conventional rule in paragraph 2 of the Preamble. The Union Parliament enacted it in the Schedule to the Status Act in which the Preamble appears. In the second place, in virtue of the same convention agreed upon in 1930, any such legislation by the Parliament of any other Dominion or of the United Kingdom, required the assent of the Parliament of the Union and the Parlia-

---

[1] *House of Assembly Debates*, vol. 23, col. 1878.

ments of all the other Members of the Commonwealth. The Statute affirmed this conventional rule in paragraph 2 of the Preamble and the Union Parliament enacted it in the schedule to the Status Act. In the third place, by virtue of the two conventions agreed upon in 1930, any such legislation by the Parliament of the United Kingdom which was to extend to the Union as part of the law of the Union required not only the assent of the Parliament of the Union and of the Parliaments of all the other Dominions, but also the request and consent of the Union. This conventional rule was affirmed in paragraphs 2 and 3 of the Preamble to the Statute, and as thus affirmed extended to the Union. It was, moreover, enacted in the Schedule to the Status Act. In addition, so much of the rule as required the request and consent of the Union was supplemented by the rule of construction in section 4 of the Statute. To this must be added section 2 of the Status Act, which, if effective, required legislation by the Union Parliament before any such legislation by the United Kingdom Parliament could extend to the Union as part of the law of the Union. On the other hand, there was a further provision of the Status Act which governed the position in South Africa. It was provided by section 5 of the Act that the words 'heirs and successors' of the King, when referred to in the South Africa Act, 1909, 'shall be taken to mean His Majesty's heirs and successors in the sovereignty of the United Kingdom of Great Britain and Ireland as determined by the laws relating to the succession of the Crown of the United Kingdom of Great Britain and Ireland'.[1] By this section any alteration in

[1] It is interesting to notice that the obsolete term 'United Kingdom of Great Britain and Ireland' is here used.

the law relating to the succession of the Crown of the United Kingdom made by the United Kingdom Parliament would automatically cause an alteration in the law of the Union, by the express provision of the Union Parliament expressed in the Status Act. It may be submitted, however, that this does not mean that any such alteration by the United Kingdom Parliament extends to the Union as part of the law of the Union. The Union law will change because the United Kingdom law has changed, but the Union law will not be changed by the extension of the United Kingdom law to the Union.[1] It is not a case of legislation of the kind contemplated either in section 4 of the Statute or section 2 of the Status Act.

There remained the legal inequality of the appeal by special leave to the Judicial Committee. Before the passing of the Statute the Union Parliament possessed power to restrict the matters in which leave to appeal might be asked, subject to reservation of such legislation, and to the proviso that the right of appeal under the Colonial Courts of Admiralty Act, 1890, should not be affected. The passing of the Statute gave full power to the Union Parliament to abolish the appeal completely. In the Status Act, however, no alteration was made in the position, and the reservation requirement was retained. An agitation to abolish the appeal arose when the Judicial Committee gave special leave in 1934 in the case of *Pearl Assurance Co.* v. *the Union Government*,[2] but the

---

[1] In the same way, if the Union Parliament had defined the words 'heirs and successors' as 'the heirs and successors of the King of Norway as determined by the law of Norway', an alteration in the law by the Norwegian Parliament would cause an alteration in the law of the Union, but it would not follow that the Norwegian Parliament possessed or was exercising power to legislate in and for the Union.

[2] [1934] A.C. 570.

Government refused to act. In January 1937 a private member's Bill providing for the abolition of the appeal was introduced in the House of Assembly,[1] but in the course of the debate it was made clear that though the Government did not regard the Judicial Committee as a completely satisfactory court of appeal from the Union,[2] it was not prepared to take action to abolish the appeal. The Bill was defeated by 70 votes to 19. It was not until 1950 that the appeal was finally abolished by an Act[3] introduced by Dr. Malan's government,[4] the repeal taking effect from April 12, 1950.

It may be added that in 1937 new Letters Patent and an Instrument of Instructions[5] were issued to the Governor-General by the King on the advice of the Prime Minister of the Union. This Instrument, unlike its predecessor, contained no instructions to reserve Bills. The statutory requirements to reserve, by section 106 of the South Africa Act and para. 25 of the Schedule, remain unimpaired however, as has been mentioned already.

[1] *House of Assembly Debates*, vol. 28, col. 30.

[2] General Smuts, Minister for Justice, *ibid.*, col. 247.

[3] No. 16 of 1950.

[4] *House of Assembly Debates*, vol. 70, cols. 916 ff. It is interesting to record that the Minister of Justice, in charge of the bill, was Mr. Swart who, as a private member, had introduced the unsuccessful bill of 1937.

[5] See *Constitutions of All Countries*, vol. 1, pp. 183 ff.

XI

THE STATUTE AND THE LEGAL STATUS OF THE IRISH FREE STATE AND EIRE

I

THE Statute of Westminster contained no provision restricting the scope of its operation in the case of the Irish Free State. The Oireachtas or legislature of the Free State, established by the Constitution of 1922, acquired the fullest powers which the Statute was capable of bestowing. This unqualified grant of power was not passed through the United Kingdom Parliament without a protest. Amendments were moved, notably by Colonel Gretton in the House of Commons[1] and by Lord Danesfort in the House of Lords[2] to provide that nothing in the Statute should be deemed to apply to the alteration, amendment, or repeal of the Irish Free State (Agreement) Act, 1922, the Irish Free State Constitution Act, 1922, or so much of the Government of Ireland Act, 1920, as continued to be in force in Northern Ireland. The object of these amendments was to ensure that the Free State legislature should possess no greater power to amend the Free State Constitution after the passing of the Statute than it had before. That is to say, it was intended to confer upon the Free State the same status in this respect as Canada, Australia, and New Zealand.

The fact that these amendments were moved at all showed that some members at least of the United Kingdom Parliament had failed to grasp or were unwilling to

[1] 260 *H.C. Deb.*, 5 s., 303.   [2] 83 *H.L. Deb.*, 5 s., 231.

accept the plain implications of the declaration of equality of status in 1926, and its elaboration in 1929 and 1930. This impression is confirmed by a study of certain of the speeches made in the course of the debate.[1] The constitutional position, however, was clear. In 1930 it had been agreed by convention that no law thereafter made by the Parliament of the United Kingdom should extend to a Dominion otherwise than at the request and with the consent of that Dominion.[2] Canada, Australia, and New Zealand had requested and consented to the insertion in the Statute of certain qualifications in so far as their Constitutions were concerned, and consequently the United Kingdom Parliament was constitutionally competent to enact the Statute as thus qualified in respect of those Dominions. But the Irish Free State, as also the Union of South Africa, had refrained from requesting the insertion of any such qualifying clauses, and therefore the United Kingdom Parliament was not constitutionally competent to enact the Statute with any such qualifications in respect of the Free State or the Union.

At the same time it is necessary to emphasize that, although the United Kingdom Parliament was not constitutionally competent to enact clauses in respect of the Free State unless the Free State had requested and consented to the enactment thereof, it was not constitutionally bound to enact any and every clause which the Free State had requested and consented to. It might

---

[1] e.g. Mr. Winston Churchill's speeches (259 *H.C. Deb.*, 5 s., 1188–99, and 260 *H.C. Deb.*, 5 s., 326–31) and Lord Salisbury's speech (83 *H.L. Deb.*, 5 s., 187–95). Contrast the maiden speech of Mr. D. Somervell (as he then was), 259 *H.C. Deb.*, 5 s., 1222–6, and Mr. Amery's speech, *ibid.*, especially 1205.

[2] Adopting para. 54 of *O.D.L. Report*.

refuse to enact such clauses unless and until the Free State agreed to some amendment in accordance with the wishes of the United Kingdom Parliament. If, and in so far as, Colonel Gretton and Lord Danesfort intended by their moving of amendments, to do no more than secure that Parliament should not pass the clauses as they stood, but should refrain from taking any action in respect of the Free State until the Free State requested and consented to the enactment of the clauses with safeguards, then their action would appear to be in accordance with constitutional convention. But in so far as they proposed the enactment of the clauses with safeguards which the Free State had not requested and consented to, they intended action contrary to constitutional convention. And in fact no such request and consent was forthcoming from the Free State. The United Kingdom Government was bound, therefore, to resist the amendments of Colonel Gretton and Lord Danesfort. When, at one stage in the discussion of the Statute of Westminster Bill, it looked as if the Secretary of State for the Dominions was proposing to consider the possibility of including some such amendment, there was an immediate protest to the Prime Minister from Mr. Cosgrave, the President of the Executive Council of the Irish Free State.[1] Finally, when the Solicitor-General had made clear the impossibility of accepting any amendment which had not been requested and consented to by the Free State, the amendment in the House of Commons was defeated by 360 votes to 50.[2] Lord

[1] The letter was quoted in full by the Secretary of State for the Dominions in the House of Commons (260 *H.C. Deb.*, 5 s., 311). It is printed in Keith, *Speeches and Documents on the British Dominions*, p. 302.

[2] 260 *H.C. Deb.*, 5 s., 354.

Danesfort's similar amendment in the House of Lords was withdrawn after debate.[1]

To what extent, then, did the unqualified application of the Statute to the Free State remove or make possible the·removal of those inequalities of status to which the Free State was subject theretofore? The question must be answered first from the standpoint of the 'Irish' view, illustrated in *Ryan's Case*, of the legal basis of the Free State Constitution, and second from the standpoint of the 'British' view, illustrated in *Moore's Case*, in the sense in which those two views have been expounded in Chapter IV above.

2

Before the passing of the Statute, the United Kingdom Parliament was bound in convention, on the Irish view, not to exercise its legal power to make laws for the Free State except with the request and consent of the Free State. That Parliament had in effect bound itself in 1922[2] not to make such laws except where, 'in accordance with constitutional practice, Parliament would make laws affecting other self-governing Dominions', and the declaration of constitutional practice finally made in 1930 therefore placed the position beyond doubt. The passing of the Statute meant the reaffirmation of the conventional rule in paragraph 3 of the Preamble, and the enactment of the new rule of construction in section 4.

Before the passing of the Statute, the Free State was subject, on this Irish view, to the overriding supremacy of United Kingdom legislation extending to the Free State by express words or necessary intendment, in

[1] 83 *H.L. Deb.*, 5 s., 245.
[2] Irish Free State Constitution Act, 1922, s. 4.

accordance with the provisions of the Colonial Laws Validity Act, 1865. But the Irish Free State (Agreement) Act, 1922, and the Irish Free State Constitution Act, 1922, of the United Kingdom Parliament, did not so extend to the Free State. The Constituent Act and its scheduled Constitution and Treaty, enacted by the Third Dáil, were unaffected by the provisions of either of these United Kingdom Acts or of the Colonial Laws Validity Act itself. The passing of the Statute had the effect of removing the fetter imposed by the Colonial Laws Validity Act upon the Oireachtas, and the Oireachtas was empowered by the Statute to repeal or amend any existing or future Act of the United Kingdom Parliament to which a Free State law, otherwise valid, was repugnant, in so far as such United Kingdom Act formed part of the law of the Free State.[1] But in as much as the Constituent Act and its Schedules did not form part of an Act of the United Kingdom Parliament extending to the Free State as part of the law of the Free State, the power of the Oireachtas to amend or repeal the Constituent Act, the Constitution, and the Treaty was not directly increased or diminished by the passing of the Statute. The constituent power of the Oireachtas was confined as before to 'amendments of this Constitution within the terms of the Scheduled Treaty'.[2] It followed therefore that the Constitution (Removal of Oath) Act, passed by the Oireachtas in 1933,[3] in so far as it purported to repeal section 2 of the Constituent Act was *ultra vires*, and in so far as it purported to delete the

---

[1] By s. 2, and adopting the conservative interpretation.

[2] Article 50 of the Constitution.

[3] No. 6 of 1933. The Bill is printed in Keith, *Speeches and Documents on the British Dominions*, pp. 469-70.

words 'within the terms of the Scheduled Treaty' from Article 50 of the Constitution was ineffective.[1] The supremacy of the Treaty was asserted in section 2 of the Constituent Act, and the Oireachtas obtained no power to amend the Constituent Act from the passing of the Statute.

On the other hand, in so far as the passing of the Statute made any alteration in the position of Canada 'in relation to the Imperial Parliament and Government and otherwise', and in particular, in so far as the passing of the Statute made any alteration in 'the law, practice, and constitutional usage governing the relationship of the Crown or the representative of the Crown and of the Imperial Parliament to the Dominion of Canada', to that extent, it might be argued, the passing of the Statute altered the position of the Irish Free State 'in relation to the Imperial Parliament and Government and other-wise', and altered 'the law, practice and constitutional usage governing the relationship of the Crown or the representative of the Crown and of the Imperial Parlia-ment' to the Irish Free State. For, as has been seen, Article 2 of the Treaty had conferred upon the Irish Free State the same status as the Dominion of Canada in these respects. Unless, therefore, it was to be argued that the status of the Free State was the status of Canada in 1921 'put into cold storage',[2] to use Mr. Amery's words, any development in the status of Canada which was brought about by the passing of the Statute would extend also to the Free State. Thus, if as a result of the passing of the Statute, certain of the inequalities of status to which Canada had been subject theretofore were re-

[1] Cf. FitzGibbon J. in *The State (Ryan)* v. *Lennon,* [1935] I.R. 170 at pp. 226–7. [2] 259 *H.C. Deb.,* 5 s., 1205.

moved or made possible of removal by Canada, the Irish
Free State would acquire power to remove such inequalities and could exercise it in complete conformity
with the Constituent Act and the Constitution, for any
such amendments would be within the terms of the
Scheduled Treaty.

The consequences of this argument may be seen when
the power of reservation is considered. Before the passing
of the Statute the Free State was subject to discretionary
reservation,[1] as Canada was also, and to obligatory
reservation under the terms of the Merchant Shipping
Act, 1894, and the Colonial Courts of Admiralty Act,
1890. The inequality involved in the exercise of the
former power was abolished by convention in 1930.[2]
But in law it was not abolished. The Oireachtas, therefore, lacked power to repeal reservation from the Constitution, so long as reservation remained in Canada.
In 1930 an undertaking was given, moreover, that the
United Kingdom Government would ask Parliament to
pass legislation abolishing reservation, if so requested by
Canada. But the adoption of a convention did not alter
the law. The passing of the Statute made no alteration
in the position. The Canadian Parliament obtained no
power under the Statute to amend the British North
America Act, 1867, in which the requirement for reservation was enacted. In law reservation remained, and
until it was removed from the Canadian Constitution the
Free State must, in law, remain subject to it. On this
view, therefore, the Act of the Oireachtas in 1933[3] which
purported to delete from the Constitution the power of

---

[1] Article 41 of the Constitution.
[2] The power had in fact never been exercised. Keith, *J.C.L.*, 3rd series,
vol. xvi, p. 137.   [3] No. 44 of 1933.

reservation, and also the power of the Representative of the Crown to refuse assent to Bills, was invalid. In respect of reservation requirements under the Merchant Shipping Act and the Colonial Courts of Admiralty Act, however, the Statute removed these legal inequalities completely.[1] On the other hand, if the Oireachtas lacked power to legislate with extra-territorial effect (which was doubtful), the Statute removed the lack.[2] No inequality of status had been involved in any case.[3]

In exercising its legislative power the Oireachtas was subject, on the Irish view, to rules similar to those which bound the other Dominions. Thus, in virtue of the convention agreed upon in 1926, projected legislation by the Oireachtas which might affect the interests of other Members of the Commonwealth, should be preceded by consultation between the Free State Government and the Governments of the other affected Members of the Commonwealth. The Statute made no alteration in this conventional rule. Then there were the three rules regulating the passing of legislation to alter the law touching the Succession to the Throne or the Royal Style and Titles. In the first place, in virtue of the convention agreed upon in 1930, any such legislation by the Oireachtas must receive the assent of the Parliaments of all the other Dominions and of the United Kingdom. The Oireachtas approved this convention. The Statute affirmed it in paragraph 2 of the Preamble, so far as the United Kingdom Parliament was concerned. In the second place, in virtue of the same convention of 1930, any such legislation passed by the Parliament of any other Dominion or of the United Kingdom must receive the assent of the Oireachtas and of the Parlia-

[1] By ss. 5 and 6.   [2] By s. 3.   [3] See p. 119 above.

ments of all the other Members of the Commonwealth. The Oireachtas approved this convention also. The Statute affirmed it in paragraph 2 of the Preamble, so far as the United Kingdom Parliament was concerned. In the third place, in virtue of the above convention combined with a further convention of 1930, any such legislation passed by the United Kingdom Parliament which was intended to extend to the Free State as part of the law of the Free State would require not only the assent of the Oireachtas and of the Parliaments of all the other Dominions, but also the request and consent of the Free State. The Oireachtas had approved this rule. It was affirmed also in paragraphs 2 and 3 of the Preamble, so far as the United Kingdom Parliament was concerned. Moreover, in so far as the rule required 'the request and consent of the Free State', the Statute supplemented it with the rule of construction enacted in section 4.

It would seem that the Oireachtas possessed power to regulate the Succession to the Throne, but it lacked power to pass a law to abolish the monarchy completely in respect of the Free State, to secede from the Commonwealth or to abolish the office of Representative of the Crown, so long as Canada accepted the Monarchy, and the Governor-General, as such legislation would be contrary to the Articles of Agreement. It must be maintained, therefore, that, on the above line of argument, the Act[1] of the Oireachtas in 1936 which purported to abolish the office of Governor-General was invalid, though the Act[2] which recognized and regulated the functions of the King in the external relations of the Free State was valid.

[1] Constitution (Amendment No. 27) Act, 1936. No. 57 of 1936.
[2] Executive Authority (External Relations) Act, 1936. No. 58 of 1936.

Before the passing of the Statute, the Free State was subject, as was Canada also, to the appeal by special leave to the Judicial Committee.[1] The Oireachtas lacked power, so long as the appeal existed in respect of Canada, to restrict or abolish the appeal. The Statute made a change in this position. For it conferred power on the Canadian Parliament to abolish the appeal so far as Canada was concerned, since the appeal was regulated not by the British North America Acts, 1867 to 1930, but by the Acts of 1833 and 1844. The Canadian Parliament abolished the appeal in criminal cases in 1933.[2] The subsequent Act of 1933[3] by which the Oireachtas purported to abolish the appeal was, accordingly, valid, at any rate so far as criminal cases were concerned. The amendment was within the terms of the Scheduled Treaty, on the view that the status of Canada to which the Irish Free State was to conform was not the status of Canada in 1921 but the status of Canada in 1933.

In respect of foreign relations the Free State had been in complete control since its acquisition in 1931 of its own Great Seal and the right of direct access to the King. No formal intervention by a Secretary of State in the United Kingdom was necessary for the conclusion of international conventions between the Free State and foreign countries, and complete equality of status was thus secured.

It is submitted, then, that if one starts from the view of the legal basis of the Free State Constituent Act and its Scheduled Constitution and Treaty which was explicitly or implicitly adopted by the Supreme Court of

---

[1] *Performing Rights Society* v. *Bray Urban District Council*, [1930] A.C. 377.
[2] The Canadian legislation was upheld in *British Coal Corporation* v. *the King*, [1935] A.C. 500.   [3] No. 45 of 1933.

the Free State in *Ryan's Case*, then some such consequences as those outlined above must follow from the enactment of the Statute of Westminster and its application to the Free State. On such a view the Statute of Westminster did not remove or make possible the removal of all the legal inequalities of status to which the Free State was subject theretofore. The legal status of the Free State, on this view, is something less than the legal status of South Africa, in relation to the United Kingdom Parliament and Government. It may be well to repeat here that this particular Irish view, which involved the acceptance of Dominion Status and an Irish Free State of 26 counties, had never been accepted by Mr. de Valera and his supporters, who demanded Republican Status and a United Ireland, and who regarded the Constitution and the Treaty as invalid in so far as they failed to embody this ideal. On Mr. de Valera's view, therefore, the Acts referred to above, which purported to abolish inequalities from the Constitution, and which were passed during his term of office, were all valid in spite of their conflict with the Treaty, because they brought the Constitution into conformity with Republican Status.

3

It is proposed to consider next the effect of the Statute on the legal status of the Free State if the matter is approached from the view of the legal basis of the Free State Constitution which was adopted in *Moore's Case*. Put shortly, the view in that case was that the Constituent Act, the Constitution, and the Articles of Agreement obtained force of law in Great Britain and Ireland by reason of the passing of an Act of the Imperial Parliament, and that they owed their validity to the same authority. Section 2 of the Constituent Act and Article 50 of the Constitution confined the Oireachtas to the making of laws and the amendment of the Constitution within the terms of the Scheduled Treaty. There were two obstacles which prevented the Oireachtas from removing this restriction upon its powers. First such legislation would have gone beyond the *area* of its powers, for the Oireachtas was confined to amendments of the Constitution, and was not empowered therefore to amend the Constituent Act. Second, within this area, it was confined to amendments of the Constitution in accordance with the terms of the Scheduled Treaty. The first obstacle was not fully discussed in *Moore's Case*, though it appears to have been implied in the judgment. But it might be argued perhaps that their Lordships did not recognize an obstacle of area in the way of the Oireachtas. There is no doubt, however, that they did recognize the second obstacle. In their view any legislation of the Oireachtas which conflicted with the Articles of Agreement was repugnant to the terms of an Imperial Act, viz. the Irish Free State Constitution Act, 1922, and to the extent of such repugnancy was, by the Colonial Laws Validity Act, void and inoperative.

What was the effect of the passing of the Statute? There must be two answers to the question, corresponding to the two views which may be taken of the effect of section 2 (2) of the Statute. On the conservative view, that the area of power was unaltered, all that section 2 (2) of the Statute did was to empower the Oireachtas to repeal or amend any Act of the United Kingdom Parliament (so far as it was part of the law of the Free State), to which an Act of the Oireachtas, passed after the enactment of the Statute and otherwise valid, was repugnant. It did not empower the Oireachtas to repeal or amend every Act whatsoever of the United Kingdom Parliament so far as it was part of the law of the Free State. Now an Act of the Oireachtas to be valid must be within the area of its powers, i.e. it must not purport to amend the Constituent Act and thus go beyond the bounds of the Constitution. On this view, therefore, the Oireachtas remained confined, after the passing of the Statute as before, to making laws and to amending the Constitution within the terms of the Scheduled Treaty, but within this area the fetter imposed by the Colonial Laws Validity Act was removed. The effect of the Statute upon the legal status of the Free State was, on this interpretation of section 2 (2), similar to its effect if the Irish view in *Ryan's Case* were adopted. The Oireachtas acquired from the passing of the Statute no increased power to remove legal inequalities except in so far as the passing of the Statute had removed, or had conferred upon Canada a power to remove, the same legal inequalities in respect of Canada.

On this line of argument, it would follow that the Constitution (Removal of Oath) Act, 1933,[1] was invalid, on the ground that, as it was already *ultra vires*, the provisions of section 2 (2) of the Statute did not avail to make it valid; the Act of 1933,[2] which purported to abolish the power of reservation, and the Act of 1936,[3] which purported to abolish the office of Governor-General, were invalid on the ground that they conflicted with the Articles of Agreement; but the Act of 1933,[4] which purported to abolish the appeal by special

[1] No. 6 of 1933.   [2] No. 44 of 1933.
[3] No. 57 of 1936.   [4] No. 45 of 1933.

leave to the Judicial Committee, was valid, at any rate in so far as appeals in criminal cases were concerned, because Canada had acquired from section 2 of the Statute power to abolish such appeals, and had exercised that power.[1]

But when the Judicial Committee came to decide in *Moore's Case* whether this Act of the Oireachtas of 1933, purporting to abolish the appeal by special leave, was a valid enactment or not, it did not follow the above line of argument, although the validity of the Canadian legislation of 1933 was before the Board for decision in the *British Coal Corporation Case* at the same time, and a decision of the Irish question based upon a decision in the Canadian case would have been natural. Instead, their Lordships adopted what appears to be the liberal interpretation of section 2 (2) of the Statute. They held that the Statute gave power to the Oireachtas to repeal or amend the Constituent Act and that Acts of the Oireachtas, passed since the enactment of the Statute, which contained amendments of the Constitution which were not within the terms of the Treaty, were, in virtue of the Statute, valid enactments. 'The effect of the Statute of Westminster', they said, 'was to remove the fetter which lay upon the Irish Free State Legislature by reason of the Colonial Laws Validity Act. That Legislature can now pass Acts repugnant to an Imperial Act. In this case they have done so.' The language here is ambiguous. If by 'Imperial Act' is meant any Imperial Act, then it is possible that the Judicial Committee regarded section 2 (2) of the Statute as extending the area of the powers of the Dominion legislature, and abolishing the

[1] Cap. 53 of 1932–3. The contrary view was expressed by Lord Hailsham, Dec. 6, 1933, in 90 *H.L.Deb.*, 5 s., 337.

former restrictions upon area. On the other hand, it may equally well be that they did not recognize that any restriction upon area had existed for the Oireachtas before the passing of the Statute. In that case, whether they took the wider view of section 2 (2) or the narrower, the result would be the same. There is nothing in the judgment to show conclusively what their Lordships intended. The question of area is nowhere explicitly discussed. If one may hazard a guess, it looks as if no restriction of area was recognized by their Lordships. If that is so, we are still left without any indication whether they preferred the wider or the narrower interpretation of section 2 (2). Here again, one may guess that they favoured the wider view.

On the view of section 2 adopted by the Judicial Committee in *Moore's Case*, the effect of the Statute upon the legal status of the Free State was sweeping. Put shortly, the Statute removed or made possible the removal of all the inequalities of status in strict law to which the Free State was subject theretofore, with the exception, of course, of the inequality involved in the continued existence of a power in the United Kingdom Parliament to legislate for the Free State. It was true that the Free State was bound by a convention as an international obligation in the Articles of Agreement, which imposed certain inequalities upon the Free State. But in strict law—municipal law—those obligations were removable in virtue of the powers conferred by the Statute.

In consequence of section 2 of the Statute, the Constitution (Removal of Oath) Act, 1933, which purported to repeal section 2 of the Constituent Act and to delete the words 'within the terms of the Scheduled Treaty' from Article 50 of the Constitution, was a valid enactment. And since 'the Statute of Westminster gave to the Irish Free State a power under which they could abrogate the Treaty, and . .. as a matter of law, they have availed themselves of that power',[1] the Act of 1933[2] repealing reservation and the power of the Governor-General to refuse assent to Bills, the Act of 1933[3] abolishing the appeal by special leave, and the Act of 1936 abolishing the office of Governor-General,[4] though repugnant to the Articles of Agreement, were valid enactments. It would follow, too, that any enactment of the Oireachtas to abolish the monarchy, or to provide for secession from the Commonwealth,[5] or to declare neutrality, would in strict law be valid.

On either British view of the effect of section 2 of the Statute, it would be accepted that the Free State was subject before the passing of the Statute to the inequalities involved in the undefined lack of power to legislate with extra-territorial effect, and in the reservation requirements of the Merchant Shipping Act and the Colonial Courts of Admiralty Act, and that these inequalities were removed by sections 3, 5, and 6 of the Statute.

In the same way the equality of the Free State in the conduct of foreign relations as a result of the acquisition of a Great Seal for the Free State was acknowledged on either British view, while the rules regulating projected legislation by the Oireachtas which might affect the interests of some other Member of the Commonwealth, and legislation altering the law touching the Succession

---

[1] *Moore's Case* [1935] A.C. 484 at p. 499.   [2] No. 44 of 1933.
[3] No. 45 of 1933.   [4] No. 57 of 1936.
[5] A contrary view is expressed in *Murray* v. *Parkes*, [1942] 2 K.B. 123

to the Throne or the Royal Style and Titles, would be stated in identical form with that in which they have already been stated for the Irish view.

4

It remains to consider what were the legal powers of the Free State, under the Constitution of 1922, to abolish the Constitution and to replace it with a new Constitution. The question is one of practical importance, for in 1937 a new Constitution was prepared by the Free State Government under Mr. de Valera; it was approved by Dáil Eireann; and it was accepted by a majority of the electorate at a referendum. This new Constitution established a new state called Éire, or, in the English language, Ireland,[1] the national territory of which consisted of the whole island of Ireland, its islands and the territorial seas.[2] However, pending the re-integration of the national territory, though without prejudice to the right of the Parliament and Government established by the new Constitution to exercise jurisdiction over the whole of that territory, the laws enacted by that Parliament are to have the like area and extent of application as the laws of the Irish Free State and the like extra-territorial effect.[3] And further, the new state of Ireland is declared to be 'a sovereign, independent, democratic state'.[4] The Constitution provides for a President of Ireland,[5] to be elected by a direct vote of the people, and to hold office for seven years, with the right to stand for re-election once only. The President appoints the Prime Minister (or Taoiseach) on the nomination of the Dáil, and the other ministers on the nomination of the Prime

[1] Article 4.   [2] Article 2.   [3] Article 3.
[4] Article 5.   [5] Article 12.

Minister with the previous approval of the Dáil.[1] The
Oireachtas consists of the President and two Houses, a
Dáil and a Senate; the sole and exclusive power of
making laws for the state is vested in the Oireachtas; no
other legislative authority has power to make laws for
the state. Every law enacted by the Oireachtas which
is in any respect repugnant to the Constitution shall, to
the extent only of such repugnancy, be invalid.[2] A system
of responsible government is set up and defined, and it is
expressly stated that the Government shall be responsible
to Dáil Eireann.[3]

But while it is clear that the Constitution of 1937
confers upon Ireland the status of a sovereign, independent state, it is also clear that it does not necessarily exclude the acceptance by this sovereign, independent
state of Dominion Status, at any rate in so far as Dominion Status has been defined in conventional terms. The
three conventional requirements of Dominion Status
were, it will be recalled, first, common allegiance along
with Great Britain to the same King; secondly, equality
of status with Great Britain; and thirdly, free association
with Great Britain in the British Commonwealth of
Nations. There is no doubt that under the Constitution
of 1937 Ireland possesses equal status with Great
Britain; it is in no way subordinate in any aspect of its
domestic or external affairs. But is it freely associated
with Great Britain in the British Commonwealth? And
does it owe allegiance to the same King? It was
possible, until April 18, 1949, to answer Yes. For the
Constitution provided[4] that 'for the purpose of the
exercise of any executive function of the State in or in

[1] Article 13. [2] Article 15.
[3] Article 28. [4] Article 29 (4) ii.

connexion with its external relations, the Government may, to such extent and subject to such conditions, if any, as may be determined by law, avail of or adopt any organ, instrument or method of procedure used or adopted for the like purpose by the members of any group or league of nations with which the State is or becomes associated for the purpose of international co-operation in matters of common concern'. This Article, which authorized the participation by the Irish Government in such institutions as the Council of the League of Nations or the Imperial Economic Committee or the International Postal Union, appears to authorize also the use by the Government in external affairs of the same King as Great Britain. For the law, as enacted in the Executive Authority (External Relations) Act, 1936, provided that so long as the Irish Free State was associated with the other nations of the British Commonwealth, and so long as the King recognized by those nations as the symbol of their co-operation continued to act on behalf of each of them (on the advice of their several governments), for the purposes of the appointment of diplomatic and consular representatives and the conclusion of international agreements, 'the King so recognized may and is hereby authorized to act on behalf of the Irish Free State for the like purposes as and when advised by the Executive Council so to do'.

So the position stood until April 18, 1949. Eire was freely associated with the members of the Commonwealth and recognized the King as the symbol of their co-operation. This was rather diluted 'allegiance' but it was not complete separation or complete republicanism. Eire still seemed to be either a republican kingdom or a monarchical republic. It was not until April 18, 1949, when the Executive Authority (External Relations) Act, 1936, was repealed by the coming into force of the Republic of Ireland Act, 1948, that it was possible to say that Eire was a republic and that she was no longer a member of the Commonwealth. (See further pp. 290 ff. below.) None the less, by agreement among the members of the Commonwealth and Eire, it was proposed that Eire should not be regarded as a foreign country or its citizens as aliens. So, after April 18, 1949, a new anomaly replaced an old. Instead of 'include me out' it was now 'exclude me in'.

It is clear that the Constitution of 1937 conflicts with the terms of the Treaty of 1921. It is necessary to ask therefore what authority the Free State possessed to enact such a Constitution. On the Irish view of the legal basis of the Constitution of 1922, which was expounded in *Ryan's Case*, it would seem that the Supreme Court considered that the Third Dáil's authority to enact the Constitution came from the people.[1] It would follow therefore that the people themselves, or a Constituent Assembly authorized by the people, possessed authority to establish a new Constitution. On this argument the Constitution of 1937, since it received the approval of a majority of the people, is lawful and supreme, in spite of the fact that it conflicts with the Treaty of 1921. This line of argument seems to be accepted by the Supreme Court of Eire at the present time. It accepts the Constitution of 1937 as supreme, and recognizes that it has been 'enacted' by the people. (See, for example, Sullivan C.J. in [1940] I.R. 470 at p. 478.)

[1] FitzGibbon J., [1935] I.R. 170 at p. 226.

On the Irish view which Mr. de Valera and his supporters have maintained since 1922, supreme authority to enact a Constitution is derived similarly from the people. They differed from the view exemplified in *Ryan's Case* only upon the question whether the Constituent Assembly of 1922 was empowered by the people to enact a Constitution repugnant to the Republican Declaration of 1916. In conformity with Mr. de Valera's view the Constitution of 1937 was submitted to the people, and their approval of it by a majority gave it lawful authority. It was declared in the Preamble that 'We, the people of Éire, . . . Do hereby adopt, enact, and give to ourselves this Constitution.'[1]

What is the position from the point of view adopted on the British side? It has been maintained that, before the passing of the Statute of Westminster, the Oireachtas possessed no power to amend the Constituent Act at all, and no power to amend the Constitution itself in any way repugnant to the Articles of Agreement. On the British view the people were not recognized to possess supreme legal authority to amend or abolish the Constitution or the Constituent Act. Before the passing of the Statute, therefore, neither the Oireachtas nor the people had power to enact a Constitution in the terms which are found in the Constitution of 1937. Did the Statute confer such a power? The answer to this question depends upon the view taken of section 2 (2) of the Statute. If the Oireachtas was restricted in the area of its powers before the Statute, and if section 2 (2) does

[1] Article 6 of the Constitution declares that 'all powers of government, legislative, executive and judicial, derive, under God, from the people, whose right it is to designate the rulers of the State and, in final appeal, to decide all questions of national policy, according to the requirements of the common good'.

not extend the area of the powers of a Dominion Parliament, then the Oireachtas acquired no power from the Statute to enact a Constitution in terms repugnant to the Articles of Agreement. If, on the other hand, no restriction of area existed beforehand or if, granting such a restriction, section 2 (2) of the Statute is interpreted, as it appears to be interpreted in *Moore's Case*, as extending the area, then the Oireachtas has full power to abolish the Constitution of 1922 and to replace it with a new Constitution in such terms as it thinks fit.

But did the Oireachtas *enact* the Constitution of 1937? It did not. It merely approved it. So that the validity of the Constitution cannot be demonstrated by considering the powers of the Oireachtas to enact it. The Constitution declares itself to have been enacted by the people of Ireland. Did the Oireachtas, then, authorize the people to enact it? Apparently not. The Plebiscite (Draft Constitution) Act, No. 16 of 1937 arranged for a plebiscite but said nothing about what effect an affirmative vote would have. So here again a consideration of the powers of the Oireachtas under the Statute is irrelevant. What of the powers of the people? The Statute gave no powers to the people of a Dominion to repeal Imperial Acts. The 'enactment' of the Constitution of Eire by the people is, on the British view, a revolution in law. The result of this revolution was recognized by an executive declaration of the British and Dominion Governments at the close of 1937, and it may be assumed that this will be considered sufficient to justify courts in the United Kingdom and the Dominions in recognizing the validity of the Constitution of Eire.

XII

THE STATUTE AND THE MONARCHY

I

REFERENCE has been made in the preceding chapters to the conventions and the rules of strict law which were to regulate action taken by the Parliaments of the Dominions and of the United Kingdom to make any alteration in the law touching the Succession to the Throne or the Royal Style and Titles. It has seemed necessary in those chapters to restate the rules as each Dominion has been dealt with because, although the fundamental conventions remained the same in respect of all Members of the British Commonwealth, the rules of strict law, in so far at least as they were embodied in the Statute of Westminster, differed in their application to each Dominion. It is proposed in this chapter, now that these differences and the reasons for them have been made clear, to collect the rules together in a brief statement. There are two reasons which appear to make this desirable. In the first place, the Monarchy is the sole remaining institution the existence of which is agreed to be essential to the concept of Dominion Status. For, in the definition of Dominion Status, an essential element was found to be 'common allegiance to the Crown'—and 'the Crown', it may be assumed, meant the Monarchy. As long, therefore, as 'common allegiance to the Crown' remained an essential element in the definition of Dominion Status and of Membership of the British Commonwealth, for so long was the maintenance and regulation of the institution of Monarchy a matter of equal concern to all.[1] The maintenance and regulation of other institutions, such as the Imperial Conference or the Imperial War Graves Commission, might also be a matter of equal concern to all. Such institutions might be necessary, or useful, or desirable. But the Monarchy was the only institution the existence of which was essential. It is important, therefore, that the rules which were intended to regulate action by the Dominions and the United Kingdom in respect of this essential, common institution should be accorded separate treatment. In the second place, these rules acquired unexpected importance at the close of 1936 upon the abdication of King Edward VIII, and it is therefore of some interest to notice whether or not the action taken by the United Kingdom and the Dominions at that time was in accordance with the rules laid down.[2]

The rules appear to be three. In the first place, in virtue of a constitutional convention declared in 1930,[3] any legislation by a Dominion Parliament altering the law touching the Succession to the Throne or the Royal Style and Titles, required the assent of the Parliaments of all the other Dominions and of the United Kingdom. That convention was approved by all the Dominion Parliaments;[4] it was affirmed by the United Kingdom Parliament in paragraph 2 of the Preamble to the Statute; and as thus affirmed extended to all the Domi-

[1] *O.D.L. Report*, para. 59.

[2] Among the many discussions of this subject which have appeared since the Abdication, the reader may with most profit choose to consult the articles by Professor K. H. Bailey in *Politica*, March and June 1938. With these may be compared R. T. E. Latham, in *A Survey of British Commonwealth Affairs*, vol. i, Appendix.

[3] Adopting para. 60 of *O.D.L. Report*.

[4] When they requested the insertion of the convention in the Preamble to the Statute.

nions. It was not enacted in the Statute. When the Union of South Africa included paragraph 2 of the Preamble in the Schedule to the Status Act, the rule became, for the Union, not only a convention, but also a rule of strict law, but, as thus enacted, the rule amounted to no more than a declaration of 'the established constitutional position'. Apart from this exception, the rule remained a convention.

In the second place, in virtue of the same constitutional convention declared in 1930, any legislation by the United Kingdom Parliament altering the law touching the Succession to the Throne or the Royal Style and Titles, which was not intended to extend to the Dominions as part of the law of the Dominions, required the assent of the Parliaments of all the Dominions. This convention likewise was approved by all the Dominion Parliaments; it was affirmed by the United Kingdom Parliament in paragraph 2 of the Preamble; and as thus affirmed extended to all the Dominions. It was not enacted in the Statute, but, here again, in so far as South Africa was concerned, the rule was not only a convention but also a rule of strict law, through its enactment in the Schedule to the Status Act. Apart from this exception, the rule remained a convention.

The third rule begins with a combination of the convention from which the above two rules were deduced, and by which the Dominions as well as the United Kingdom were bound, with another convention[1] which bound the United Kingdom only. The third rule required, in virtue of these two conventions declared in 1930, that any legislation by the United Kingdom Parliament altering the law touching the Succession to the Throne

---

[1] Adopting para. 54 of *O.D.L. Report*.

or the Royal Style and Titles, which was intended to extend to any Dominion as part of the law of that Dominion, must obtain not only the assent of the Parliaments of all the Dominions, but also the request and consent of the Dominion to which such legislation was to extend. The conventions which combined to make this rule were approved by the Parliaments of all the Dominions; they were affirmed by the Parliament of the United Kingdom in paragraphs 2 and 3 of the Preamble to the Statute, and as thus affirmed they extended to all the Dominions.

But the third rule went further. For, so much of the rule as required the 'request and consent of the Dominion' to which such United Kingdom legislation was to extend, was supplemented by the rule of construction enacted in terms of strict law in section 4 of the Statute, which provided that no such United Kingdom Act should extend or be deemed to extend to a Dominion as part of the law of that Dominion unless it was expressly declared in that Act that that Dominion had requested and consented to the enactment thereof.

The third rule, in so far as it had been supplemented by the rule of strict law in section 4 of the Statute, did not apply to the Commonwealth of Australia, the Dominion of New Zealand, or Newfoundland until the Parliaments of those Dominions adopted section 4. And when the Commonwealth of Australia did adopt section 4, the 'request and consent' referred to in section 4 was required to be the request and consent of the Parliament and Government of the Commonwealth.[1] On the other hand, the request and consent referred to in the convention of 1930 and in paragraph 3 of the Preamble was not

[1] By s. 9 (3) of the Statute.

required, by any explicit rule, to be the request and consent of the Parliament and Government. In 1936, no action had yet been taken by the Parliament of the Commonwealth or of New Zealand to adopt section 4, and the rule applied to those Dominions, therefore, as a convention only. No action to adopt section 4 had been taken by the Parliament of Newfoundland either, but as that Parliament had ceased to exist in 1933, it was impossible to operate the rule in respect of Newfoundland in 1936.

Canada, South Africa, and the Irish Free State were in a different position. The third rule, as supplemented by the rule of strict law in section 4 of the Statute, extended to Canada, South Africa, and the Free State. For those Dominions it had the force, therefore, not only of a convention but also of, in part, a rule of strict law. In the case of South Africa three further propositions must be advanced. First, in so far as paragraphs 2 and 3 of the Preamble to the Statute were enacted in the Schedule to the Status Act, it might be argued that the whole of the third rule had the force of strict law in so far as the Union was concerned, and not merely that part of it which was enacted in section 4 of the Statute. At the same time, as has been mentioned above, the two paragraphs as thus enacted did no more than declare the 'established constitutional position'. Secondly, in virtue of section 2 of the Status Act, no Act of the United Kingdom Parliament might extend to the Union as part of the law of the Union unless it was extended thereto by an Act of the Union Parliament. There was, therefore, in the case of the Union, an additional requirement which must be fulfilled before an Act of the United Kingdom Parliament, altering the law touching the Succession to the Throne or the Royal Style and Titles, could be deemed to extend to the Union as part of the law of the Union. Not only must the assent of the Parliament of the Union and of the Parliaments of all the other Dominions be obtained, and not only must the request and consent of the Union be declared in the Act, but also that Act must be extended to the Union by an Act of the Parliament of the Union. Thirdly, in virtue of section 5 of the Status Act, the 'King' in the Union was to mean that person who was the heir and successor of Edward VII 'in the sovereignty of the United Kingdom of Great Britain and Ireland as determined by the laws relating to the succession of the Crown of the United Kingdom of Great Britain and Ireland'. It would appear to follow from this section that any alteration by the United Kingdom Parliament in the law touching the Succession to the Throne in respect of the United Kingdom,[1] would automatically take effect in the Union by the law of the Union as enacted in section 5 of the Status Act, though it would not extend to the Union as part of the law of the Union until expressly extended thereto by an Act of the Union Parliament.

Four small points may be mentioned before passing to consider the application of these rules in 1936. In the first place, it will have been noticed that, except in the case of Australia, and then only when section 4 of the Statute is adopted by the Commonwealth Parliament, 'the request and consent of the Dominion' to which reference was made in the third rule, was nowhere

---

[1] Assuming that 'Great Britain and Ireland' meant 'Great Britain and Northern Ireland', for that is the only 'United Kingdom' known since 1927 to the law touching the Succession to the Throne or the Royal Style and Titles.

explicitly required to be the request and consent of the Parliament or of the Government or of the Parliament and Government of the Dominion.[1] The agency through which the request and consent of the Dominion were to be expressed was left undefined.

In the second place, the 'assent' of the Parliaments of the United Kingdom and of the Dominions, which was required to any alteration in the law touching the Succession to the Throne or the Royal Style and Titles, was not necessarily to be prior or previous assent. On the contrary, all that the rule required was that if an alteration was made by any Parliament the assent of all the other Parliaments must be obtained. It was immaterial whether the formal assent was given prior or subsequent to the making of an alteration by any one Parliament, though it was obviously essential that it should be known informally and beforehand whether a proposed alteration would be likely to obtain the assent of all the Parliaments. If the alteration was made, and the assent was refused, then by constitutional convention the alteration must be repealed.

In the third place, it was nowhere required in the rules that the 'assent' of the other Parliaments to such an alteration in the law by any one Parliament should be recited or declared in the Act making the alteration.

In the fourth place, in so far as 'request and consent' of a Dominion was required only by convention before the United Kingdom Parliament might pass such an Act so as to extend to the Dominion as part of the law thereof, there was no necessity that this 'request and consent' should be declared in that Act. It was only in virtue of

[1] In the case of South Africa, however, s. 2 of the Status Act involved consent by an Act of the Union Parliament.

section 4 that no such Act should be deemed to extend to a Dominion unless there was an express declaration in the Act that that Dominion had requested and consented to the enactment thereof.

2

To what extent were these rules applied at the abdication of Edward VIII in 1936? The initial fact was that an alteration in the law touching the Succession to the Throne was about to be made by the United Kingdom Parliament. The reaction of each Dominion must be treated in turn.

The Government of the Dominion of Canada was in agreement with the United Kingdom Government that a change in the law regulating the Succession to the Throne, in order to exclude the issue, if any, of Edward VIII, and the descendants of that issue, was desirable and necessary. It was prepared to advise the Parliament of Canada, which was not then in session, to assent to such an alteration by the United Kingdom Parliament. But it desired also that the alteration in the law by the United Kingdom Parliament should extend to Canada as part of the law of Canada. The third of the rules stated above therefore applied. By convention the assent of the Parliament of Canada was required; by convention the request and consent of Canada was necessary if this alteration was to extend to Canada; and by section 4 of the Statute this request and consent must be declared in the Act of the United Kingdom Parliament. For this purpose the request and consent of the Government of Canada was adequate. In pursuance of these desires on the part of the Government of Canada, and in conformity with the conventional and legal rules, the Preamble to

His Majesty's Declaration of Abdication Act, 1936, recited:

And whereas, following upon the communication to his Dominions of his Majesty's said declaration and desire, the Dominion of Canada, pursuant to the provisions of section 4 of the Statute of Westminster, 1931, has requested and consented to the enactment of this Act. . . .

The Act therefore applied to Canada as part of the law of Canada, and would be so construed by a Court. Finally, there remained the necessity by constitutional convention for the assent of the Parliament of Canada to be signified to the alteration. This was carried out by a short Act passed upon the resumption of the Dominion Parliament in 1937. It is submitted, therefore, that the action of the Dominion of Canada was in complete accordance with the rules of convention and of strict law which applied to its case.[1]

The Government of the Commonwealth of Australia was in agreement with the United Kingdom Government that the alteration should be made, and it was prepared to advise the Commonwealth Parliament to give its assent to the alteration. It desired further that the Act of the United Kingdom should extend to the Commonwealth as part of the law of the Commonwealth. By constitutional convention, and by constitutional convention alone,[2] two things were therefore necessary. It

[1] Professor Kennedy has maintained that the recital of 'the request and consent' of Canada in the Abdication Act was unnecessary. (See *University of Toronto Law Journal*, vol. ii, pp. 117–19.) In his view para. 3 of the Preamble and s. 4 of the Statute have no reference to laws touching the Succession to the Throne, which are governed solely by para. 2 of the Preamble. For reasons given above the present writer is of opinion that para. 2 alone is not sufficient to cover all cases, and that para. 3, and s. 4 must be amalgamated with it in certain cases.

[2] For s. 4 of the Statute had not yet been adopted.

was necessary that the assent of the Commonwealth Parliament should be signified to the proposed alteration; and it was necessary further, if the Act making the alteration was intended to extend to the Commonwealth, that the request and consent of the Commonwealth should be signified. The former was done by a resolution of the Commonwealth Parliament on December 11, 1936, the same day upon which the Abdication Act was passed by the United Kingdom Parliament. The Preamble to the Abdication Act speaks of the assent of the 'Commonwealth of Australia', which was meant to include, evidently, the assent of the Parliament of the Commonwealth, although, as has been said, no such recital of assent was necessary. But there was no reference, in public at any rate, to the 'request and consent' of the Commonwealth, and no recital in the Preamble to the Act of such request and consent. However, such a recital was, admittedly, not required by any rule. It is not possible to say until all the correspondence has been made public whether or not the United Kingdom Parliament legislated for the Commonwealth without the request and consent of the Commonwealth. As, however, the rule was merely a convention, its non-observance would not prevent the extension of the Abdication Act to the Commonwealth as part of the law of the Commonwealth.

In the case of New Zealand, the Dominion Government were prepared to ask the Dominion Parliament to assent to the alteration, and at the same time they desired that the United Kingdom Act should extend to New Zealand as part of the law of the Dominion. The Parliament of New Zealand was called together and gave its assent to the alteration after the Abdication Act had been passed by the United Kingdom Parliament. This, it is submitted, was in complete accordance with convention. In the Preamble to the Abdication Act the 'assent' of New Zealand is recited, though such a recital was not required by any rule. The assent here referred to must mean the assent of the Government of New Zealand, though such assent was neither required to be given by any rule nor required to be recited by any rule. As in the case of Australia there is no reference to the request and consent of New Zealand, and it is as yet impossible to know whether the United Kingdom Parliament legislated without such request and consent. But the fact that such 'request and consent' is not recited in the Preamble to the Abdication Act proves nothing and breaks no rule.

The Government of the Union of South Africa was in agreement with the United Kingdom Government that an alteration in the law touching the Succession to the Throne was necessary in order to exclude the heirs of Edward VIII, though it did not think that legislation was necessary to give effect to his abdication.[1] The Union Government was prepared to ask the Union Parliament to assent to the alteration, but it did not desire that the Act of the United Kingdom Parliament making the alteration should extend to the Union as part of the law of the Union.[2] No question of 'request and consent', according to rules of convention or of strict law, arose

[1] General Hertzog, *House of Assembly Debates*, vol. 30, col. 575. On this view it was possible for George VI to be proclaimed King in the Union immediately upon the signature by Edward VIII of his Deed of Abdication, since the Throne thereby became vacant, and the Duke of York succeeded by law. It was not necessary to await legislation either by the United Kingdom Parliament or by the Union Parliament.

[2] *Ibid.*, col. 576.

therefore in the case of the Union. On the view of the Union Government there was needed the 'assent' of the Parliament of the Union to the alteration, and there was needed legislation by the Parliament of the Union to alter the Succession to the Throne so far as the Union was concerned. The Union Parliament was not in session at the time of the abdication, but the Union Government signified to the United Kingdom Government its assent to the proposed alteration 'in anticipation of parliamentary approval' and 'in so far as a change of the law of succession was involved'.[1] The assent of the Union of South Africa was recited in the Preamble to the Abdication Act, but, as has been said, such assent by a Government of a Dominion was not required by any rule, nor was its recital, whether the assent came from a Parliament or a Government, required by any rule. On the view of the effect of section 5 of the Status Act put forward in Chapter X above, the passing of the Abdication Act by the United Kingdom Parliament caused an automatic change in the occupant of the Throne so far as South Africa was concerned. It would seem, however, that this view was not accepted by the Union Government. In 1937 the Union Parliament passed an Act which gave assent to the alteration, and made such changes in the law of the Succession as were deemed necessary. Moreover, since, in the view of the Union Government, Edward VIII's abdication dated from the moment when he signed the instrument of abdication, and not from the moment when the Abdication Act of the United Kingdom Parliament received the Royal Assent, it was declared in the Union Act that the accession of George VI should date from the time

[1] Mr. Pirow, Minister of Railways and Harbours, *ibid.*, cols. 758-9.

when the instrument of abdication was signed. Retrospectively, then, the Union Act declared that George VI was King in South Africa from December 10.[1]

The Government of the Irish Free State gave no formal indication of their assent to, or dissent from, the alteration proposed to be made by the United Kingdom Parliament in the law touching the Succession to the Throne. But they indicated that they did not desire the extension of the United Kingdom Act to the Free State as part of the law of the Free State. All that was required of the Free State, therefore, was the assent of the Oireachtas to the change. There was no need for the 'request and consent' of the Free State to be recited in the Preamble to the United Kingdom Act, and there was no need for the 'assent' of the Oireachtas or of the Government to be so recited. There was, in fact, no reference to the Free State in the Preamble to the Abdication Act, and it is submitted that this was in complete accordance with the conventional and the legal rules. After the passing of the Abdication Act, the Oireachtas, on December 12, passed an Act[2] making *inter alia* the necessary change in the law of the succession so far as the Free State was concerned, and thereby indicated their assent to the alteration.[3] George VI thus succeeded to the Throne in the Free State on December 12, 1936.

[1] On the view of s. 5 of the Status Act just referred to, this legislation by the Union Parliament was necessary only in so far as it expressed the assent of the Union Parliament to the alteration, and pre-dated the accession of George VI to Dec. 10.

[2] Executive Authority (External Relations) Act.

[3] The Act of Settlement extended to the Free State in virtue of Article 73 of the Constitution and, on the Irish view, was part of the law of the Free State and alterable by the Oireachtas. (See Mr. de Valera's Speech, *Dáil Debates*, Dec. 12, 1936.)

If George VI was King in South Africa on December 10, and Edward VIII was King in the rest of the Commonwealth on that date; and if Edward VIII was King in the Irish Free State on December 11–12 and George VI was King in the rest of the Commonwealth at that time; it would appear that between December 10 and 12, 1936, the British Commonwealth was partly dismembered, though fortunately on December 12, when the Irish Free State Act received the assent of the Chairman of the Dáil, the Commonwealth was reunited by a common allegiance to the same King, George VI.

Whereas the abdication of 1936 raised questions involving legislation touching the succession to the Throne, the grant of Dominion status to India and Pakistan in 1947 involved an alteration in the Royal Style and Titles. By a Royal Proclamation on June 22, 1948, the words 'Emperor of India' were removed from the Royal Title. The assent of the Parliament of the United Kingdom was given to this change in section 7 (2) of the Indian Independence Act, 1947,[1] and it was announced in the House of Commons on July 1, 1948, that there had been 'full discussion and legislation passed by the Dominions'[2] before the Proclamation was issued.[3]

3

Towards the end of 1948 and in the early months of 1949 the position of the Monarchy in the Commonwealth became the subject of discussion when the Oireachtas passed the Republic of Ireland Act and when India announced that, in its new Constitution, it

[1] 10 & 11 Geo. 6, c. 30.
[2] Mr. Attlee's words, 452 *H.C. Deb.*, 5 s., 2379.
[3] See futher in Appendix VII below.

would adopt the republican form of government. It is necessary to consider rather carefully the significance of the decisions taken at that time so far as they affected the Crown and the Commonwealth.

When we look at the words of paragraph 2 of the Preamble to the Statute of Westminster we find that the United Kingdom and the Dominions committed themselves to three statements about their relationship to each other and to the Monarchy. In the first place they said that they were all freely associated members of the British Commonwealth of Nations. In the second place they said that they were united by a common allegiance to the Crown. It is not easy to say just precisely what each of them meant by this. 'Allegiance' is a legal term. It describes the mutual bond and obligation between the King and his subjects, or, in certain circumstances, aliens. It has a central position in the law of treason.[1] It was true, as a matter of law, that people in the Dominions and in the United Kingdom in 1931 did all owe allegiance to the King. What that allegiance involved in terms of law might not be identical in each member; it would be determined by the law of that member. What all members would agree upon, however, was that they were all kingdoms, and all kingdoms of the same king. In that sense they had a common allegiance to a Crown. In the third place they said in 1931 that they recognized the Crown as the symbol of their free association as members of the Commonwealth.

These three statements described the position of the United Kingdom and the Dominions in relation to the Crown and the Commonwealth in 1931. They were

[1] See *Joyce* v. *Director of Public Prosecutions*, [1946] A.C. 347.

not declared to be unalterable, but until they were altered, they governed the position. It should be noticed, however, that although these three statements are connected, they are distinct. The one need not necessarily involve the other two. Thus it is conceivable that the United Kingdom and the Dominions could be freely associated as members of a Commonwealth and regard the fact that they were or were not all monarchies as beside the point. Or they might believe that it was not necessary to have a 'symbol' of their free association at all, or that if they were to have a symbol the Crown or a monarchy was not the best kind of symbol. Or they might say that it was essential to recognize the Crown as the symbol of the association, but that it was not necessary that all of the members should be kingdoms. The Crown as symbol is distinct from the Crown as the object of allegiance in the legal sense. There might be thought to be a limit to this. Could one conceive of a Commonwealth with the Crown as a symbol of its members' free association, and yet all those members republics? Could there be a King without any kingdoms? It might approach the inconceivable, but it would be rash to conclude that so absurd an anomaly could not happen in the Commonwealth.

It is not suggested that all or any of the members of the Commonwealth speculated along these lines in 1926 and 1931. It is important to realize, however, that such speculation was justifiable logically. And it was not long before one member, Eire, began to demonstrate some of the possible permutations and combinations which might be attempted upon the three statements about the Crown and the Commonwealth which found a place in the Preamble to the Statute.

The Executive Authority (External Relations) Act of 1936 and the Constitution of 1937 between them could be construed to amount to an attempt by Eire to say that she would be a member of the Commonwealth and that she would recognize the King as the symbol of her free association with the other members, since that was the symbol they recognized,[1] but that she would not continue to be a kingdom, nor would her people continue to owe allegiance to the King. It is true that Eire did not completely remove the King from the system of government, nor did she formally call herself a republic in the Constitution of 1937. Yet she went almost the whole way in asserting that she could accept two of the statements of 1931 but not the third. And the fact that the other members of the Commonwealth agreed to regard Eire as continuing to be in the Commonwealth by the terms of their declaration at the close of 1937 may be regarded as some measure of acquiescence in Eire's assertion.[2]

What happened when the Republic of Ireland Act was passed? It repealed the Executive Authority (External Relations) Act of 1936 and thus removed the Monarchy from any exiguous or ambiguous position it may ever have had in the Irish system of government. At the same time it was made quite clear by the Irish government that they did not intend Ireland to be a member of the Commonwealth. It was no concern of theirs, therefore, what symbol the members might

[1] Some Irishmen would contest this interpretation and say that Eire did not accept either membership of the Commonwealth or the Crown as the symbol of free association; she merely recorded the fact that other members did. See Nicholas Mansergh, *The Commonwealth and the Nations*, pp. 202 ff.

[2] See p. 276 above.

adopt for their free association. It seems clear that Eire meant by her action in passing the Republic of Ireland Act to repudiate all three statements of 1931—she did not wish to be a kingdom, she did not wish to accept the Crown as the symbol of the free association as a member of the Commonwealth, and, most important of all, she did not wish to be a member. It is essential that this should be realized. Eire did not wish to reject one or two of the statements; she wished to reject all three. At the same time it seems almost certain that in the other members of the Commonwealth, and perhaps in Eire itself also, it was generally assumed that the fact that Eire had decided not to be a kingdom, and thus not to owe allegiance to the King, meant that she could not, even if she would, recognize the Crown as the symbol of her free association in the Commonwealth, nor could she continue to be a member of the Commonwealth. To do so, it was felt, was not only against the rules as they stood—which was true enough—but also was logically or practically impossible. How could a republic accept the Crown as a symbol? And if you cannot accept the Crown as a symbol, how can you remain a member of the Commonwealth? There was a tendency here to regard the symbol of the association as more important and logically superior to the association itself.

These arguments did not have to be pressed very far because it was clear that whatever a Republic of Ireland might conceivably be able to do, it clearly did not want to do it. It meant to leave. The members of the Commonwealth accepted this fact and proceeded to make reciprocal arrangements with Eire. But when the case of India came up at a Conference of Commonwealth

Prime Ministers in April, 1949, the distinctions made above came to be discussed and pressed to a logical conclusion. India clearly meant to reject one of the statements of 1926 and 1931. She would not continue to owe allegiance to the Crown; she intended to be a republic. Equally clearly she wanted to accept one of the statements of 1926 and 1931. She wanted to retain her free association with the other members of the Commonwealth. Could she do these two things? And if so, could she or should she continue to accept the Crown as the symbol of her free association? The answer from India's side was that she could accept the Crown as the symbol of her free association; the answer from the side of the other members of the Commonwealth was that in their view India could continue to be a member, although she would no longer be a kingdom. Thus allegiance to the Crown ceased to be regarded as an essential pre-requisite of membership of the Commonwealth. The Crown's essential position now is that of the symbol of the association. As the rules stand now, if you wish to be a member of the Commonwealth you must accept the Crown as the symbol of your association. For the time being the questions: 'Does the Commonwealth need a symbol of the free association of its members, and if so, what should it be?' are answered 'Yes. The Crown.'

The statement which was issued by the Prime Ministers' Conference after their discussions in April, 1949, deserves careful study and is set out below. In the first paragraph it will be noticed that the position as defined in 1926 and 1931 is summarized. In the second paragraph is recited India's wish to become a republic and reject allegiance to the Crown, with her desire to remain a member of the Commonwealth and to recognize the King as the symbol of its free association and as such the Head of the Commonwealth. In the next paragraph there is emphasized the fact that the other members of the Commonwealth still subscribe to all three statements of 1931, while accepting India's membership as a republic. The Declaration of 1949 is as follows:

The governments of the United Kingdom, Canada, Australia, New Zealand, South Africa, India, Pakistan and Ceylon, whose countries are united as Members of the British Commonwealth of Nations and owe a common allegiance to the Crown, which is also the symbol of their free association, have considered the impending constitutional changes in India.

The government of India have informed the other governments of the Commonwealth of the intention of the Indian people that under the new Constitution which is about to be adopted India shall become a sovereign independent republic. The government of India have however declared and affirmed India's desire to continue her full membership of the Commonwealth of Nations and her acceptance of the King as the symbol of the free association of its independent member nations and as such the Head of the Commonwealth.

The governments of the other countries of the Commonwealth, the basis of whose membership of the Commonwealth is not hereby changed, accept and recognize India's continuing membership in accordance with the terms of this declaration.

Accordingly the United Kingdom, Canada, Australia, New Zealand, South Africa, India, Pakistan and Ceylon, hereby declare that they remain united as free and equal members of the Commonwealth of Nations, freely cooperating in the pursuit of peace, liberty and progress.

When the new Constitution of India came into force on January 26, 1950, then, the Commonwealth became a Commonwealth of seven kingdoms and one republic, with the King as the head of the State in the law of the seven kingdoms but with no position in the State in the law of the republic. There was, however, a common recognition by all eight members of the King as the symbol of their free association and as such Head of the Commonwealth. This new title had no legal basis and the Head of the Commonwealth had, as such, no legal powers. The title and the office were created by the Declaration of 1949 which, like the Declaration of 1926, was not a legal document but a convention. If the Declaration of 1926 had been rewritten in 1950 it might have run: 'United by a common recognition of the King as the symbol of their free association and, as such, the Head of the Commonwealth'.

So the position stood when George VI died on February 6, 1952. In the Accession Proclamation made in London on February 8, Queen Elizabeth II was described as 'by the grace of God, Queen of this Realm and of all Her other Realms and Territories, Head of the Commonwealth, Defender of the Faith'. The phrase 'Head of the Commonwealth' was used also in the proclamations issued in Australia, New Zealand, Pakistan, and Ceylon. In India there was no proclamation, but the Prime Minister addressed a message to the Queen welcoming her as 'the new Head of the Commonwealth'. In Canada and South Africa, however, the phrase 'Head of the Commonwealth' was not used. Instead she was proclaimed 'Elizabeth the Second, by the grace of God, of Great Britain, Ireland, and the British Dominions beyond the Seas, Queen, Defender of the Faith', and in addition, in the case of Canada, 'Supreme Liege Lady in and over Canada', and, in the case of South Africa, 'Sovereign in and over the Union of South Africa'. There was some comment both at the use of the title 'Head of the Commonwealth' in certain of the proclamations and at the lack of uniformity, more particularly when it was noticed that two of the members of the Commonwealth which have been most anxious to assert their national independence—Canada and South Africa—should have adopted what looked like the old-fashioned formula.

It should be emphasized, perhaps, that the Accession proclamations do not determine what the Sovereign's Titles are to be. These proclamations do not make or alter law. The Queen's Titles at her accession were those settled by proclamations under the Royal Titles Act, 1927, one issued in 1927[1] and the other (removing the words 'Emperor of India') in 1948.[2] Thus her title was 'Elizabeth the Second, by the Grace of God, of Great Britain, Ireland, and the British Dominions beyond the Seas, Queen, Defender of the Faith'. This was the form which Canada and South Africa followed. But they added, in each case, a phrase to describe the Queen's special relationship to themselves. The form of proclamation adopted in the other members of the Commonwealth had no statutory origin or authority, but it is right to add that no such origin or authority was needed. On the other hand it seemed certain that, in the light of this new way of describing the Sovereign, the old form of the title as proclaimed under the Royal Titles Act, 1927, could hardly survive long. If it were

[1] See p. 125.
[2] See p. 290 above.

to be amended, however, the consent of the parliaments of all the members of the Commonwealth, including India, would be required, in terms of the convention declared in paragraph 2 of the Preamble to the Statute of Westminster.

XIII

THE END OF DOMINION STATUS?

'THE House will observe in the Royal Proclamation', said Mr. Churchill in the House of Commons at Westminster on February 11, 1952, in moving addresses of sympathy on the death of George VI,

the importance and significance assigned to the word 'Realm'. There was a time—and not so long ago—when the word 'Dominion' was greatly esteemed. But now, almost instinctively and certainly spontaneously, the many States, nations and races included in the British Commonwealth and Empire have found in the word 'Realm' the expression of their sense of unity, combined in most cases with a positive allegiance to the Crown or a proud and respectful association with it.[1]

The dropping of the word 'Dominion' in the Accession Proclamations in certain members of the Commonwealth has seemed to some students of Commonwealth relations to be one more step towards what is sometimes spoken of as 'The End of Dominion Status'.[2] It is time to consider what force there is in this phrase. If the matter is to be rightly understood, however, it is necessary to consider separately the question whether there has been a decline in the use of the words 'Dominion Status' and the question whether what those words stood or stand for is now considered out of date. Is it the

[1] 495 *H.C. Deb.*, 5 s., col. 963.
[2] This is the title of an article published in 1944 by Professor F. R. Scott, of McGill University, in 38 *American Journal of International Law* (January 1944), pp. 35 ff. Considerably rewritten, it was republished in 23 *Canadian Bar Review* (November 1945, pp. 725 ff.).

label on the bottle that is objected to or the liquid inside?

We may begin by reminding ourselves that the word 'Dominions' to distinguish the more or less self-governing parts of the Empire from the non-self-governing parts had its origin in a resolution of the Colonial Conference of 1907 which associated Great Britain with the 'self-governing Dominions' as members of the Conference for the future. The phrase 'self-governing Dominions' was soon shortened to 'Dominions', with the word 'self-governing' understood but undefined.[1] In the years that passed between 1907 and 1926 'self-governing' became more and more to mean free from control by the United Kingdom or by any other government, and in 1926 equality of status was declared to be one of the marks of Dominion Status. The legal consequences of that declaration were carried some stages farther in the Statute of Westminster, as has been explained in preceding chapters.

Quite distinct from this use of 'Dominion' to describe any or all of the self-governing parts of the Commonwealth overseas, a use whose history begins in 1907, was the use of the word as part of the title of a member of the Commonwealth, as, for example, 'the Dominion of Canada', a use whose history begins not in 1907 but forty years before, in 1867. From the passing of the British North America Act of 1867, when certain of the British North American colonies federated, Canada was known as 'the Dominion of Canada', a title chosen by the Canadians. Yet it is interesting to notice that although that title became generally accepted, it is not the title given to Canada in the British North America Act itself. Section 3 of that Act provides that the

[1] See above, p. 22.

provinces 'shall form and be one Dominion under the name of Canada'. 'Canada' was the name given to the new political community in its birth certificate.

It should be noticed also that although, contrary to the Act of 1867, Canada was usually known as 'the Dominion of Canada', not all the other 'Dominions' (in the sense in which that term was chosen in 1907) used the term in their title. Though New Zealand was called 'the Dominion of New Zealand', Australia took the title of 'the Commonwealth of Australia' in 1901, and South Africa the title of 'the Union of South Africa' in 1909. When in 1922 Ireland was to become a member of the Commonwealth, she chose the title of 'the Irish Free State'. So it was that in Australia, for example, though people spoke of 'the Dominions' and regarded Australia as one of them, they would not speak of Australia as 'this Dominion' or 'the Dominion' but as 'this Commonwealth'. Nor would they speak of the relations between the Commonwealth of Australia and the States as 'Dominion–States relations' but as 'Commonwealth–States relations'. In Canada, on the other hand, it was usual to speak of the government of Canada as 'the Dominion government' and of its relations with the provincial governments as 'Dominion–Provincial Relations'.[1]

It is against this sort of background that we must consider our question. 'Dominion' might mean any member of the Commonwealth other than Great Britain, or it might mean also Canada as a whole or New Zealand. What were the objections that came to

[1] The Rowell–Sirois Commission was a Commission on Dominion–Provincial Relations. The meetings of ministers of the different governments were called Dominion–Provincial Conferences.

be levelled against the use of the word in one sense or the other? There were several and they deserve separate consideration.

To consider Canada first and on narrow ground, it was possible for Canadians to object that they were calling themselves and were being called by an incorrect name. This was perfectly true. As often happens to human beings, Canada was being called by a name different from that in its birth certificate. If it did not like that name, it was perfectly entitled to ask that it be called by its proper name. In doing so it was doing nothing particularly revolutionary or secessionist; it was placing itself in the same position as, say, Australia.

A second difficulty peculiar to Canada was that the word 'Dominion' did not appeal to French Canadians as a name to describe Canada or the Canadian Government. They seldom used it; they usually spoke of 'la Confédération', and they preferred to speak of the 'Dominion-Provincial Conference' as 'La Conférence Fédérale-Provinciale'. Their objection to the word 'Dominion' arose not so much from the fact that the word was not easily translated into French or from the fact that it was not Canada's proper name as from their desire to assert the independence of the Province of Quebec inside the union of Canada. They wished to assert that Canada was not a unitary state and that the government at Ottawa had limited powers and must not transgress those limits; it must respect provincial powers. This they could assert more effectively by speaking of 'La Confédération' and of the 'federal' government at Ottawa than by speaking of 'the Dominion' and 'the Dominion government'.

But the Canadian attitude must be considered on wider grounds than these and in association with attitudes which were shared by some other members of the Commonwealth. There were at least five grounds upon which objection was taken to the use of 'Dominion' as a collective word to describe the oversea members of the Commonwealth. There was first the view that the word suggested domination, that the Dominions were territories over which Britain had 'dominion'. This implication seemed to be contained particularly in such phrases as 'the British Dominions' or 'Britain and her Dominions'. Historically there was something to be said for this view, though the dominion was the King's dominion, not Britain's, and usage, since 1907 at least, had established the position that the Dominions were not subject to Britain's dominion. However, a flavour of inequality could attach to the word.

This possible implication was strengthened, it was felt, by the fact that the word 'Dominion' did not apply to the United Kingdom. Although the United Kingdom might have equal status with the Dominions, it was not a Dominion. Historically 'Dominion' was a contraction from 'the self-governing British Dominions beyond the Seas'. It referred to the oversea members of the Commonwealth. It was convenient, in the United Kingdom at least, to have some word to describe the oversea members. Some people thought,[1] however, that it implied a difference which might be misinterpreted into a difference of status between the United Kingdom and the oversea members.

[1] This was one of Professor Scott's objections. 38 *American Journal of International Law*, p. 47.

A third objection was that 'Dominion' had been used
to describe so many different degrees of self-government
that it was too ambiguous a term. Though it might
include a fully self-governing member of the Commonwealth it had, since 1907, been used to describe countries which, in defence and foreign affairs for example,
had been under the control of the United Kingdom.
Although in 1926 it had been declared that the Dominions were equal in status with Great Britain, the word
'Dominions' still had about it suggestions of its history
of inequality. It still seemed possible to conceive of a
Dominion Status which might mean, in law at any
rate, unequal status. To describe the members of the
Commonwealth as enjoying Dominion Status was to
use an obsolete term. It was like calling an adult an
adolescent.

When the time came to invite Ireland to accept
membership of the Commonwealth a further difficulty
about 'Dominion' revealed itself. The Dominions,
historically speaking, were all grown-up or growing-up
daughter nations of the United Kingdom. They had been
subordinate colonies; their peoples had come from the
British Isles, though in Canada and South Africa they
had united themselves with people of non-British stock,
so that they were daughter nations or, at least, daughter-
in-law nations. The word 'Dominions' had about it
this history of growing up as daughters of a mother
country. Ireland could not accept these historical
implications. She was not a daughter nation but a
mother country. She had not begun as a colony but as
an ancient kingdom; she was not a daughter but a sister
kingdom with Great Britain. For the Irish Free State
the term 'Dominion Status' was not appropriate; she

was a member of the Commonwealth. If this was true of Eire, it was clearly true also of India, Pakistan, and Ceylon, who, though for long subordinate to Britain, were not peopled by British stock and had had a history of independence in the past. 'Dominion' was hardly appropriate for them.

But, and this is the fifth objection, there was something unsatisfactory about the word 'Dominion' even for those who were, in truth, grown-up daughter or daughter-in-law nations. When people have grown up, they do not like to be referred to always as 'the daughter of so-and-so'. They have an adult existence in their own right. The time comes when the fact that they have grown up must be taken for granted. So the word 'Dominion' must be superseded by 'Member of the Commonwealth' which applies alike to mother and daughter and stresses neither the family relationship nor the days of childhood.

These objections to the use of 'Dominion' and 'Dominion Status' were not all held by all oversea members of the Commonwealth, and those that held them did not hold them all with equal intensity. Nor were they even set out in a schedule of objections. From time to time, however, actions were taken which showed that some members at any rate felt the force of these objections, and it would be true to say that the use of the terms has declined since 1945. Yet it would be a mistake to assume that the words were consistently avoided. A good example of the variety of usage occurred in 1947. When steps were being taken to grant full self-government to India and Pakistan in 1947, it was announced in the United Kingdom that the name of the Secretary of State for Dominion Affairs was to be changed to that of Secretary of State for Commonwealth Relations, and that of the Dominions Office to Commonwealth Relations Office.[1] This looked like an acceptance or anticipation of the fact that India and Pakistan did not propose to have themselves called 'Dominions' but 'Members of the Commonwealth'. Yet two days later the Indian Independence Bill was presented to the House of Commons and it provided for the establishment of two 'Dominions'. India continued to be a Dominion until it became a republic on January 26, 1950; Pakistan is still a Dominion. Ceylon accepted the term 'Dominion' when it obtained full self-government in 1948.

On the other side it is interesting to see the action which Canada has taken, and here it must be remembered that the Canadians had the two questions to deal with—first the usage 'the Dominion of Canada' and secondly the usage 'the Dominions' to describe the oversea members of the Commonwealth of which Canada was one. Canada's action has been confined to the question of its own name, but it may be assumed that in taking this action it has been impelled by objections to the word 'Dominion' in the second sense. It is because it objects to being called 'a Dominion' that it has wished to cease being called 'the Dominion of Canada'. In 1947 new letters patent[2] were issued in Canada constituting the office of Governor-General, and in them the word 'Canada' replaces 'Dominion of Canada' or 'Dominion' where they had occurred in the

[1] 439 H.C. Deb., 5 s. col. 1320. The announcement was made on July 2.
[2] Issued September 8, 1947, and in effect on October 1, 1947. The new and the old documents are printed in 7 *University of Toronto Law Journal*, pp. 475 ff.

former letters patent. At a meeting of the Dominion-Provincial Conference of January 1950 it was decided that in future it should be called 'the Federal-Provincial Conference', and its report and later reports appeared under that title. Thus was the French-Canadian attitude recognized. As opportunity offers in the Canadian parliament the words 'Dominion of Canada' and 'Dominion' are removed from previous acts of parliament and replaced by 'Canada'. It is now the official usage in Canada.

It may seem surprising that Canada, having taken such care to remove 'Dominion' from its legal documents, should have chosen to describe Elizabeth II, in the Accession Proclamation, as 'of the British Dominions beyond the Seas, Queen' instead of adopting the new formula 'Queen of this Realm and of all Her other Realms and Territories, Head of the Commonwealth'. On reflection, however, it can be seen that there is no necessary inconsistency in what Canada did. The legal changes she has been making have concerned her own name, and in the Accession Proclamation the Queen is spoken of as 'Supreme Liege Lady in and over Canada', not 'the Dominion of Canada'. So far as the reference to 'the British Dominions beyond the Seas' is concerned, that phrase was part of the legal title of the Sovereign, as determined under the Royal Titles Act, 1927, and Canada's repetition of it in her Accession Proclamation did not imply approval of it or disapproval of it. It remains open to Canada, if it chooses, to propose an alteration in the title of the Queen in the future.

The outcome of these discussions about 'Dominion' has been that the terminology in Commonwealth relations is changing. The various parts of the Commonwealth, whatever their constitutional status, are coming to be called 'Commonwealth countries'. The Dominions and the United Kingdom are all called 'members' of the Commonwealth. They have 'member status', a status which includes Dominion Status and the status of the United Kingdom. Those parts of the Commonwealth which are not of equal status with the members are, like the members, Commonwealth countries, and they are called, variously, colonies, protectorates, dependent territories, non-self-governing territories, and so on. 'Dominion Status' is apparently to be replaced by 'Member Status' or 'Realm Status'.

But is it accurate to speak of this as 'the end of Dominion Status'? In one sense it clearly is accurate. The use of the terms 'Dominion' and 'Dominion Status' is coming to an end. The end may come quickly or the terms may die hard. On the other hand, is what 'Dominion Status' stood for coming to an end? The answer to this question cannot be given without some qualifications. In so far as there was attached to 'Dominion Status' some remaining notion of inferiority to the United Kingdom, some historical memory of subordinate status, of adolescence, of the Mother Country's apron-strings, it is true that 'Member Status' in the Commonwealth means a change. 'Member Status' has no such associations; it contains no embarrassing reminders of past subjection. It applies and can only apply to fully self-governing nations. Yet it would be an exaggeration to suggest that it means much more than 'Dominion Status' did in 1926. 'Dominion Status' was a growing and developing concept. Independence and equality were its essential characteristics.

It is true that it implied independence within the Commonwealth, but that surely is precisely what 'Member Status' must mean. The new terminology is very little, if anything, more than new labels on the old bottles, new names for old things. It should not be underestimated on that account. Names are of great importance, as the history of the Commonwealth has shown. If it was wise to replace 'Colony' by 'Dominion' who can doubt that it is wise to replace 'Dominion' by 'Realm', or by 'Member of the Commonwealth'?

APPENDIX I

THE COLONIAL LAWS VALIDITY ACT, 1865

(*28 & 29 Vict., c. 63*) [*June 29, 1865*]

AN Act to remove Doubts as to the Validity of Colonial Laws.

Whereas Doubts have been entertained respecting the Validity of divers Laws enacted or purporting to have been enacted by the Legislatures of certain of Her Majesty's Colonies, and respecting the Powers of such Legislatures, and it is expedient that such Doubts should be removed:

Be it hereby enacted by the Queen's most Excellent Majesty, by and with the Advice and Consent of the Lords Spiritual and Temporal, and Commons, in this present Parliament assembled, and by the Authority of the same, as follows:

1. The Term 'Colony' shall in this Act include all of Her Majesty's Possessions abroad in which there shall exist a Legislature, as herein-after defined, except the Channel Islands, the *Isle of Man*, and such Territories as may for the Time being be vested in Her Majesty under or by virtue of any Act of Parliament for the Government of *India*:

The Terms 'Legislature' and 'Colonial Legislature' shall severally signify the Authority, other than the Imperial Parliament or Her Majesty in Council, competent to make Laws for any Colony:

The Term 'Representative Legislature' shall signify any Colonial Legislature which shall comprise a Legislative Body of which One Half are elected by Inhabitants of the Colony:

The Term 'Colonial Law' shall include Laws made for any Colony either by such Legislature as aforesaid or by Her Majesty in Council:

An Act of Parliament, or any Provision thereof, shall, in construing this Act, be said to extend to any Colony when it is made applicable to such Colony by the express Words or necessary Intendment of any Act of Parliament:

The Term 'Governor' shall mean the Officer lawfully administering the Government of any Colony:

The Term 'Letters Patent' shall mean Letters Patent under the Great Seal of the United Kingdom of *Great Britain* and *Ireland*.

2. Any Colonial Law which is or shall be in any respect repugnant to the Provisions of any Act of Parliament extending to the Colony to which such Law may relate, or repugnant to any Order or Regulation made under Authority of such Act of Parliament, or having in the Colony the Force and Effect of such Act, shall be read subject to such Act, Order or Regulation, and shall, to the Extent of such Repugnancy, but not otherwise, be and remain absolutely void and inoperative.

3. No Colonial Law shall be or be deemed to have been void or inoperative on the Ground of Repugnancy to the Law of *England*, unless the same shall be repugnant to the Provisions of some such Act of Parliament, Order or Regulation as aforesaid.

4. No Colonial Law, passed with the Concurrence of or assented to by the Governor of any Colony, or to be hereafter so passed or assented to, shall be or be deemed to have been void or inoperative by reason only of any Instructions with reference to such Law or the Subject thereof which may have been given to such Governor by or on behalf of Her Majesty, by any Instrument other than the Letters Patent or Instrument authorising such Governor to concur in passing or to assent to Laws for the Peace, Order, and good Government of such Colony, even though such Instructions may be referred to in such Letters Patent or last-mentioned Instrument.

5. Every Colonial Legislature shall have, and be deemed at all Times to have had, full Power within its Jurisdiction to establish Courts of Judicature, and to abolish and reconstitute the same, and to alter the Constitution thereof, and to make Provision for the Administration of Justice therein; and every Representative Legislature shall, in respect to the Colony under its Jurisdiction, have, and be deemed at all Times to have had, full Power to make Laws respecting the Constitution, Powers, and Procedure of such Legislature; provided that such Laws shall have been passed in such Manner and Form as may from Time to Time be required by any Act of Parliament, Letters Patent, Order in Council, or Colonial Law for the Time being in force in the said Colony.

6. The Certificate of the Clerk or other proper Officer of a Legislative Body in any Colony to the Effect that the Document to which it is attached is a true Copy of any Colonial Law assented to by the Governor of such Colony, or of any Bill reserved for the Signification of Her Majesty's Pleasure by the said Governor, shall be *prima facie* Evidence that the Document so certified is a true Copy of such Law or Bill, and, as the Case may be, that such Law has been duly and properly passed and assented to, or that such Bill has been duly and properly passed and presented to the Governor; and any Proclamation purporting to be published by Authority of the Governor in any Newspaper in the Colony to which such Law or Bill shall relate, and signifying Her Majesty's Disallowance of any such Colonial Law, or Her Majesty's Assent to any such reserved Bill as aforesaid, shall be *prima facie* Evidence of such Disallowance or Assent.

And whereas Doubts are entertained respecting the Validity of certain Acts enacted or reputed to be enacted by the Legislature of *South Australia*: Be it further enacted as follows:

7. All Laws or reputed Laws enacted or purporting to have been enacted by the said Legislature, or by Persons or Bodies of Persons for the Time being acting as such Legislature, which have received the Assent of Her Majesty in Council, or which have received the Assent of the Governor of the said Colony in the Name and on behalf of Her Majesty, shall be and be deemed to have been valid and effectual from the Date of such Assent for all Purposes whatever; provided that nothing herein contained shall be deemed to give Effect to any Law or reputed Law which has been disallowed by Her Majesty, or has expired, or has been lawfully repealed, or to prevent the lawful Disallowance or Repeal of any Law.

[*Note*: It may be worth mentioning that in 1937 section 1 of this Act was amended by the substitution of the words 'British India and British Burma' for 'and such territories . . . India'. The object of this amendment was to bring the Act into line with the provisions of the Government of India Act, 1935, which *inter alia* separated Burma from India. The amendment was made by statutory order issued under the authority of the Government of India Act, 1935, s. 311 (5). See Government of India (Adaptation of Acts of Parliament) Order, 1937. S.R. and O. No. 230 of 1937, art. 2, Sched., Part II, p. 966.]

APPENDIX II

THE STATUTE OF WESTMINSTER, 1931

*An Act to give effect to certain resolutions passed by Imperial
Conferences held in the years 1926 and 1930.*

(22 Geo. 5, c. 4)   *[11 Dec. 1931]*

WHEREAS the delegates of His Majesty's Governments in the
United Kingdom, the Dominion of Canada, the Commonwealth of Australia, the Dominion of New Zealand, the
Union of South Africa, the Irish Free State and Newfoundland, at Imperial Conferences holden at Westminster in the
years of our Lord nineteen hundred and twenty-six and
nineteen hundred and thirty did concur in making the
declarations and resolutions set forth in the Reports of the
said Conferences:

And whereas it is meet and proper to set out by way of
preamble to this Act that, inasmuch as the Crown is the
symbol of the free association of the members of the British
Commonwealth of Nations, and as they are united by a
common allegiance to the Crown, it would be in accord with
the established constitutional position of all the members of
the Commonwealth in relation to one another that any
alteration in the law touching the Succession to the Throne
or the Royal Style and Titles shall hereafter require the
assent as well of the Parliaments of all the Dominions as of
the Parliament of the United Kingdom:

And whereas it is in accord with the established constitutional position that no law hereafter made by the
Parliament of the United Kingdom shall extend to any of
the said Dominions as part of the law of that Dominion
otherwise than at the request and with the consent of that
Dominion:

And whereas it is necessary for the ratifying, confirming and establishing of certain of the said declarations and resolutions of the said Conferences that a law be made and enacted in due form by authority of the Parliament of the United Kingdom:

And whereas the Dominion of Canada, the Commonwealth of Australia, the Dominion of New Zealand, the Union of South Africa, the Irish Free State and Newfoundland have severally requested and consented to the submission of a measure to the Parliament of the United Kingdom for making such provision with regard to the matters aforesaid as is hereafter in this Act contained:

Now, therefore, be it enacted by the King's most Excellent Majesty by and with the advice and consent of the Lords Spiritual and Temporal, and Commons, in this present Parliament assembled, and by the authority of the same, as follows:—

1. In this Act the expression 'Dominion' means any of the following Dominions, that is to say, the Dominion of Canada, the Commonwealth of Australia, the Dominion of New Zealand, the Union of South Africa, the Irish Free State and Newfoundland.

2.—(1) The Colonial Laws Validity Act, 1865, shall not apply to any law made after the commencement of this Act by the Parliament of a Dominion.

(2) No law and no provision of any law made after the commencement of this Act by the Parliament of a Dominion shall be void or inoperative on the ground that it is repugnant to the law of England, or to the provisions of any existing or future Act of Parliament of the United Kingdom, or to any order, rule or regulation made under any such Act, and the powers of the Parliament of a Dominion shall include the power to repeal or amend any such Act, order, rule or regulation in so far as the same is part of the law of the Dominion.

3. It is hereby declared and enacted that the Parliament of a Dominion has full power to make laws having extra-territorial operation.

4. No Act of Parliament of the United Kingdom passed after the commencement of this Act shall extend, or be deemed to extend, to a Dominion as part of the law of that Dominion, unless it is expressly declared in that Act that that Dominion has requested, and consented to, the enactment thereof.

5. Without prejudice to the generality of the foregoing provisions of this Act, sections seven hundred and thirty-fiv and seven hundred and thirty-six of the Merchant Shipping Act, 1894, shall be construed as though reference therein to the Legislature of a British possession did not include reference to the Parliament of a Dominion.

6. Without prejudice to the generality of the foregoing provisions of this Act, section four of the Colonial Courts of Admiralty Act, 1890 (which requires certain laws to be reserved for the signification of His Majesty's pleasure or to contain a suspending clause), and so much of section seven of that Act as requires the approval of His Majesty in Council to any rules of Court for regulating the practice and procedure of a Colonial Court of Admiralty, shall cease to have effect in any Dominion as from the commencement of this Act.

7. —(1) Nothing in this Act shall be deemed to apply to the repeal, amendment or alteration of the British North America Acts, 1867 to 1930, or any order, rule or regulation made thereunder.

(2) The provisions of section two of this Act shall extend to laws made by any of the Provinces of Canada and to the powers of the legislatures of such Provinces.

(3) The powers conferred by this Act upon the Parliament of Canada or upon the legislatures of the Provinces

shall be restricted to the enactment of laws in relation
to matters within the competence of the Parliament of
Canada or of any of the legislatures of the Provinces
respectively.

8. Nothing in this Act shall be deemed to confer any
power to repeal or alter the Constitution or the Constitution
Act of the Commonwealth of Australia or the Constitution
Act of the Dominion of New Zealand otherwise than in
accordance with the law existing before the commencement
of this Act.

9.—(1) Nothing in this Act shall be deemed to authorize
the Parliament of the Commonwealth of Australia to make
laws on any matter within the authority of the States
of Australia, not being a matter within the authority of
the Parliament or Government of the Commonwealth of
Australia.

(2) Nothing in this Act shall be deemed to require the
concurrence of the Parliament or Government of the Commonwealth of Australia in any law made by the Parliament
of the United Kingdom with respect to any matter within
the authority of the States of Australia, not being a matter
within the authority of the Parliament or Government of
the Commonwealth of Australia, in any case where it would
have been in accordance with the constitutional practice
existing before the commencement of this Act that the
Parliament of the United Kingdom should make that law
without such concurrence.

(3) In the application of this Act to the Commonwealth
of Australia the request and consent referred to in section
four shall mean the request and consent of the Parliament
and Government of the Commonwealth.

10.—(1) None of the following sections of this Act, that
is to say, sections two, three, four, five and six, shall extend
to a Dominion to which this section applies as part of the

law of that Dominion unless that section is adopted by the Parliament of the Dominion, and any Act of that Parliament adopting any section of this Act may provide that the adoption shall have effect either from the commencement of this Act or from such later date as is specified in the adopting Act.

(2) The Parliament of any such Dominion as aforesaid may at any time revoke the adoption of any section referred to in subsection (1) of this section.

(3) The Dominions to which this section applies are the Commonwealth of Australia, the Dominion of New Zealand and Newfoundland.

11. Notwithstanding anything in the Interpretation Act, 1889, the expression 'Colony', shall not, in any Act of the Parliament of the United Kingdom passed after the commencement of this Act, include a Dominion or any Province or State forming part of a Dominion.

12. This Act may be cited as the Statute of Westminster, 1931.

APPENDIX III

THE STATUS OF THE UNION ACT, 1934

No. 69 of 1934.

*(Assented to by His Majesty the King on the 22nd June, 1934.
Date of commencement, August 22, 1934.)*

To provide for the declaration of the Status of the Union of
South Africa; for certain amendments of the South Africa
Act, 1909, incidental thereto, and for the adoption of certain
parts of the Statute of Westminster, 1931.

Whereas the delegates of His Majesty's Governments in
the United Kingdom, the Dominion of Canada, the Commonwealth of Australia, the Dominion of New Zealand, the
Union of South Africa, the Irish Free State and Newfoundland, at Imperial Conferences holden at Westminster in the
years of our Lord 1926 and 1930, did concur in making the
declarations and resolutions set forth in the Reports of
the said Conferences, and more particularly in defining the
group of self-governing communities composed of Great
Britain and the Dominions as 'autonomous communities
within the British Empire, equal in status, in no way
subordinate one to another in any aspect of their domestic
or external affairs, though united by a common allegiance
to the Crown and freely associated as members of the
British Commonwealth of Nations';

And whereas the said resolutions and declarations in so
far as they required legislative sanction on the part of the
United Kingdom have been ratified, confirmed and established by the Parliament of the United Kingdom in an Act
entitled the Statute of Westminster, 1931 (22. Geo. V. c. 4);

And whereas it is expedient that the status of the Union
of South Africa as a sovereign independent state as herein

before defined shall be adopted and declared by the Parliament of the Union and that the South Africa Act, 1909 (9. Edw. 7. c. 9) be amended accordingly;

And whereas it is expedient that the said Statute of Westminster, in so far as its provisions are applicable to the Union of South Africa, and an Afrikaans version thereof, shall be adopted as an Act of the Parliament of the Union of South Africa;

Now, therefore, be it declared and enacted by the King's Most Excellent Majesty, the Senate and the House of Assembly of the Union of South Africa, as follows:—

1. In this Act the expression 'the South Africa Act' means the South Africa Act, 1909 (9. Edw. 7. c. 9) as amended from time to time.

2. The Parliament of the Union shall be the sovereign legislative power in and over the Union, and notwithstanding anything in any other law contained, no Act of the Parliament of the United Kingdom and Northern Ireland passed after the eleventh day of December, 1931, shall extend, or be deemed to extend, to the Union as part of the law of the Union, unless extended thereto by an Act of the Parliament of the Union.

3. The parts of the Statute of Westminster, 1931 (22. Geo. V. c. 4) and the Afrikaans version thereof, set forth in the Schedule to this Act, shall be deemed to be an Act of the Parliament of the Union and shall be construed accord. ingly.

4. (1) The Executive Government of the Union in regard to any aspect of its domestic or external affairs is vested in the King, acting on the advice of His Ministers of State for the Union, and may be administered by His Majesty in person or by a Governor-General as his representative.

(2) Save where otherwise expressly stated or necessarily implied, any reference in the South Africa Act and in this Act to the King shall be deemed to be a reference to the King acting on the advice of his Ministers of State for the Union.

(3) The provisions of subsections (1) and (2) shall not be taken to affect the provisions of sections *twelve*, *fourteen*, *twenty* and *forty-five* of the South Africa Act and the constitutional conventions relating to the exercise of his functions by the Governor-General under the said sections.

5. Section *two* of the South Africa Act is hereby amended by the insertion after the word 'implied' of the words—

'heirs and successors' shall be taken to mean His Majesty's heirs and successors in the sovereignty of the United Kingdom of Great Britain and Ireland as determined by the laws relating to the succession of the Crown of the United Kingdom of Great Britain and Ireland.

6. Sections *twenty-six* and *forty-four* of the South Africa Act are hereby amended by the deletion of the words 'a British subject of European descent' in paragraphs (*d*) and (*c*) respectively of the said sections and the substitution therefor of the words 'a person of European descent who has acquired Union nationality whether—

(i) by birth or
(ii) by domicile as a British subject or
(iii) by naturalization, or otherwise, in terms of Act 40 of 1927 or of Act 14 of 1932.'

7. Section *fifty-one* of the South Africa Act is hereby amended by the deletion of the words 'of the United Kingdom of Great Britain and Ireland' where they occur in the oath and in the affirmation prescribed by the said section, and by inserting the words 'King or Queen (as the case may be)' immediately after the words 'His Majesty'.

8. Section *sixty-four* of the South Africa Act is hereby repealed and the following section substituted therefor:—

64. When a Bill is presented to the Governor-General for the King's assent he shall declare according to his discretion, but subject to the provisions of this Act, and to such instructions as may from time to time be given in that behalf by the King, that he assents in the King's name, or that he withholds assent. The Governor-General may return to the House in which it originated any Bill so presented to him, and may transmit therewith any amendments which he may recommend, and the House may deal with the recommendation.

9. Section *sixty-seven* of the South Africa Act is hereby amended by the deletion of the words, 'or having been reserved for the King's pleasure shall have received his assent'.

10. Nothing in this Act contained shall affect the provisions of section *one hundred and six* of the South Africa Act, relating to an appeal to the King-in-Council, or the provisions of sections *one hundred and fifty* and *one hundred and fifty-one* of the said Act.

11. (1) Sections *eight* and *sixty-six* of the South Africa Act are hereby repealed.

(2) Section *sixty-five* shall be repealed as from a date to be fixed by the Governor-General by proclamation in the *Gazette*.

12. This Act shall be known as the Status of the Union Act, 1934.

Schedule

The entire Preamble and sections 1, 2, 3, 4, 5, 6, 11, and 12 of the Statute (with the modifications in sections 1, 4, and 11 referred to on p. 243 above) were enacted.

APPENDIX IV

STATUTE OF WESTMINSTER ADOPTION BILL, 1937

To provide for the adoption of sections two, three, four, five, and six of the Statute of Westminster, 1931, and for other purposes.

WHEREAS the delegates of His Majesty's Governments in the United Kingdom, the Dominion of Canada, the Commonwealth of Australia, the Dominion of New Zealand, the Union of South Africa, the Irish Free State and Newfoundland, at Imperial Conferences holden at Westminster in the years of Our Lord One thousand nine hundred and twenty-six and One thousand nine hundred and thirty, did concur in making the declarations and resolutions set forth in the Reports of the said Conferences, and more particularly in defining the group of self-governing communities composed of Great Britain and the Dominions as 'autonomous communities within the British Empire, equal in status, in no way subordinate one to another in any aspect of their domestic or external affairs, though united by a common allegiance to the Crown and freely associated as members of the British Commonwealth of Nations':

And whereas the said resolutions and declarations in so far as they required statutory force and effect on the part of the United Kingdom have been ratified, confirmed and established by an Imperial Act entitled the Statute of Westminster, 1931 (22 Geo. V. c. 4):

And whereas it is amongst other things enacted by section ten of the said Act that none of the following sections of that Act, that is to say, sections two, three, four, five, and six, shall extend to the Commonwealth of Australia as part of the law of the Commonwealth unless that section is adopted

by the Parliament of the Commonwealth and any Act of
that Parliament adopting that section may provide that the
adoption shall have effect either from the commencement
of the said Statute of Westminster, 1931, or from such later
date as is specified in the adopting Act:

And whereas it is desirable that sections two, three, four,
five, and six of the said Statute of Westminster, 1931, shall
be adopted by the Parliament of the Commonwealth of
Australia:

Be it therefore enacted by the King's Most Excellent
Majesty, the Senate, and the House of Representatives of
the Commonwealth of Australia, as follows:

1. This Act may be cited as the Statute of Westminster
   Adoption Act, 1937.
2. Sections two, three, four, five, and six of the Imperial
   Act entitled the Statute of Westminster, 1931 (which
   Act is set out in the Schedule to this Act), are adopted
   and the adoption shall have effect from the first day of
   January, One thousand nine hundred and thirty-eight.

APPENDIX V

THE STATUTE OF WESTMINSTER ADOPTION ACT

No. 56 of 1942

(Assented to October 9, 1942.)

An Act to remove doubts as to the validity of certain Commonwealth legislation, to obviate delays occurring in its passage, and to effect certain related purposes, by adopting certain sections of the Statute of Westminster, 1931, as from the commencement of the War between His Majesty the King and Germany.

Whereas certain legal difficulties exist which have created doubts and caused delays in relation to certain Commonwealth legislation, and to certain regulations made thereunder, particularly in relation to the legislation enacted, and regulations made, for securing the public safety and defence of the Commonwealth of Australia, and for the more effectual prosecution of the War in which His Majesty the King is engaged: And whereas these legal difficulties will be removed by the adoption by the Parliament of the Commonwealth of Australia of sections two, three, four, five and six of the Statute of Westminster, 1931, and by making such adoption have effect as from the commencement of the War between His Majesty the King and Germany:

Be it therefore enacted by the King's Most Excellent Majesty, the Senate, and the House of Representatives of the Commonwealth of Australia, as follows:

1. This Act may be cited as the Statute of Westminster Adoption Act, 1942.
2. This Act shall come into operation on the day on which it receives the Royal Assent.

3. Sections two, three, four, five and six of the Imperial Act entitled the Statute of Westminster, 1931 (which Act is set out in the Schedule to this Act) are adopted and the adoption shall have effect from the third day of September, One thousand nine hundred and thirty-nine.

Schedule

The whole of the Statute of Westminster, 1931.

APPENDIX VI

THE STATUTE OF WESTMINSTER ADOPTION ACT, 1947 (NEW ZEALAND)

THE Governor-General of New Zealand, in his speech at the opening of the New Zealand Parliament on February 22, 1944, announced that his ministers proposed 'to place before Parliament the question of the adoption of the Statute of Westminster, the enactment of which would bring New Zealand into line with the other self-governing dominions'. 'The adoption of this measure', he said, 'will remove doubts in the eyes of foreign powers regarding the sovereign status of New Zealand, and will at the same time have the practical effect of removing existing legal administrative difficulties both in New Zealand and in the United Kingdom.'[1]

New Zealand had encountered the same difficulties as Australia (see pp. 216 a–e above), particularly during wartime, through the doubts of its power to legislate with extra-territorial effect and of the extent to which its laws in relation to shipping were repugnant to the Merchant Shipping Act, 1894, and therefore void. And it was obliged, as was Australia, to reserve bills and to submit to some delay.[2] It was obstacles of this kind, as well as reasons of status, which prompted the Labour Government of Mr. Fraser to decide to follow the Australian example and to adopt the relevant sections of the Statute. However, the matter dropped and no action was taken until 1947.

In the meantime New Zealand had to rely, as had Australia until its adoption of the sections in 1942, upon

---

[1] *New Zealand Parliamentary Debates*, vol. 264, p. 7.
[2] See R. O. McGechan in J. C. Beaglehole (ed.), *New Zealand and the Statute of Westminster*, pp. 85–97.

ad hoc legislation by the United Kingdom Parliament to extend its powers. The Whaling Industry (Regulation) Act, 1934, gave extra-territorial force to New Zealand legislation for the regulation of the whaling industry so far as such legislation applies to ships registered in New Zealand or to territory administered by New Zealand. Similarly the Emergency Powers (Defence) Act, 1939, and the Army and Air Force (Annual) Act, 1940, gave powers of extra-territorial legislation to New Zealand for certain specified matters. The Prize Act, 1939, also extended to New Zealand. These Acts all applied to New Zealand, under the rule of construction in the Colonial Laws Validity Act, by express words. On the other hand, by the constitutional convention agreed upon in 1930 and recited in paragraph 3 of the Preamble to the Statute, the request and consent of New Zealand to the passing of these Acts was required,[1] and it would appear that it was in fact obtained, but so long as section 4 of the Statute had not been adopted there was no legal requirement that this request and consent should be recited in the Acts and it is accordingly not recited. It would appear that one or two other Acts, like the Regency Acts of 1937 and 1943, might be held to apply by necessary intendment to New Zealand as part of the law of New Zealand.[2] Though it does not appear that the request and consent of New Zealand to their passage was explicitly sought, there was consultation between the United Kingdom and the Dominions and no objection to the passage of the Acts was made by New Zealand or any other Dominion.[3]

The only tangible product of the announcement in the Governor-General's speech of February 22, 1944, was the initiation of some valuable public discussion in New Zealand of the effect of the Statute upon the Dominion and the

[1] See above, pp. 231–2.

[2] See Appendix B to A. E. Currie, *New Zealand and the Statute of Westminster*, 1931.

[3] 319 *H.C Deb.*, 5 s., 1452–3 and 392 *H.C. Deb.*, 5 s., 1251.

publication of two books in 1944: A. E. Currie's *New Zealand and the Statute of Westminster, 1931*, a careful legal analysis of the position; and a collection of lectures by J. C. Beaglehole, F. L. W. Wood, L. Lipson, and R. O. McGechan, edited by J. C. Beaglehole, and entitled *New Zealand and the Statute of Westminster*. The lecture by R. O. McGechan deals with the legal consequences of the adoption of the Statute,[1] but the other lectures deserve equal attention, for they combine to place the Statute in its broader political environment.

In 1947 some new factors came into play.[2] A bill to abolish the second chamber of the New Zealand Parliament —the Legislative Council—was introduced in the House of Representatives on August 5 by the Leader of the Opposition, but on the second reading the Attorney-General raised the question whether the New Zealand Parliament had power to pass such legislation. Section 32 of the New Zealand Constitution Act of 1852, which provided for a bicameral legislature, was one of those sections which was exempted from the amending power granted in the Act of 1857.[3] The only way in which all doubt could be removed was to request the Parliament at Westminster to pass an act to remove the restrictions remaining in the Act of 1857. This procedure could have been followed, had the New Zealand Parliament wished, without introducing any question of adopting sections 2–6 of the Statute of Westminster. However, the Prime Minister intervened with a proposal that, before any attempt should be made to alter the Constitution, the New Zealand Parliament should adopt sections 2–6 and thereafter, following the procedure envisaged by section 4, request and consent to the enactment by the

[1] Reference may be made also to Mr. McGechan's article in *New Zealand Law Journal*, Feb. 1944, pp. 18 ff.

[2] See *New Zealand Parliamentary Debates*, vol. 277, pp. 123–9, 197–222, 320–41; vol. 279, pp. 531–44, 547–64, 870–86; and New Zealand Parliamentary Paper A-13 of 1947.

[3] See above, p. 228.

Parliament of the United Kingdom of legislation to remove
the restrictions embodied in the Act of 1857 and safeguarded by section 8 of the Statute. The Prime Minister
explained that New Zealand's reluctance to proceed with
the adoption of sections 2–6 as proposed in 1944 arose from
a feeling that if such action had been taken during the war
it might have been misrepresented by enemy propaganda
as evidence that the British Commonwealth was being dismembered. No such charge could now be made and it
seemed most satisfactory, if additional freedom was to be
sought in regard to the power of constitutional amendment,
to complete the job and remove all possible doubts about
the general legislative competence of the Parliament of New
Zealand by adopting sections 2–6 of the Statute. The Prime
Minister's proposal, put forward as an amendment on the
second reading of the opposition bill to abolish the legislative
council, was carried in a division on party lines by 39 to 37.
Thereafter the Statute of Westminster Adoption Bill and the
New Zealand Constitution (Request and Consent) Bill were
passed without a division in the House of Representatives
and received the royal assent on November 25, 1947.[1] Soon
after, the Parliament of the United Kingdom passed the
New Zealand Constitution (Amendment) Act, 1947,[2] which
received the royal assent on December 10. The Act[3]
repealed the New Zealand Constitution (Amendment) Act
of 1857 and declared that 'it shall be lawful for the Parliament of New Zealand by any Act or Acts of that Parliament
to alter, suspend, or repeal, at any time, all or any of the
provisions of the New Zealand Constitution Act, 1852'. In
paragraph 4 of its Preamble it declares that New Zealand

[1] They became Acts Nos. 38 and 44 of 1947 respectively.
[2] 11 Geo. 6, c. 4. See 152 *H.L. Deb.*, 5 s., 1018–22, and 445 *H.C. Deb.*,
5 s., 801–6, 859–60.
[3] It may be noted that the Act as passed is identical in its terms with
the Draft which the Parliament of New Zealand had submitted as a
Schedule to its Request and Consent Act.

has requested and consented to the enactment of the Act, and by virtue of this declaration it extends to New Zealand under the rule of construction embodied in section 4 of the Statute of Westminster.

One or two points may be noted about the Adoption Act itself. In the first place it provides, in section 2, that the adoption of the relevant sections of the Statute shall have effect from the commencement of the Adoption Act—which proved to be November 25, 1947. New Zealand did not choose, as Australia did,[1] to use its power under section 10 (1) of the Statute to make adoption date back to any time after the commencement of the Statute, viz. December 11, 1931. The result is that any law passed by the United Kingdom Parliament between December 11, 1931, and November 25, 1947, that purports to apply to New Zealand —and examples of such laws are given on p. 322 above— continues to do so, unaffected by the adoption of sections 2–6 of the Statute, for so long, at any rate, as the Parliament of New Zealand chooses. In order to remove any doubts on this point, there is included in the Adoption Act[2] a declaration that all such acts shall be deemed to apply and extend to New Zealand and to have always applied and extended.

An opportunity was taken in the Adoption Act also to clarify the meaning of the term 'Dominion' in section 4 of the Statute where there is the reference to the request and consent of a Dominion. Australia, it will be remembered,[3] had asked in 1931 that, so far as she was concerned, the request and consent referred to in section 4 should be the request and consent of the Parliament and Government of the Commonwealth and this rule appeared in section 9 (3) of the Statute. New Zealand has decided that it shall be the request and consent of the Parliament of New Zealand and has embodied this rule in section 3 (1) of the Adoption Act.

[1] See pp. 216 f–g.
[2] Section 3 (2).
[3] pp. 209–10 above.

THE STATUTE OF WESTMINSTER ADOPTION ACT, 1947

No. 38 of 1947

(Assented to November 25, 1947.)

AN Act to adopt certain Sections of the Statute of Westminster, 1931.

Be it enacted by the General Assembly of New Zealand in Parliament assembled, and by the authority of the same, as follows:

1. This Act may be cited as the Statute of Westminster Adoption Act, 1947.

2. Sections two, three, four, five and six of the Act of the Parliament of the United Kingdom cited as the Statute of Westminster, 1931 (which Act is set out in the Schedule to this Act), are hereby adopted, and the adoption of the said sections shall have effect from the commencement of this Act.

3. (1) For the purposes of section four of the said Statute of Westminster, 1931, the request and consent of New Zealand to the enactment of any Act of the Parliament of the United Kingdom shall be made and given by the Parliament of New Zealand, and not otherwise.

   (2) Every Act of the Parliament of the United Kingdom passed after the commencement of the Statute of Westminster, 1931, and before the commencement of this Act, that purports to apply to New Zealand, or to extend to New Zealand as part of the law of New Zealand, shall be deemed so to apply and extend and to have always so applied and extended according to its tenor, notwithstanding that it may not be expressly declared in any such Act that New Zealand has requested, and consented to, the enactment thereof.

Schedule

The whole of the Statute of Westminster, 1931.

APPENDIX VII

THE STATUTE AND THE INDIAN AND CEYLON INDEPENDENCE ACTS, 1947

IT might have seemed at first sight that the simple and obvious way in which to grant Dominion status to India, Pakistan, and Ceylon would have been to add their names, by way of an amendment, to the list of Dominions in section 1 of the Statute of Westminster. When the time came in 1947, however, the situation was not so simple as that. Partition in India meant that special and complicated legislation was needed and it was proper, therefore, that the powers of complete autonomy which were to be conferred on the new Dominions should find a place in the act of partition. In Ceylon also certain special provisions had to be made for setting up the Dominion and a simple reference to section 1 of the Statute would have been inadequate. Moreover, so far as India and Pakistan were concerned, a simple reference to the Statute would have been inappropriate, quite apart from the problems surrounding partition. For the Colonial Laws Validity Act, 1865, had never applied to India[1] and therefore section 2 (1) of the Statute which repeals that Act so far as the Dominions were concerned, would have had no operation for India. Finally, the new Dominions appear to have desired an immediate abolition of reservation and disallowance, a provision which the Statute did not embody.

But although Dominion status has been conferred on India, Pakistan, and Ceylon by distinct acts and although the Indian Independence Act itself contains no express mention of the Statute of Westminster by name, yet it will be found that most of the fundamental sections of the Independence Acts—the 'emancipating' sections, so to speak—

[1] Section 1.

are 'lifted', though with modifications, from the Statute. It
is of some interest therefore to compare briefly the Independence Acts and the Statute in these respects.

A comparison may begin most easily with the Ceylon
Independence Act.[1] In this Act sections 2–6 and 11 of the
Statute are reproduced with the substitution of 'Ceylon' for
'Dominion' in the appropriate places. Section 4 of the
Statute appears as section 1 (1) of the Ceylon Independence
Act and section 11 of the Statute as section 4 (2). Then
sections 2, 3, 5, and 6 of the Statute are grouped together
as a First Schedule to the Ceylon Act, under the heading
'Legislative Powers of Ceylon' and it is enacted by section
1 (3) of the Act that they shall have effect with respect to the
legislative powers of Ceylon from the day when Ceylon
acquires Dominion status. Ceylon has obviously received,
therefore, the fullest powers which the Statute could confer
and in this respect resembles South Africa, for example.

For India and Pakistan section 2 (1) of the Statute,
repealing the Colonial Laws Validity Act, was not appropriate, as already explained. But section 2 (2) with its repeal
of the rule of repugnancy—a rule which did apply to India
—was relevant to the situation and it finds a place as section
6 (2) of the Indian Independence Act.[2] Section 3 of the
Statute appears in section 6 (1) of the Act; while the limited
repeal of reservation in sections 5 and 6 of the Statute is
swallowed up in section 6 (3) of the Act by a complete
repeal of reservation and disallowance. Section 4 of the
Statute, however, is not adopted in the Independence Act.
Instead, the form of words which South Africa introduced
into section 2 of the Status of the Union Act, 1934,[3] is
introduced into the Indian Act and section 6 (4) runs:

'No Act of Parliament of the United Kingdom passed on
or after the appointed day shall extend, or be deemed to

[1] 11 Geo. 6, c. 7.
[2] 10 & 11 Geo. 6, c. 30.
[3] See above, pp. 244–6.

extend, to either of the new Dominions as part of the law of that Dominion unless it is extended thereto by a law of the Legislature of the Dominion.'

This is one instance of a tendency in the Indian Independence Act to introduce a more precise definition of the safeguards of Dominion legislative autonomy than is found either in the Statute of Westminster or in the Ceylon Independence Act. Thus while the Ceylon Act follows the Statute in speaking of the powers of the Parliament of a Dominion to repeal any 'existing or future Act of Parliament of the United Kingdom',[1] the Indian Act speaks of '*this* or any existing or future Act of Parliament of the United Kingdom'.[2] Does this mean that the legislatures of India and Pakistan can amend the Indian Independence Act but that the legislatures of Ceylon and the old Dominions cannot amend the Ceylon Independence Act or the Statute of Westminster respectively? It can be argued convincingly that 'existing' includes the Ceylon Act and the Statute, but if it does, why introduce 'this' into the Indian Act? And if it does not, why make a difference between India and Ceylon?[3] Again, while the Ceylon Act and the Statute confine themselves to a declaration that no United Kingdom Act shall extend to the Dominion unless it is expressly declared in that Act that the Dominion has requested and consented thereto, the Indian Act not only adopts the formula of the Status Act, as explained already, but also enacts that no Order in Council or other statutory instrument made on or after the day appointed for establishing the two Dominions shall extend to either Dominion.[4] These differences should not be exaggerated. Ceylon can itself enact similar provisions, if it chooses to do so, by virtue of the powers granted in the

[1] Ceylon Independence Act, First Schedule, para 1 (2); Statute of Westminster, section 2 (2).

[2] Section 6 (2). My italics.

[3] It may well be that the difference amounts to no more than a difference of draftsmen. [4] Section 6 (5).

Ceylon Independence Act, just as South Africa has done.[1]

Two further points of interest to the student of the Statute of Westminster may be briefly mentioned. First of all, it would seem that the legislatures of India and Pakistan were not intended to be sovereign legislatures in the sense in which that term is applied to the Parliament of the United Kingdom. For it is provided in sections 6 (1) and (6) of the Indian Independence Act—no doubt at the request of those entitled to speak for the proposed new Dominions—that the legislature of each of the two Dominions shall have full power to make laws for that Dominion and that this power 'extends to the making of laws limiting for the future the powers of the Legislature of the Dominion'. Now the sovereignty of the Parliament of the United Kingdom is often illustrated by the proposition that it cannot bind itself or its successors; in this sense the legislatures of India and Pakistan are not sovereign. Ceylon, on the other hand, would appear to have a sovereign legislature in the same sense as the United Kingdom. The power of the Ceylon legislature to bind itself contained—to take no wider ground—in section 5 of the Colonial Laws Validity Act[2] was removed by the Ceylon Independence Act. Ceylon thus attains a legislative sovereignty like that of the Parliament of the Union of South Africa.[3]

The second point of interest is found in section 7 (2) of the Indian Independence Act where the assent of the Parliament of the United Kingdom is given to the omission from the Royal Style and Titles of the words 'Indiae Imperator' and 'Emperor of India'. This action is in accordance with the rules discussed in Chapter XII above. It was announced on

[1] One further small difference may be noted. The Indian Independence Act, sections 6 (4) and (5) and the Ceylon Act, section 1 (1) speaks of 'on or after the appointed day'; the Statute, section 4, says 'after the commencement of this Act'.

[2] See pp. 224–5 above and *Attorney-General for New South Wales* v. *Trethowan* [1932] A.C. 526.

[3] But see Appendix VIII.

July 1, 1948, in the British House of Commons[1] that legislation had been passed by the Parliaments of the Dominions
also, though it was not specified whether this included India,
Pakistan, and Ceylon. Ceylon is bound by these conventions,
for in an agreement made with the United Kingdom Government, it affirmed its readiness to accept common allegiance
to the Crown and to adopt and follow the resolutions of past
Imperial Conferences.[2] It is not so clear that India and
Pakistan are bound, for they were not members of the
Imperial Conference and in any case the resolutions adopted
on these matters concerned only the United Kingdom and
the Dominions existing at that time. Yet it is reasonable to
infer that inasmuch as and for so long as India and Pakistan
accept the name of Dominion, they accept also the rights
of the Dominion Parliaments in this matter. In fact, however, when the change of title was proclaimed on June 22,
1948, legislation had been passed by Canada, Australia, New
Zealand, and South Africa, only.

[1] 452 *H.C. Deb.*, 5 s., 2379.
[2] Cmd. 7257, Appendix II.

APPENDIX VIII

THE STATUTE AND THE ENTRENCHED SECTIONS OF THE SOUTH AFRICA ACT

It has been maintained in successive editions of this book that the passing of the Statute of Westminster destroyed the legal efficacy of the provisions of section 152 of the South Africa Act which prescribed a certain procedure for amending sections 35, 137, and 152 of the Act, the so-called 'entrenched sections'.[1] This opinion, which had been generally held by commentators on the Statute,[2] was subjected to a most careful examination by Professor D. V. Cowen, of the University of Cape Town, in a work entitled *Parliamentary Sovereignty and the Entrenched Sections of the South Africa Act* published in 1951. It appeared to the present writer that the argument adduced by Professor Cowen showed conclusively that the view previously maintained in this book was ill founded and must be revised. Before this task could be undertaken, however, a further event occurred. In March, 1952, the Appellate Division of the Supreme Court of South Africa decided in the case of *Harris and others* v. *Minister of the Interior and another*[3] that, in spite of the passing of the Statute of Westminster, the entrenched sections were still binding and that any attempt to alter them contrary to the procedure laid down in section 152 was void. The full significance of this decision cannot be grasped until some time has passed. It is obvious, however, that it is of the greatest importance not only in the law of South Africa but also in the law of the rest of the Commonwealth. In this short appendix an attempt is made to comment briefly upon

[1] See above, pp. 240–2.

[2] See, for example, Wade and Phillips, *Constitutional Law*, 4th ed., pp. 425–6; A. B. Keith, *The Dominions as Sovereign States*, p. 177; and H. J. May, *The South African Constitution*, pp. 32–3.

[3] 1952 (2) A.D. 428 and [1952] 1 T.L.R. 1245.

the decision with special reference to its effect upon our interpretation of the Statute of Westminster.

It may be best to set out the grounds upon which the author was led to conclude that the entrenched sections were no longer effective after the passing of the Statute and then to explain how these grounds are affected by the judgement of the Appellate Division. First of all, it was asserted that the entrenched sections were binding before the passing of the Statute because they were contained in an Act of the United Kingdom Parliament which, according to the rules embodied in the Colonial Laws Validity Act, must prevail over any legislation repugnant to it. With the repeal of the Colonial Laws Validity Act in 1931, it was suggested, this safeguard disappeared. In particular any amendment of the entrenched sections carried out by a procedure other than that laid down in section 152 would be a law repugnant to section 152 and therefore, by section 2 of the Colonial Laws Validity Act, void. Such a law would infringe also section 5 of the Colonial Laws Validity Act which provided that laws altering a constitution must have been 'passed in such manner and form as may from time to time be required by any Act of Parliament . . .', and it would be void on that count also. When the Colonial Laws Validity Act was repealed, it was argued, both these safeguarding sections disappeared.

The Appellate Division has dealt with this first contention by holding that the Colonial Laws Validity Act was not relevant to a consideration of the effectiveness of the entrenched sections. They noted that section 152 of the South Africa Act gave to the Union Parliament a power to amend any section of that Act, provided of course that the provisions of section 152 itself were followed. 'A repeal or alteration of the South Africa Act', they held, 'enacted by an Act of the Union Parliament in accordance with the provisions of section 152 would be repugnant to the provisions so repealed or altered. Those provisions are, it is true,

contained in a British Act of Parliament, namely, the South
Africa Act, but that repugnancy is specifically authorized by
that very British Act which is a later Act than the Colonial
Laws Validity Act and must therefore in case of conflict over-
ride the earlier Act. Section 2 of the Colonial Laws Validity
Act could, therefore, have no application to a repeal or an
amendment of the South Africa Act.'[1] With the conclusion
stated here the author has no quarrel. It must be conceded
that if the Union Parliament, acting in terms of the South
Africa Act, should amend any part of that Act section 2
of the Colonial Laws Validity Act would have no material
upon which to operate. But would it not be preferable to
state this by asserting not that amendments to the South
Africa Act, duly passed, were valid though repugnant, but
that they were valid because not repugnant? Surely an
authorized amendment is not repugnant to the South Africa
Act but consistent with it? The point is more than a matter
of words, but it need not detain us here, for there is no
disagreement about the inapplicability of section 2 of the
Colonial Laws Validity Act so far.

But what about amendments to the South Africa Act
passed contrary to the provisions of Section 152? Would
they not be void by virtue of section 2 of the Colonial Laws
Validity Act and by virtue of section 5 also? The Court's
answer to this question is that it is not necessary to bring the
Colonial Laws Validity Act into the matter at all. There
is section 152 which lays down the manner and form in
which the Act may be altered; it governs the situation and
the Colonial Laws Validity Act need not be invoked. That
was the position before the passing of the Statute. It follows
therefore that the repeal of the Colonial Laws Validity Act
by the Statute made no difference to the position. Section
152 was there before and it was there afterwards.

It must be conceded, of course, that the Statute of Westminster did not repeal section 152. But did it not weaken

[1] 1952 (2) A.D. 428 at p. 461.

its effectiveness? The author has maintained that it did. He has argued that the repeal of the Colonial Laws Validity Act coupled with the words of section 2 (2) of the Statute of Westminster meant that section 152 was now on the same footing in South African law as any other law in the Union. And here we move on to the second ground upon which it seemed proper to conclude that the entrenched clauses were no longer effective. If we consider the concluding words of section 2 (2) of the Statute—'the powers of the Parliament of a Dominion shall include the power to repeal or amend any such Act, order, rule or regulation in so far as the same is part of the law of the Dominion'—does that not mean that the Statute made a positive grant of power to the Union Parliament to alter the South Africa Act just as if it were any other Act of the Union Parliament, and could it not therefore alter section 152 without following the special procedure laid down there?

The Court's answer to this contention was that when section 2 (2) of the Statute of Westminster refers to 'a law made by a Dominion, such law means in relation to South Africa a law made by the Union parliament functioning either bicamerally or unicamerally in accordance with the requirements of the South Africa Act'.[1] The Court here gives its authority to a line of argument which was set out with great cogency by Professor D. V. Cowen in the work already referred to, and it may be added that for the clearest and most convincing statement of that argument Professor Cowen's book still stands alone. Shortly stated the argument is that, although it is accepted that there are no limits to the power of the Union parliament to amend the South Africa Act and to amend or abolish the entrenched sections, and although it might be argued that section 2 (2) of the Statute of Westminster relieved the Union parliament of all legal restrictions imposed upon it by any British law, the prior and fundamental question was: 'What is the Union Parliament?'

[1] At p. 462.

Granted that an act of the Union parliament is always valid, when is the Union parliament to be deemed to have passed an act of parliament? And the answer to this question, says the Court, is that whereas in relation to most matters the Union parliament consists of the Governor-General and the two houses sitting separately and it is deemed to have passed an act when the consent of all three of these elements is obtained, in relation to matters contained in the entrenched sections the Union parliament consists of the Governor-General and the two houses sitting together and it is deemed to have passed an act when the consent of the Governor-General and of two-thirds of the two houses sitting together is obtained.[1] If the proper procedure is not followed no act of parliament has been passed, and therefore the provisions of the Statute of Westminster relating to the powers of the Union parliament do not begin to apply.

This is a strong argument. Moreover it is equally effective in meeting the contention that the repeal of the Colonial Laws Validity Act abolished the efficacy of the entrenched sections as it is in disposing of the argument based upon the words in section 2 (2) of the Statute of Westminster. For a measure passed contrary to the entrenched sections would not be an act of parliament at all and therefore no question of repugnancy would arise and the provisions of the Colonial Laws Validity Act would not come into operation. Their repeal by the Statute of Westminster does not therefore affect the question of the entrenched sections. It is upon this ground rather than upon the ground adopted by the Court that it seems preferable to establish the proposition that the Colonial Laws Validity Act may be disregarded.

[1] And this does not exhaust the possibilities. For section 63 of the South Africa Act provides that a case of deadlock between the two houses shall be decided by a joint sitting with a simple majority. This provision strengthens the view that the South Africa Act does not conceive of the parliament of the Union as an exclusively bicameral body.

It seems clear that in the discussions of the effect of the
Statute of Westminster upon the entrenched sections which
went on before the publication of Professor Cowen's book
and before the judgement of the Appellate Division, a
fundamental question has been steadily ignored, namely:
What is the parliament of the Union? It has been assumed
that the parliament of the Union is the three elements of
Governor-General, Senate and House acting separately and
that it was to such a parliament and its acts that the Colonial
Laws Validity Act and the Statute of Westminster exclusively referred so far as the Union was concerned. This, it
should be admitted, was an unwarranted assumption,
ignoring as it did the provisions of the Constitution of
the Union which created the law-making authority of the
Union, and determined its structure and mode of legislating
no less than its powers. The procedure referred to in the
entrenched sections was part of the definition of the Union
parliament and was not a limitation upon the powers of
an exclusively bicameral parliament. The Colonial Laws
Validity Act and the Statute of Westminster affected the
powers of the Union parliament but they did not affect its
definition; they regulated the effect of an act of the Union
parliament but they did not determine when it should be
deemed to have passed an act. So it was that, in the judgement of the Court, a measure passed contrary to the entrenched sections, both before the passing of the Statute
and since, is of no effect not because it is an invalid act but
because it is not an act of parliament at all. And it must be
confessed that this argument is convincing and reveals the
fundamental mistake in the views, expressed in earlier
editions of this book, concerning the ineffectiveness, since
the passing of the Statute, of the entrenched clauses.

It may be worth while to mention two further considerations which appeared to the author to support the view that
the passing of the Statute of Westminster destroyed the
efficacy of the entrenched sections. The first was that

whereas saving clauses were inserted in the Statute in respect
of the Canadian (section 7), New Zealand and Australian
(section 8) Constitutions no such clauses were inserted in
respect of the Constitution of the Union. It seemed reasonable to assume that these saving clauses were inserted
because it was thought that without them the parliaments
of Canada, Australia and New Zealand would have
obtained an unrestricted power to alter the constitutions
of these Dominions and this result was not desired by
those Dominions.[1] Here again, however, as the Court has
pointed out, whatever may have been the need for such
saving clauses in the case of Canada, Australia and New
Zealand, no such clauses were needed for the Union. The
parliament of the Union had power to amend the South
Africa Act in any particular before the passing of the
Statute; no increase upon the area of its powers could be
granted by the passing of the Statute. Nor did the Statute
make any change in the rules which determined how parliament should express its will. ' "Parliament" ', said the
Court, 'means Parliament functioning in accordance with
the South Africa Act.'[2]

The second consideration which seemed to confirm the
view that the entrenched clauses lacked force was the
decision of the Appellate Division itself in 1937 in the case
of *Ndlwana* v. *Hofmeyr*.[3] That case the Court itself has now
overruled in its decision in *Harris's Case*. It pointed out that
its predecessors had evidently assumed—as many students of
the subject had done before and since—that the parliament
of the Union could mean only the Governor-General and
the two houses sitting separately, and that any document
produced by that body and purporting to be an act of

[1] There is good reason to believe, however, that such a saving clause
was not necessary in Australia to safeguard the amending process. See
Cowen, *op. cit.*, p. 32.

[2] At p. 465.

[3] 1937 A.D. 229.

parliament must be accepted by the Court as such. But, said the Court in 1952, 'this Court is competent to inquire whether, regard being had to the provisions of section 35, an act of Parliament has been validly passed'. It was true, no doubt, to say, as the Court had done in *Ndlwana* v. *Hofmeyr*, that 'Parliament's will, as expressed in an Act of Parliament, cannot now in this country as it cannot in England be questioned by a Court of Law whose function it is to enforce that will not to question it'.[1] But that statement, true as it is, does not conclude the matter. It is necessary to go farther and ask whether the document that purports to be an act of parliament expressing the will of parliament is in reality such. This is what the Court did in *Harris's Case*, thus bringing the discussion down to the fundamental question. It was because the Court in *Ndlwana* v. *Hofmeyr* had not addressed itself to this prior question that the argument in its judgement was largely irrelevant.

It will be seen that the judgement in *Harris's Case* over-rules—and it is respectfully submitted rightly overrules—the opinions expressed by the author concerning the effect of the Statute of Westminster upon the entrenched sections. It is not possible here to follow up in detail the consequences of the decision for South African constitutional law or for the constitutional law of other members of the Common-wealth if the same line of reasoning were to be applied by their courts.[2] One remark only may be made. The Court's judgement makes it clear that the validity of the entrenched clauses and their priority in determining what is an act of parliament in the Union depend in no way upon their being part of a superior Imperial act. Their priority depends not upon origin but upon logic. The efficacy of the provisions in the South Africa Act describing how parliament is constituted and how it legislates for different purposes

[1] At p. 237.
[2] Some of these consequences are opened up by Professor Cowen in an article in the *Modern Law Review*, July and October 1952.

follows from the nature of a constitution, and it would so follow even if laws made by the parliament of the United Kingdom had never had the power to prevail over colonial laws repugnant to them. The judgement in *Harris's Case* does not assert the imperial supremacy of British law over South African law; it asserts the logical priority of a constitution over the institutions which it has created and whose nature and powers it describes and determines.

INDEX

Abdication of Edward VIII, *see* Edward VIII.

Admiralty, Courts of, *see Table of States under* Colonial Courts of Admiralty Act, 1890.

Africa, South, Union of, *see* South Africa, Union of.

Alberta, Canadian Province, responsible government established in, 51. *See also* Canadian Provinces.

Allegiance, to the King, an essential of Dominion Status, 29–30, 34, 277–8.
  Oath of, abolished in Irish Free State, 259, 267, 269–70.

Allen, Dr. C. K., 98 n.[3]

American Colonies, United Kingdom Parliament renounces intention to tax, 79.

Amery, Mr. L. S., 166 n.[6], 256 n.[1], 260.

Anson, Sir W. R., on relation of King to his ministers, 57–8.

Appeals, to Judicial Committee of Privy Council, *see* Judicial Committee of Privy Council.

Asquith, Mr. H. H., *see* Oxford and Asquith, 1st Earl of.

Atkin, Lord, 98 n.[3]

Australia, Commonwealth of, and abdication of Edward VIII, 285–6; constitution of, 50–1, 81, 112; amendment of constitution of, 202 ff.; defined as Dominion in Statute of Westminster, 139–40; and appeals to Judicial Committee, 91–8, 132, 222–3; and disallowance, before 1926, 71–4, after 1926, 128–9, 219–20; and reservation, before 1926, 62–70, after 1926, 126–7, 129–32, 219, 220; High Court of, power to restrict appeals from, 92–3; Parliament of, and power to legislate with extra-

territorial effect, 219; and laws touching succession to throne, 220–2, c. xii; and power to adopt ss. 2–6 of Statute, 152, 214–16; and s. 4 of Statute, 146–7, 151–2, 209–14; effect of Statute on, 161–3, 164–5, 182–3, c. viii, 227–31, 256.

Australia, South, Colony of and State of, *see* South Australia, Colony of, *and* State of.

Australia, Western, Colony of, and State of, *see* Western Australia, Colony of, *and* State of.

Australian Colonies, and appeals to Judicial Committee, 91–8; and disallowance, 70–4; and reservation, 63–5, 68–9; drew up their own constitutions in 1850–5, 112.

Australian States, status of, 60 n.[2], 201–2, 223–6; and disallowance, 71–4, 224; and reservation, 63–70, 224; and appeal to Judicial Committee, 91–8, 224; legislatures of, and lack of power to pass extra-territorial legislation, 211–12, 224; general constituent powers of, 224–5; how affected by Statute, 162, 185–6, c. viii; and requests for Imperial legislation, 210–14, 217–18; position in relation to amendment of Commonwealth Constitution, 210–11, 217–18; affected by s. 6 of Statute, 226; validation of laws of, 80.

Bailey, Professor K. H., 68 n.[5], 69 n.[1, 2], 201 n.[1], 223 n.[1], 278 n.[2]

Baker, P. J. Noel, *The Present Juridical Status of the British Dominions in International Law*, 133 n.[1]

Baldwin, Robert, advocates establishment of responsible government, 53.

INDEX

INDEX

INDEX